TUSITALA OF THE SOUTH SEAS

TUSITALA OF THE SOUTH SEAS

THE STORY OF ROBERT LOUIS STEVENSON'S LIFE IN THE SOUTH PACIFIC

By

JOSEPH W. ELLISON

HASTINGS HOUSE, PUBLISHERS *NEW YORK*

Printed in the United States of America
by the Vail-Ballou Press, Inc., Binghamton, N.Y.

Library of Congress Catalog Card No.: 53-7850

TO TRUDI

FOR HER DISCRIMINATING JUDGMENT AND HER HELPING HAND

ACKNOWLEDGMENTS

For permission to include quotations in this volume grateful acknowledgment is made to:

Chatto & Windus: *Recollections of Robert Louis Stevenson* by Arthur Johnstone, Copyright, 1905 by Chatto & Windus.

Doubleday & Company, Inc.: *Reminiscences of the South Seas,* by John La Farge, Copyright, 1912 by Doubleday Page and Co.

Grant, John Booksellers Ltd.: *Stevensoniana,* Edited by J. A. Hammerton, Copyright, 1910 by John Grant.

Houghton Mifflin Company: *Letters of Henry Adams, 1858–1891.* Copyright, 1930 by Worthington C. Ford.

Longmans, Green and Co.: *This Life I've Loved,* by Isobel Field, Copyright, 1937, Longmans, Green and Co.

Macmillan Company: *Partial Portraits,* by Henry James, Copyright, 1888, Macmillan Company.

Merrill Company: *With Stevenson in Samoa,* by H. J. Moors, Copyright by Small, Maynard & Company.

Charles Scribner's Sons: *The Life of Robert Louis Stevenson,* by Graham Balfour, Copyright, 1915 by Charles Scribner's Sons.

Charles Scribner's Sons: *An Intimate Portrait of R.L.S.* by Lloyd Osbourne, Copyright, 1924 by Charles Scribner's Sons.

Charles Scribner's Sons: *The Life of Mrs. Robert Louis Stevenson,* by Nellie Van De Grift Sanchez, Copyright, 1920 by Charles Scribner's Sons.

Charles Scribner's Sons: *The Letters of Robert Louis Stevenson,* Vols. III, IV, Edited by Sir Sidney Colvin, Copyright, 1925 by Charles Scribner's Sons.

Charles Scribner's Sons: *The South Seas,* by Robert Louis Stevenson, Edited by Sir Sidney Colvin, Copyright, 1925 by Charles Scribner's Sons.

Charles Scribner's Sons: *Weir of Hermiston,* by Robert Louis Stevenson, Copyright, 1925 by Charles Scribner's Sons.

The portrait of Robert Louis Stevenson on the jacket and the photographs used on the end papers are by courtesy of Charles Scribner's Sons.

I wish to thank the General Research Fund of Oregon State College for subsidizing, in part, my research in international relations in the Pacific, of which this study is an outgrowth, and also Mr. William H. Carlson, Director of Libraries of the Oregon State System of Higher Education, and Mr. Henry G. Alsberg, Editor, Hastings House.

To my wife I owe a special debt for her unflagging patience in reading the manuscript and offering valuable suggestions.

INTRODUCTION

THIS IS THE picturesque and dramatic story of Robert Louis Stevenson's years among the fabulous, enchanted isles of the South Pacific. It is an account of a most charming, glamorous literary personality embarked on a strange Odyssey—in flight from grim, ever pursuing death. It is an Arabian Nights tale of the exploits of this beloved writer whose adventure stories had already charmed millions, as he criss-crossed the Pacific, always only one jump ahead of the grim reaper, in small chartered vessels, sailing through sudden storms and hurricanes or becalmed in tropic seas, visiting high and low islands, fraternizing with native "kings" and "queens," chiefs, lepers and ex-cannibals, in the Marquesas, Tahiti, Hawaii, the Gilberts and Samoa.

On the treasure island of Upolu, the surf-lapped, palm-crowned, "expurgated heaven," this frail Odysseus built high on a mountain ledge his "flash-house," the sensation of the Islands. These last years —six of them—in the South Seas were Stevenson's most happy, most adventurous, and most productive. For the first time this "weevil in a biscuit" lived an active life, a life that fully satisfied him. For the first time this frail wanderer in search of the will-o'-the wisp, health, found a home, "wealth," and happiness. It was a life that gave rise to the famous Stevenson legend which captivated the imagination of the reading world, surpassing in romantic interest even that of Lord Byron.

The volumes of letters to his friends in England and America provide one of the most valuable sources for the Stevenson South Sea story. Originally they were written without any thought of publication. It was not until June, 1892 when Stevenson wrote to Sidney Colvin, his critic and mentor, that it occurred to him that "this diary of mine to you would make good pickings after I am dead, and a man could make some kind of a book out of it without much trouble." After Stevenson's death, Colvin edited and published the letters, allowing the books to form themselves.

These volumes stamp their author as one of the greatest letter writers. They are not only good literature; they are also excellent documents of the life and times of Stevenson in the South Seas and in the western world. In them we follow their author from month to month, from year to year, from stage to stage. In these detailed, frank, spontaneous and personal documents the author lays bare his soul, and paints a portrait of a man of genius—kind, generous, Bohemian, a lover of justice, a friend to his fellow men, irrespective of race, color or religion, whether saint or sinner. There is no envy or jealousy in him; he was always ready to cheer, to encourage fellow writers, young and old. Even his egotism was amiable and infectious.

The letters reveal an undying optimism, a buoyancy of life, the ability to smile in face of overshadowing odds. "I believe," he said, "in the ultimate decency of things, aye and if I woke in hell, should still believe it!" Like the brave old sea-dog, Andrew Barton, who while lying stricken on deck, his life-blood flowing out, insisted:

> A little Ime hurt, but yett not slaine;
> Ille but lye downe and bleed a while,
> And then Ille rise and fight againe.

Stevenson likewise declared: "Vital—that's what I am at first, wholly vital, with a buoyancy of life to smile against fearful odds," and: "Well we will not give in that we are beaten; I still mean to get my health again; I still propose this book or the next, to launch a masterpiece."

For over four years the "happy warrior," lived the life of a family patriarch, ruled as laird of a clan of native retainers in Stuart tartans; was the gay cavalier, as guest and host at native feasts, *kava* ceremonies, dances, songs, and parties. He was counselor to warring factions, champion of the natives against German, British and American consuls, officers and men-of-war. He was justly acclaimed by the natives as the man with the loving heart, the teller of tales—TUSITALA!

Stevenson had to live romance as well as to write romance. Just when he was at the height of his fame, when he was working, as though racing with death, on the *Weir of Hermiston,* the climax of his life's ambition, death caught up with him. While preparing the dinner salad, after a day of inspired dictation, he suddenly cried out: "My head—oh, my head," and sank insensible at the feet of his wife. On the following day, the chiefs who only a short time before had built and dedicated to him the "Road of the Loving Heart," were hacking out a path to the peak of Mount Vaea where he was to be carried and laid to rest. Like President Lincoln, General Wolfe and Admiral Nelson, Stevenson too died just when ultimate victory was in sight.

This is also the story of "God's sweetest," handsome, hospitable, and poetic Polynesians, whose cause Stevenson championed. It is a story of their migrations, their mythology, their ceremonies in war and in peace, their dances and songs, their national struggles, and their resistance to the intrusion and intrigue of the *Papalangi* (foreigners). In this too Tusitala played a leading role.

More than half a century has passed since the Tusitala–South Sea drama was enacted. During this time both the Stevenson legend and the South Pacific picture have undergone a transformation. With the impact of Western civilization, much of the native culture has vanished. Many of the beautiful and colorful native customs and ceremonies have faded out. Were Tusitala to revisit these islands, he would be amazed, perhaps disappointed, to find roads, air transport, radio, western clothes, and possibly jazz.

The Stevenson legend, too, had suffered an eclipse. Three score years ago the magic initials, "R.L.S.," were the hall-mark of literature, representing the most admired and most loved literary personality of the age. His name was a household word. He exercised greater personal sway over his public than any other contemporary writer. His admirers and disciples acclaimed him the greatest romancer and the greatest storyteller, the greatest artist of the age, a sublimated Sir Walter Scott. This over-praise, this adulation of Stevenson the artist, and Stevenson the "seraph in chocolate," soon brought about a severe reaction.

A more dispassionate estimate reveals that Scott and Stevenson differ in kind as well as in degree. Scott never achieved Stevenson's superb technical skill; the fine diction, the neat phrasing, the mellifluous sentences. On the other hand, Scott surpassed his successor in sweep of imagination, in fertility of invention; to compare the one with the other is to compare a full symphony orchestra with a string quartet. Moreover, Scott surpassed Stevenson in the power to characterize women. Professor William Lyon Phelps remarked: "Stevenson's romances are Paradise before the creation of Eve. The snake is there, but not the woman." Stevenson, however, was versatile. He wrote stories, novels, poems, essays, dramas and even prayers, in which, according to one critic: "Their author seems to be presenting the Deity with specimens of his literary skill." Then, too, let us bear in mind that if Scott and Dickens had died at the age of forty-four, there would not have been the *Waverly Novels* or *A Tale of Two Cities.* The depth, however, of the writing in the *Weir of Hermiston,* which has the elements of one of the greatest novels, is a good indication that Stevenson had at last attained maturity and a remarkable power of psychological analysis. What might he not have achieved had he been granted more years in his art.

Stevenson's reputation in the literary world shrank even more after the First World War, when a wave of disillusionment and pessimism swept over the Western World. It was the age of Spengler's *Decline of the West,* of Hemingway, Dos Passos, and Steinbeck, of realism and naturalism. In such an atmosphere Stevenson's optimism and romance expressed in the high, heroic vein, and in meticulously polished style, the very opposite of the "literature of woe," appeared shallow, artificial, the work of a mere stylist. He was called a case of arrested development, an adolescent. Since the Second World War, however, a re-evaluaton of the personality and work of Stevenson has begun. Perhaps tastes in art and literature change as do fashions in clothes. Perhaps the prominent part played by the Pacific in the last war helped to revive interest in Stevenson and Melville, the writers who helped popularize this part of the world. A veritable Stevenson revival has been taking place in England and the United States. His works are appearing in new editions and are discussed on radio programs; his stories and novels, such as *Treasure Island, Dr. Jekyll and Mr. Hyde, Kidnapped, David Balfour, Beach of Falesá, Ebb-Tide* and *St. Ives,* have been filmed. His life, too, is being re-examined and re-appraised. And though he has emerged, not as a "seraph in chocolate," but as a man with his full complement of human frailties, he nevertheless shines forth again, a radiant, gallant, magnetic personality. Robert Louis Stevenson lives again!

JOSEPH W. ELLISON

OREGON STATE COLLEGE
JANUARY, 1953

CONTENTS

TUSITALA OF THE SOUTH SEAS

CHAPTER I

THE SILVER SHIP

"IF YOU *should* find a yacht out there, mind you take it," Robert Louis Stevenson jokingly advised his wife Fanny, when she left Saranac for California. Six weeks later he received this telegram:

"Can secure splendid sea-going schooner yacht *Casco* for seven hundred and fifty a month with most comfortable accommodation for six aft and six forward. Can be ready for sea in ten days. Reply immediately. Fanny."

"Blessed girl, take the yacht and expect us in ten days. Louis." This was the elated reply from the semi-invalid author of *Treasure Island, Dr. Jekyll and Mr. Hyde* and *Kidnapped.*

While convalescing from catarrhal consumption at Saranac, in the Adirondacks, near the Canadian border, Stevenson spent many a cold winter evening dreaming of yachting cruises in warm waters, of islands clothed with palms, and maidens draped only in smiles. He and his family sat around the lamp as the wind and snow lashed against the windows, and pored over outspread maps and Findlay's *Directories of the World.* These massive volumes warned mariners against the treacherous character of some island natives and the "licentious character of these island women, many of an extreme beauty and all as unclothed as Eve."

Additional stimulus and inspiration came from S. S. McClure, the youthful, energetic representative of a syndicate of newspapers. McClure's *Autobiography* reveals that he and Stevenson spent considerable time discussing the South Sea cruise and that he sent Stevenson a number of books about the South Seas, including a *South Pacific Directory*. When McClure revisited Saranac he found Stevenson, his imagination thoroughly aroused, shaping plans "to take a phonograph along and make records of the sounds of the sea and wind, the songs and the speech of the natives." These recordings were to illustrate lectures which Stevenson planned to deliver on his return from the South Seas.

McClure backed up his enthusiasm for Stevenson's proposed South Pacific adventure with tempting offers. "We are on the lookout for the very best we can get, and we are always ready to pay the highest price," pleaded McClure. "Now if you write me weekly letters, describing your experiences in the Pacific, I could have them published all over the land, and a great audience would enjoy them. Can you do this work, and if so what will you ask for it?"

"How many letters do you want?" asked Stevenson.

"As many as you like—say fifty; that will keep us going for a year. Just interesting jotting. Write about whatever interests you most and send it along. Will you do it?"

"Well, I don't know what to ask for a class of work I have never done before. I am not sure I can please you, but I am willing to try. What do you think would be a fair price, Mr. McClure?"

"Name your own terms—I am prepared to pay anything that is reasonable."

"I will do it for $100 a letter, or $5000 for the fifty letters, which is making no reduction for a quantity."

"Shake hands, Stevenson! I'll give you twice as much; I'll give you $200 for each letter of from a column to a column and a half in length —$10,000 for the fifty letters! And if you want any of the money now you can have it!"

Stevenson had yearned unceasingly for a South Sea cruise, but when little chance of finding a desirable schooner on the Pacific Coast seemed likely, he was reconciled to a cruise in the Indian Ocean.

Energetically McClure combed all ports on the Atlantic; he submitted lists of vessels, irrespective of size and character. Imagine Stevenson's high spirits when a South Sea cruise was no longer a wish, no longer a dream. To sail the South Seas in his own yacht! It may be he will chart some unknown islands! It may be he will set foot where no white man had as yet ventured.

His friend, Lady Taylor, was the first to hear. "I have to announce our great news. On June 15th we sail from San Francisco in the schooner *Casco* for a seven month's cruise in the South Sea. You can conceive what a state of excitement we are in . . . But this is an old dream of mine which actually seems to be coming true, and I am sunstruck. It seems indeed too good to be true . . . From Skerryvore to the Galapagos is a far cry! And from poking in a sick-room all winter to the deck of one's own ship, is indeed heavenly change."

Even Mother Stevenson was as excited as a youngster. She well remembered the lines she used to repeat as a little girl in school:

> Full many are the beauteous isles,
> Unseen by human eye,
> That, sleeping 'mid the ocean's smiles,
> In sunny silence lie.

On June 7, 1888, Stevenson, his mother and step-son, Lloyd Osbourne, arrived in San Francisco. They were overjoyed at the sight of the *Casco*, a graceful-looking, swift-racing yacht of some seventy-four tons register, ninety-four feet long and twenty-two feet beam. Those graceful lines, those lofty masts and white sails! A beautiful ship resting like a swan upon the water!

Stevenson's enthusiasm mounted when he boarded the yacht; those luxurious fittings: the glittering, polished brass-work; the white and gold panels and mirrors; the velvet-upholstered seats in the cabins; the crimson carpets and soft rugs on the floor of the saloon. It was a floating palace! Little wonder the natives of the Paumotus called her *Pahi Muni*—Silver Ship!

The owner of the *Casco*, Dr. Merrit, a very stout Oakland millionaire physician had qualms about entrusting his expensive craft to this long-haired, eccentric, invalid author. A conversation with Stevenson, however, dispelled any misgivings. "I'll go ahead with the yacht. I'd read things in the papers about Stevenson, and thought he was a kind of a crank; but he's a plain, sensible man that knows what he's talking about just as well as I do." Turning to Otis, skipper of the yacht, he remarked, "Why, Captain, Mr. Stevenson is all right; he seems quite as sensible a man as either you or I." The doctor's fears about permitting an old lady like Mother Stevenson to travel on his ship likewise vanished when he saw her. "You're a healthy-looking woman!" he remarked as he grasped her hand appraisingly.

Dr. Merrit humorously confessed that he had built his yacht in the hope of reducing his weight, that cruising gratifyingly had made him sixty pounds lighter. "But," exclaimed Mother Stevenson, "we don't want it to have that effect on Mr. Stevenson, or there would be nothing left of him!" Turning to Fanny, the doctor warned that the yacht, named after Casco Bay in his native state of Maine, "Is the apple of my eye—you may think your husband loves *you,* but I can assure you that I love my yacht a great deal better, and I am just afraid you will run away with her and never bring her back."

According to the contract agreement Stevenson was to pay a rental of $500 a month and assume all the expenses of the crew and provisions. Captain Otis was to be in full control; his approval would be required for a visit to any place in the South Seas.

The next question to be settled was their destination. Stevenson favored a long cruise in the warm sea waters that would either cure him or hasten his death. If the latter, he wished to be far enough from land so that he would be buried at sea. He must have wished to emulate the glamorous Sir Francis Drake who died at sea and was buried in the waters of the Caribbean. At first he expressed preference for the Galapagos. But when he informed Fanny that the islands were barren of vegetation, and that they might have to pass through a belt of calms and be held up for weeks, she insisted on the Marquesas. And to the Marquesas they accordingly went.

For three weeks Stevenson reveled in the stir and excitement of supervising the preparations for the long voyage. Frequently he slept on the yacht. At last, on June 27, 1888, when all was ready and the cabin was filled with fruits and flowers sent by friends, the *Casco* was towed across the Bay from Oakland to North Beach, where she was anchored for the night.

At dawn, as the first rays of the warm June sun were breaking through, and the slumbering city of San Francisco was beginning to stir, the *Casco,* flying the Stars and Stripes, the Union Jack, and the flag of the yacht club of which Stevenson was a member, was towed by the *Pelican* through the Golden Gate and into the Pacific. She proudly dipped her flag when saluted by a government cutter and a number of newspapermen. The San Francisco yacht club considered providing an escort through the Golden Gate, but Stevenson and his friends discouraged the plan. Fanny and Mother Stevenson, however, believed it would have been a "pretty and cheerful sight."

When the *Casco* crossed the bar and felt the heaving swell of the Pacific, she turned her bow southward, and with her white sails unfurled, raced like a bird released from a cage. She seemed dwarfed by the enormous waves and when she frequently put her rail under water, she looked frail indeed for the long voyage ahead.

Standing on the deck of the swiftly sailing schooner, Stevenson watched excitedly and proudly the race of his heroic little ship, victorious over the mountainous waves. As he gazed shoreward until the land mass faded in the haze, finally completely vanishing from view, little did he realize that he was destined never again to set foot on his native land, never again to visit America, never again to see his close friends. Little did he dream that he was going into "exile"; that he would spend his remaining six years in the Pacific and be buried on the summit of one of the island peaks.

It was a far cry, indeed, from Skerryvore to the Marquesas. But this was no longer a wish or dream. He had succumbed long ago to the age-old spell of the sea. Now, at last, he was to have his fill.

For over four centuries, since Balboa first waded in its blue waters; since Magellan and Drake navigated its vast spaces, and since Cook, Bougainville and a host of other explorers had charted its far-flung islands, the Pacific Ocean had cast a romantic spell. Stevenson could not escape it. During the nineteenth century it became the fashion to extol the primitive fascination of the South Sea islands and their people. Artists and writers, seeking an escape from "an excess" of civilization: from government, church, industrialization, and the dull routine of modern life, were lured by the siren of the South Seas. They dreamed of atolls with their placid, mysterious, sapphire lagoons. They envisaged the rugged peaks of the volcanic Marquesas, Tahiti, and Samoa, with their silver waterfalls, milk-warm tropic nights, scented breezes, and waving palm-trees, that "giraffe of vegetables." They imagined themselves witnessing seductive dances by sylphlike, dusky, velvet-skinned maidens, clad in garlands and wreathed in smiles; or being lulled to sleep by soothing waters washing the coral reefs, only to cascade back again in white silvery foam. Here they hoped to find a refuge, a peaceful, idyllic existence.

"Your civilization is your disease, my barbarism is my restoration to health!" exclaimed the French painter, Paul Gaugin, when he left Paris to live and die in the Marquesas. Melville, Pierre Loti, Stoddard, to recall only a few of the many romantics, as well as missionaries, traders, and sailors have hymned the fascinations of the South Seas and the gentle, unspoiled natives. From Samoa Henry Adams wrote: "If one must go to the sea, these are the seas to go to."

Stevenson had an inordinate love for the sea, a love which stemmed from his father and grandfather, builders of lighthouses. "Whenever I smell salt water, I know I am not far from the works of my ancestors," he declared. As a boy he was fascinated by the tales of travelers from the South Seas. He wanted to see those islanders who wore red flowers in their hair, whose life was oratory and etiquette. His eyes and heart followed the ships as he watched them going windward. Later he thrilled to Stoddard's *South Sea Idylls* and Melville's *Typee*. He never forgot the prediction of a drunken Highland sibyl: "You too will some day sail the seas."

Of the eleven persons who comprised the entire human cargo on the *Casco,* seven were members of the cosmopolitan crew. Captain Albert H. Otis, the "Nares" in the novel *The Wrecker,* was an American—adventurous, blue-eyed, often scornful and sullen, but a skilful master. There was a Swede, a Finn, a Russian, a Japanese cook, and Valentine Borch, a Swiss cabin boy.

The head of this sea-going family, the moving spirit of the cruise, was Robert Louis Stevenson, whose fame as an author was growing rapidly. His alert, slender figure made him look younger than thirty-eight years and taller than five feet and ten inches. His spidery, thin arms, spindly legs, narrow chest, thin face, veined oval forehead, flaccid muscles, and unmistakable stoop immediately labeled him a consumptive. When Captain Otis first met him at Dr. Merrit's home, he found him "so painfully thin that his clothes seemed a burden to him; his brown hair falling to his shoulders around a face of death-like whiteness." The captain doubted whether it would be possible for his illustrious passenger "to make the trip and return alive," and thought he had better make the "necessary arrangements for his death at sea."

Everyone who met Stevenson agreed that his most striking features were his compelling eyes. They were brown, brilliant, set wide-apart in his long, narrow, "horsey" face, and singularly sensitive to emotions, making his entire face radiate with charm. But when he was angry or agitated, they flashed, glowed, and blazed. His full-formed lips were bordered by an oversized moustache. His mouth sensitively registered alternating expressions: humor, scorn, sarcasm, sympathy.

In temperament Stevenson was more Southern European than Scotch. In fact he was often taken for a Frenchman: restless, impulsive, volatile, vivacious, quixotic. His movements were nervous as if his being were packed with quicksilver. In conversation he was seldom still, pacing up and down the room, waving his long arms above his head, gesticulating and talking in a vigorous, racy style.

His ordinary talk was deliberate, with a Scotch intonation, rolling the "r"s. It was a crisp Edinburgh accent. He spoke not only with his lips but with his whole person and very graphically. Words came readily to his tongue, which made him a splendid story-teller. "His resonant voice and full rich tone," opined his step-son, Lloyd Osbourne, "would have done justice to the greatest actors." When he was angry, however, his voice often became a "thin treble." Nor was it difficult to upset him. He might be sitting at the table or lounging in his chair, relaxed, with his hands around his knee, when suddenly a letter or a word of contradiction would throw him into a rage. Like a wild animal in a cage he would then pace up and down the room.

Though physically weak, Stevenson was buoyant and courageous, fearing neither risk nor danger and refusing to be coddled. "Oh, hell! What does it matter? Let me die with my boots on," he used to plead. Men of action and physical courage he greatly admired and envied. When he visited Honolulu, he was asked by Professor Scott of Tokyo University: "How is it that in all your fiction you are so powerless to draw a convincing picture of a woman, but an old pirate you are more skilled in delineating than either Marryat or Cooper?" Stevenson replied: "I suppose we are attracted mostly by contrast. And poor devil that I am," he, placing his hand on his chest, exclaimed, "see! Here am I, tall as you, weigh ninety-eight pounds, and can span my chest with my hand! I have always admired great strength, even in a pirate. Courage has interested me more than anything else."

Even a severe critic like Henry Adams found Stevenson intellectually inspiring. Moreover, Louis injected a great deal of vitality into everything he discussed. His courtesy and readiness to listen to others endeared him to his fellows, white or colored, civilized or native. Adams felt, however, that Stevenson would be a trying companion.

Stevenson indulged freely in the use of tobacco, maintaining that smoking was an essential attribute of a husband. There could be a shortage of food but not of tobacco, and he was always well supplied with cans of his favorite, Willis' *Three Castles* brand. He scorned smoking anything but cigarettes rolled by himself. "The genuine cigarette smoker rolls his own," he boasted. When he finished one cigarette, his long, tapering, tobacco-stained fingers immediately shaped a fresh one.

In the eyes of some Stevenson's eccentricities, such as wearing a velvet jacket, red sash, and his long hair parted in the middle and combed back, smacked of posing. His former friend, Henley, believed that Stevenson "could not be in the same room with a mirror but he must invite its confidences each time he passed it." There was undoubtedly much of the poseur in him. However, his habit of wearing his hair long might have been not an affectation but rather as a protection against cold. When he reached the tropics he was often happy to wear his hair short.

The second passenger of the quartet was Stevenson's wife,

Her father's friend, Reverend Henry Ward Beecher, baptized and christened her Frances Matilda, but she was commonly called Fanny. Though born a Van de Grift, an American of Dutch-Scandinavian stock, she was in size and complexion of the Latin-European type. Her small stature, tiny hands and feet and easy step made her look younger than forty-eight. A mass of black curly hair, dusky complexion, flashing, sparkling brown eyes, thin lips, strong jaw and chin bespoke a personality of unconquerable will and force. Stevenson called her "The Stormy Petrel," "The Tiger Lily."

Fanny was married at the age of seventeen to the handsome, improvident, twenty-year-old Samuel Osbourne, by whom she had three children, one of whom died in early childhood; the other two, Isobel and Lloyd lived to survive both her and Stevenson. Accusing her debonair husband of infidelity, she decided in 1875 to move to Gretz, France, to give Isobel instruction in art. It was there that the gay, open-hearted, bohemian Robert Louis Stevenson fell in love with her at first sight. Against the wishes of his ardent Presbyterian parents, Stevenson and Fanny were married after she had divorced her first husband. Though at first opposed to his son's marrying a divorcee, even the dour Tory Covenanter, Father Thomas, greatly admired the good judgment and intellectual attainments of his only daughter-in-law. "I doot yer a besom," he told her. Father Thomas or "Uncle Tom" or "Mr. Tom" as she called him made his erratic son promise "never to publish anything without" Fanny's approval. He was a good judge of character.

The third member of the family on the *Casco* was Margaret Stevenson, mother of Robert Louis. Aunt Maggie, as she was often called, looked younger than her sixty-two years. She was a little above medium height, slender, graceful. Her oval face was framed by silky ringlets; her complexion was fair, her nose aquiline. In her younger days she was gay, vivacious and buoyant, the very antithesis of her wilful, violent, somber, Calvinist husband, Thomas, whom she had married when she was only nineteen. Though still sweet and of sympathetic nature, she became more reserved and dignified after the passing of her husband in 1887. She usually dressed in black and wore a starched white organdy cap with its streamers floating down her back. Mother Stevenson took great pride in her distinguished author-son, her only child.

The last of the group was the six-foot, blond, lean, twenty-year-old Lloyd Osbourne, Stevenson's step-son. Though of American ancestry, Lloyd looked, spoke, and behaved like an Englishman. He was witty and well-mannered, but haughty.

The first three days of the cruise were hard on Fanny. She spent much time in bed and Lloyd also kept to his cabin. Even the skipper did not appear for meals for two days. Stevenson and his mother, however, were good sailors, and had all the food for themselves. Nevertheless Aunt Maggie confessed that she missed the first breakfast because after being on deck several hours she "was not able to face red herrings and mutton chops."

As long as the weather was delightful and the ocean smooth the women spent their time knitting and reading Gibbon's *Decline and Fall of the Roman Empire.* They also spent happy hours on deck watching the pilot birds alighting on the waves and the flying fish landing on the schooner. However, the isolation from the civilized world, the tedious monotony of sunlight, moonlight, and starlight began to weigh upon them. Often during a calm the sails flopped lazily and the schooner barely made two knots an hour. Rarely a passing ship lifted its sail above the horizon. When the ocean became squally and the sensitive schooner buried its low rail under water, the women were greatly alarmed. Fanny asked the skipper what he would do if Mother Stevenson were to fall overboard. Nonchalantly he replied: "Put it in the log!"

Fanny was a poor sailor and suffered from the phobia that she would drown. "I hate the sea," she once wrote, "and am afraid of it though no one will believe that because in time of danger I do not make an outcry." Though she was a good cook and prided herself on her housekeeping, she complained that "to keep house on a yacht is no easy matter. When I was deathly sick, the question was put to me by the cook, what shall we have for the cabin dinner."

Stevenson, on the other hand, a thorough sailor and an incorrigible adventurer, scoffed at the frightened women. He enjoyed everything about the cruise; everything was a new experience. He was always the first one up in the morning and the last to retire at night. Tanned like a native, barefooted and in shirt and trousers and white cap, he would saunter on deck, ever on the alert for excitement. During the day he would write, play the flute, lounge or survey the endless expanse of water. The scenes around him never dulled: the little waves sparkling in the sun, the interminable rollers, the silver wake churned up by the swiftly-racing yacht. Even on rainy days he stood on deck watching the rain-whipped water or listening to the creaking of the rigging. Like a youngster, he was excited by a shoal of flying fish, leaping into the air and dropping in a silver shower into the sea: the albacore sailing along in arch-fashion and then disappearing in the water. At the cry of "shark!" he would rush to the rail and watch the beast snap at the schooner and soon sink again into the unbroken blue water. And often he would sweep the horizon hoping to spot the sail of a passing ship.

In the evening Stevenson would lie on deck and gaze raptly at the Southern Cross, the procession of stars which appeared larger and brighter than "those back home in the northern climes." When all was quiet, with scarcely a sound but the rippling of the parting waters, he would like to think of the world he had left behind: of Scotland, Edinburgh, High Street, and old friends. But he shuddered at the thought of the penetrating inhospitable chill of Scotland and Edinburgh, that "gusty, rainy, smelly, grimy old city." The warm, soothing air of the South Sea was like a tonic to his sick lungs. Captain Otis noticed that Stevenson grew stronger during the first week on the water. He walked with more physical energy and his color vastly improved.

At first the skipper had a poor opinion of his master passenger. However, as the journey progressed, they became good friends, more so after the following incident had taken place. Once being questioned by Mother Stevenson as to his opinion of her son's writings, the Skipper blurted out: "My dear madam, I have already told you that I have read but one of your son's books, and since you have urged me to express an opinion, I will say that, from the casual examination I have given some of the others, I do not think I would care to read them." Needless to say the good woman was startled, actually offended by the captain's candid, uncomplimentary opinion.

Stevenson, overhearing the skipper's remarks through the skylight, rushed to the deck, exclaiming: "Captain, you have raised yourself in my estimation by your frank statement to my mother that you had only read one of my books through, and that you did not care for the others; if you had told her that you had read them all and liked them, as most people tell me whether or not, I will be as frank and tell you that I would have thought you lied!" That episode sealed a warm friendship; the skipper and the writer spent many hours lying on deck and exchanging sea yarns.

During the months the *Casco* sailed the Pacific, she experienced fair weather and foul: calms, squalls and storms. When the breeze was favorable she raced at a steamer's speed, covering about 240 miles a day; dipping and rising as gracefully as a seagull. But when she encountered calms she made little progress, barely thirty-five miles a day. She would lie idle with her tall white sails hanging listlessly against the mast, a mere speck on a seemingly endless painted sea. Scarcely a sound could be heard; not a murmur, not a bird. All around them was the silent vastness of blue-green water below; the cloudless, clear blue sky above. Daily the air grew more soothing. At sunset the ocean was a sea of fire; the sky became a revolving color disk: grey, violet, purple, red, and blue. In the evening the moonlight and starlight were clear and illuminating. South of the Equator the stars looked large and bright; the sea became more mysterious; the air felt soft and warm. Peace and contentment settled on the yacht and her passengers.

However, even Stevenson had to admit that often the "sea is a terrific place, stupefying to the mind and poisonous to the temper —the motion, the lack of space, the cruel publicity, the villainous tinned foods, the sailors, the captain, the passengers." Often during his long cruises on the South Seas he used to complain about the monotonous diet which came out of the pickle-tub or out of tins. "Oh, for a beefsteak, an onion, and an Irish potato!" he sighed nostalgically.

For nine days the weather was pleasant. On the tenth the sky and the sea gave warning of an approaching storm. The air became raw and cheerless; a heavy gale roared and the schooner rolled and pitched. Captain Otis suspected that they were sailing near one of those dangerous revolving storms of the Pacific from which it would be difficult to extricate the ship once it was sucked within the outer rim. For many hours he was puzzled. On which side of the schooner was the storm? He ordered all hands on deck; and with every bit of the schooner's canvas drawing, she tore westward.

For three and a half days the sea ran high. The wind seized the whitecaps from their mountainous waves and broke them into a sheet of spray that filled the air and deck. Visibility was nil. The gale howled; tons of crashing water broke over the deck. Into the cockpit and through the deadlights came the flood. The masts and rigging creaked. The schooner plunged her nose into the sea in the downpour. With all his strength the steersman spun the wheel. Thirty hours of men against the sea before Captain Otis was confident that his schooner had ridden out the storm. Those had been anxious days for the crew and passengers; there had been little sleep.

The *Casco* was fortunate and Captain Otis was gratified that he had ordered the ship westward. Another vessel, the *Tropic Bird,* also from San Francisco, smacked into the storm and came out crippled, stripped of her sails. Had the undermanned *Casco* run into the storm she might have perished, together with the crew and passengers. Even then her perils were not over. Shortly before she reached the Marquesas, a freakish black squall struck the schooner with massive impact, bulging her sails and spilling a torrent into her cockpit. Streams of water gushed into the cabin. Even Captain Otis considered the situation hazardous. The women were in consternation. But the captain had warned them again and again that all deadlights on the lee-side should be closed. Now when two powerful streams of water flooded the cabin, the heedless women were convinced "that there may be a grain of reason even in a 'seaman's crankiness' about dead-lights."

Finally the storm had spent itself and life on the *Casco* again became calm and peaceful. Everyone on board celebrated the escape from possible shipwreck with a special dinner. Stevenson and the skipper made appropriate toasts. After dinner the group spent the evening on deck. It was a lovely night; the ship was bathed in soft silver fairylike light and the air was mild and soothing. The *Casco* was approaching the end of the first leg of the cruise—the Marquesas.

CHAPTER II

AMONG EX-CANNIBALS

"LAND HO!" WAS the prolonged cry of the lookout at dawn on July 28, 1888. The Stevensons, arousing themselves from their slumbers, rushed to the deck in whatever clothes were handy, to thrill at the first sight of the fabled South Sea islands, the famous Marquesas!

This group was discovered in 1595 by the Spanish flotilla commissioned by the viceroy of Peru, Garcia Hurtado de Mendoza and named for the viceroy's lady, Las Islas Marquesas. Later, English, Americans and French visited the islands; they murdered natives, destroyed their villages to "put the fear of God in the niggers' hearts, and sowed a crop of deadly evils which helped to cause the extinction of the race." In 1842 the French annexed the group.

It was still early morning. By half-past five the islands could be distinguished faintly from the scattered clouds on the horizon. Through the fading darkness the blue, jagged outline of the peaks began to rise in silhouette. Ua-huna, with its lopped-off summit, appeared from the seaboard side. Nukuhiva, swathed in a veil of rapidly fading clouds, rose abeam. To the south the peaks of Uapu, glistening like pinnacles of a Gothic cathedral, pierced the morning sunlight. When the mist rolled away, peaks, cliffs, and buttes, tucked in clouds and crowned with spreading gold and rose, became more distinct. Around the island was a white necklace of surf. Down the peaks threaded the slender veins of waterfalls, silver ribbons glistening in the sunlight.

Stevenson stood on deck in complete "silence and expectation," inhaling the fragrance of the perfumed air. "The first experiences," he wrote, "can never be repeated. The first love, the first sunrise, the first South Sea island, are memories apart." This was an unforgettable first approach; he felt the excitement of the explorer.

Captain Otis focused his glass in search of an entrance through the pounding surf and reef. The sun was already high when the *Casco* cautiously nosed her way into the Bay of Anaho, on the northern coast of Nukuhiva, made famous by Melville's *Typee.* Below, in the bay, large schools of fish were going about their business, unconcerned with the arrival of strangers. Crowding the crescent beach and climbing the steep sides of the mountains which embraced the inlet, were the inevitable coconut palms. Snug in a grove of palms upon the curved beach, facing the reef and the eternally foaming surf, stood a native village. The first lesson Stevenson learned was that in the South Seas the coconut and the native hug the beach —the latter fears the spirits of the interior.

The anchor chains clanked through the hawse holes. Hardly was the *Casco* anchored, when a canoe came alongside bringing a German cotton-grower and a native chief. "Captain!" shouted the white trader, "is it permissible to come on board?" The two visitors boarded the yacht and shook hands with Stevenson and the others. The young, handsome chief, Taipi-Kikino, six feet four, broad in proportion and dressed in immaculate white linen trousers and coat, enjoyed everything on the yacht; there was a broad smile on his tattooed face.

The first canoe was only the forerunner of a whole fleet of them loaded with natives of both sexes. Soon the uninvited visitors swarmed all over the schooner. The men, tall, athletic and handsome, though strange-looking to the whites, were in various stages of "undress." Some wore shirts, others just a loin-cloth or a mere handkerchief. All were tattooed from head to foot in patterns that looked like "open-worked silk tights." There was no word of welcome, no show of civility; their knives and furtive glances looked menacing. When Stevenson declined to buy their bananas and oranges at exorbitant prices, they complained rudely of the miserliness of the strangers. Amidst jeering laughter one of them remarked cynically: "Here is a mighty fine ship, to have no money on board!"

The Marquesan women, whose figures were graceful but whose features were hard, appeared fatter and duller than the men and were more modest in their conduct. With large, melting, cowish eyes they looked in amazement at the beautiful yacht with its lofty spars, crimson upholstery, and gilt mirrors. They slouched on the chairs, pawed the velvet, and peered into the mirrors. One fat dame pulled up her dress and shouting with delight, rubbed herself bare-breeched upon the velvet cushions in the cabin.

When Stevenson conducted a tour through the yacht, the natives followed him Indian fashion; the women, held in an inferior position, were not permitted to walk too close to the men folk. Some of the photos in the albums aroused the admiration of the native visitors. When they found the picture of Queen Victoria, they exclaimed: "Victoree a! Bretano!" Even greater was their pleasure when they were served biscuits and jam. They filled the air with their *kochas!* (thank you). They dubbed Stevenson, *Le Ona,* the owner of the beautiful vessel, the rich man!

Stevenson confessed that this, his first experience with the South Sea islanders, aroused in him repugnance and even considerable alarm. As he sat in his cabin writing, he felt himself a helpless prisoner when three generations of natives squatted cross-legged on the floor around him, staring at him animal-like. "These natives may look like amiable fawning dogs," he thought to himself, "but after all only a short time before they were inveterate cannibals." And what if the dormant cannibalistic habit would awaken, and the desire for a bit of "long pig" would get the better of them? Why, the entire crew and passengers of the *Casco* would be "butchered for the table." It was doubtful if even an indiscriminating cannibal would be attracted to such a lean, juiceless morsel as Stevenson. At any rate, he soon realized that his apprehensions were absolutely groundless.

The Stevensons spent five weeks at Nukuhiva, Hivaoa, and other places in the Marquesas. They sailed around, tramped in the mountains and valleys, mingled with the natives and made many interesting observations. They reveled in the beauty of the sunsets and the huge swells of the sea breaking on the cliffs. The healthful, bland climate, the enchanting scenery, and the kindly, hospitable people intrigued them.

Of the charm of Anaho Stevenson could not speak too highly. Awakening at three in the morning he felt the gentle tossing of the *Casco* in the bay filled by the long swells, and inhaled the balmy air. Oceanward, the water reflected the stars. Shoreward, the high squalls and the black mountains took him in fancy 10,000 miles away to Scotland, to a Highland loch amidst a country of pines, heather, green ferns, and the Gaelic tongue.

When day-break came, he was deeply moved by a most resplendent sunrise: the mountains overhanging the port with "lawn, and cliff and forest," which were tinted saffron, sulphur, and rose. Along the beach men and women, boys and girls, in green and blue and red garments, were visiting the baths. Soon the glow enveloped the entire landscape. Here a native fisherman paddled his canoe; there several natives communicated by means of their traditional whistling. All else was silent, except for the eternal turbulent surf.

Stevenson expected to find the Marquesans, erstwhile cannibals, backward and barbarous. He was astonished to discover how mistaken he had been. To his friend Sidney Colvin in London, he wrote: "It is all a swindle: I chose these islands as having the most beastly population, and they are far better, and far more civilized than we. I know one old chief, Ko-o-amua, a great cannibal in his day, who ate his enemies even as he walked home from killing 'em, and he is a perfect gentleman and exceedingly amiable and simple-minded, no fool, though." Without attempting to justify cannibalism, he pointed out that "to cut a man's flesh after he is dead is far less hateful than to oppress him whilst he lives." "Furthermore," he argued, "in the eyes of Buddhists and vegetarians, we consume the carcasses of creatures of like appetites, passions, and organs with ourselves;

we feed on babes, though not our own; and the slaughter-house resounds daily with screams of pain and fear."

Stevenson considered the Marquesans the most appealing of the Polynesian race. He was especially impressed with their height, muscular strength, broad, deep chests, and rounded limbs, and their graceful erect posture while standing or walking. The women, though duller and fatter than the men, were comely, with superb rounded bosoms. He found the Marquesans kindly, sociable, frank, eager for affection like "amiable fawning dogs." They were also dignified and well-mannered; they would not accept gifts unless given an opportunity to reciprocate. When presented with a gift, they pretended to forget it; it had to be offered them again before their departure. They were usually delighted to give more than one asked for. Among the gifts with which the Stevensons were favored were pieces of tapa and old men's beards. The latter were highly regarded and were often worn as ornaments by the men. Père Siméon, a young Gascon missionary, assured Stevenson that the Marquesans were "peut-être plus civilisés que nous-mêmes" [perhaps they are more civilized than we are], of a mind far more like Christ's than any of the races of Europe. He admired their kindness, their generosity, their readiness to forgive.

When Stevenson and Frère Michel passed through a village street, friendly cries of *kaoha!* greeted them from a cotton patch. In a glen under cool foliage and near a rushing brook they came along a well-built house where a family of eight were having their evening meal. Here the shouts of *kaoha!* became a chorus. The visitors were prevailed upon to dismount and partake of the meal,—of course, without paying for it, for the Marquesans disapproved of taking money for food. The mother of the family, nude to the waist, saluted the strangers with some coquetry. "Goodbye!" she said and pressed two crimson flowers into Stevenson's hand. "I speak Inglis," she boasted. She had learned it from a whaler-man who was "a plenty good chap."

Farther along the road Stevenson and the priest observed a girl bathing naked in the little stream. It amused them to behold her alarm and the haste with which she put on her many-colored garments. Even daughters of cannibals were conscious of shame, mused Stevenson.

Another characteristic of the Marquesans that appealed to Stevenson was their fondness for children. "Happy is the man that has his quiver full of them," was a native saying. Families would vie for the adoption of a stray child. The natural ones and the adopted grew up together. The whole Stevenson family was adopted by Chief Paaaeua, the strait-laced chief of Atuona, who had been appointed by the French government. The elaborate ceremony ended with the feast-rite of adoption, which consisted of chicken, pig, and coconuts. After the banquet the audience was entertained with singing and dancing. The songs, a weird form of crooning, a monotonous, prolonged chant without tune or high notes, related the history and achievements of the Marquesans. The dancers performed with a great deal of spirit and grace; they combined their dances with calisthenics; they waved their hands, and climbed on each other's backs and shoulders. Some of the steps were reminiscent of a Highland reel. Stevenson believed that a century or so ago the Highlanders were in the same "convulsive and transitory state as the Marquesans of today."

Of course, the adoption of people so rich as to possess a floating palace enhanced the prestige of Chief Paaaeua. Not to be outdone, former Chief Moipu, who had been displaced by the French government because of his lax morals, proposed to "make brothers" with Lloyd, whom he called Mata Galahi (glass-eyed). To the feast of brotherhood, which was held on board the *Casco*, Moipu came in full pomp, accompanied by his attendants carrying gifts "from plumes of old man's beards to little, pious, Catholic engravings." Lloyd now had the right to live in the house of the chief who had adopted him. Nor was Atuona an undesirable place in which to live; it was free from mosquitos. According to a legend the absence of mosquitos was a reward from the gods whom Atuona people served better than did their neighbors. The mosquitos had been collected in a coconut shell by the gods and sent to Nukuhiva.

The beauties of the country and its agreeable people influenced many a white man to settle in the Marquesas. One of these was a Mr. McCallum, an American from the Atlantic Coast. He had read widely of the South Seas and was determined to visit these islands. When Stevenson met him, McCallum had been living in the islands a number of years and was quite satisfied to remain there until death, enjoying the society of Shakespeare, Burns, and the breakers. His only desire was to see just once more the rude wintry landscape of his native land.

The problem of depopulation of the Marquesas troubled Stevenson. Here was a people, the most viable, judging by their physical appearance, inhabiting a country justly celebrated for its beauty and healthfulness; yet they were dying out rapidly. The natives watched the extinction of their people with grave apprehension. "The coral waxes, the palm grows, and man departs," was a native proverb. "Take a little baby like this; then dead. All the Kanaques die. Then no more," lamented a sad mother with a puny babe in her arms.

The French authorities and the missionaries likewise were aware of this deplorable condition. "Oui, monsieur, cela se despèrit," remarked a French missionary, pointing to the dwindling number of children in his class-room. In the port and capital, Tai-hae, on Nukuhiva, Stevenson found the jail completely empty. The jailer explained: "Comme c'est jour de fête, je les ai laissé aller à la chasse." [since it is a festival day, I permitted them to go hunting]. They were permitted to go hunting goats in the mountains. As to the women prisoners, the jailer added cheerfully: "Je crois, Monsieur le Résident, qu'elles sont allées quelquepart faire une visite." [I believe Mr. Governor, that they went visiting]. M. Delaruelle, the French Resident, remarked indulgently: "They are dying, poor devils! The main thing is to let them die in peace." In 1842 the Marquesan population was about 20,000; in 1942 it had dwindled to 2,600. The natives faced the decline with a deep melancholy.

What could be the causes of the depopulation of the Marquesans? Stevenson agreed that it was due in part to faulty hygiene, native doctoring, bathing during fever, and unchastity. He believed, strongly, however, that the advent of the whites, foreign domination and missionaries were even more responsible for this decay and decline. White whalers and sailors introduced opium and social diseases which helped to demoralize the natives and produce sterility with a resultant high death rate. Foreign governments forced upon the natives a new mode of life by discouraging their own economic and social system. The missionaries, both Catholic and Protestant, in their misguided efforts to stamp out some of the barbarities, proscribed the native dances and songs which added so much to the zest and happiness of these simple people, and imposed upon them the standards of morality which prevailed in Europe and America. In Oceania, where breadfruit, bananas, coconuts grow wild and can be had for the mere plucking, and where the other needs are really few, the problem of securing food and shelter and clothes does not consume much time and energy. Entertainment, therefore, is of primary importance. Song and dance were a natural outlet for the emotions of these people. These ceremonials kept alive their interest in their past and gave meaning to their future. Shirts, trousers, canned goods, and religious rites they could not always appreciate. These could not possibly replace their own historic festivities, their poetry, their group amusements. Life now became dull, monotonous; the play instinct thwarted, their joy in life declined. The dispirited natives squatted outside their huts like sphinxes, no longer singing or dancing. They fell into deep despondency and the race began to die out. In Samoa, where the natives continued their songs, dances, games and pleasures, the population increased.

Easily dejected, the Marquesan was prone to suicide by hanging or poisoning from the fruit of the *eva*. This latter mode of suicide would afford the victim time for the important last hour ceremony. He could see the coffin; he could hear the cry of mourners; he could be conscious until the end. The coffin was highly prized by the native: he had it ready sometime before death. One old man sick with small pox lived in his coffin for a fortnight, eating, drinking, smoking and visiting with passers-by about his approaching end. The Marquesan honored the bodies and graves of the dead. Formerly the families often kept corpses oiled and in the sun until they dried into mummies.

A few of the more intelligent of the natives deeply deplored the impact of occidental civilization and the imposition of an alien pattern on their traditional way of life. In fluent, spirited French, Stanislao Moanatine, chief of Akaui, the adopted son of "Queen" Vaekehu, an educated gentleman who called himself a traveled savage, lamented the placing of the native customs on the expurgatorial list. "Chaque pays a ses coutumes," he complained, "tenez une danse qui n'est pas permise, je ne sais pas pourquoi, elle est très jolie" [Every country has its customs. Take the dance which is not permitted, I don't know why, it is very beautiful]. Stevenson was inclined to agree with him. He wondered whether civilization and Christianity had not done the natives much harm and brought little moral good.

Stevenson inquired from the priests how successful they had been in their efforts to Christianize these natives. The reply was, "not too much." "You can no more make Christians of them than you can mould water," confessed one. Although they went to church, chanted in a barbaric rhythm, kneeled and bowed their heads when the mystery of transubstantiation took place, they displayed little understanding of the white man's religion. It was just another form of their own magic and rites. The burning questions they frequently debated were: What caused the fall of angels? Were Adam and Eve white, or brown like us? How could God resurrect a man who had been eaten by sharks and then the same shark be consumed by another Marquesan? Why is cannibalism wrong when Christians are permitted to eat the body and drink the blood of Jesus himself?

Fanny was told that on one of the islands a man whom the entire population hated was killed in vengeance. To afford everyone a taste of the enemy without arousing the authorities, match boxes with the cooked flesh of the slain were secretly passed around. A native woman presented Lloyd with an ornament to wear which was made of woman's hair. Probably a number of women had been killed to make this decoration and their bodies had been cooked for the dancers' banquet.

A native Hawaiian missionary in the Marquesas told Stevenson that shortly after a Peruvian slave ship had kidnapped natives at the cannibal island of Hiva-Oa, an American whaler arrived. One of the men was captured by the natives and brought to the chief. The latter invited a native missionary, Kekela, to the feast. The conversation that passed between the chief and the missionary as told to Stevenson in Kanaka English was as follows: "'I got 'Melican mate,' the chief he say. 'What you go do 'Melican mate?' Kekela he say. 'I go make fire, I go kill, I go eat him,' he say; 'you come tomollow eat piece.' 'I no *want* eat 'Melican mate!' Kekela he say; 'why you want?' 'This bad shippee, this slave shippee,' the chief he say. 'One time a shippee he come from Pelu, he take away plenty Kanaka, he take away my son. 'Melican mate he bad man. I go eat him; you eat piece.' 'I no *want* eat 'Melican mate!' Kekela he say; and he *cly*—all night he cly!"

The missionaries did succeed in persuading the Marquesans to discontinue cannibalism. Père Siméon deplored, however, the fact that the natives "have no spiritual life, nor any concept of it. You see they have no cares, and that is what leads to a higher life."

Among the illustrious persons Stevenson entertained was the wife of former King Temona. Temona had been kidnapped, exiled, and worked as a cook on a whaler. He was later exhibited for a small charge in English seaports. Then he was returned to his native land, where he became a Protestant. He died an ardent supporter of Catholicism and the French. His wife, commonly called "Queen," and officially addressed as *Madame Vaekehu, Grande Chefesse,* was an extremely religious person. She spent much of her time in the company of the Sisters and with religious pictures. A special path was made from her European house to the Catholic mission. When she came to dine on board the *Casco,* in company with her son Stanislao and her granddaughter, she was dressed in a beautiful white robe, in style like a nightgown, and a white China crepe shawl, embroidered and fringed. She was so beautifully and artistically tattooed that when she was young her "leg was one of the sights of Tai-o-hae; she had been passed from chief to chief. She had been fought for and taken in war."

The Stevensons were fascinated by the exquisite manners and charm of this lady who had once presided over many a bloody sacrificial feast, who "sat on the high place . . . while the drums were going twenty strong and the priests carried up the bloodstained baskets of long pig." She probably had ordered the execution of many a witch. It was even rumored that she had become tired of her husband, the prince consort, and had him killed and eaten. Now they found her a lady of refined manners and intensely religious. Her speech was musical Marquesan; *merci* was the only French word she used. When parting, Fanny held out her hand. "Her Majesty" held it, smiled, and kissed the hostess twice. When Stevenson kissed the little granddaughter goodbye, the "Queen" uttered a cry of gratification. She pressed Stevenson's hand with feminine coquetry.

Stevenson held long conversations with the "Queen's son, Stanislao Moanatine," who was well-educated and intelligent. This Marquesan chief listened most intently to the tales of famous episodes in English history: the story of Gordon, the Indian mutiny, Lucknow, the relief of Arrah, the death of Spottiswoode. His face and his eyes glowed. Then in spirited French he told of the by-gone days of the Marquesans, of the days when the drumbeat used to assemble the folk to make a holiday. Now, he lamented, the houses are down, the people are dead or dying and the dance declining and prohibited.

In the Marquesas Stevenson learned his first lesson of the sad consequences of imperialism and the impact of white man's civilization and religion upon the natives. Stanislao's lament and reproach lingered in his mind. Like Walt Whitman, whom he admired, Stevenson had always been a man with a strong sense of justice and a champion of the cause of the underdog, a hater of sanctimonious hypocrisy. Once in the Highlands Stevenson severely chided a man who was beating his dog. "It's not your dog," protested the owner. "No," snapped back Stevenson, "but it's God's dog, and I am not going to see you ill use it!" In 1881 he severely criticized Britain for her shameful attack on weak and liberty-loving Transvaal. He was ashamed to belong to a nation which, to gain a superficial triumph and prestige, had lost genuine glory and honor.

Now Stevenson became the champion of the cause of the Polynesian race. He was always ready to battle for its rights. He did not idealize the natives; his was a genuine sympathy for them. He did not refer to them as savages; he did not deprecate their code of morals. In the Marquesas, later in Hawaii, and in Samoa the natives felt that they had found in him a true friend and vehement champion. "Ah, vous devriez rester ici, mon cher ami! Vous êtes les gens qu'il faut pour les Kanaques; vous êtes doux, vous et votre famille; vous seriez obeis dans toutes les îles." [You should remain here, my dear friend! You are the man who is needed for the Kanakas. You are kind, you and your family; you would be obeyed in all the islands.] Thus spoke Stanislao when parting from Stevenson. Thus spoke later many other Polynesian chiefs in Hawaii, Tahiti and Samoa.

Before the *Casco* left the Marquesas, Stevenson entertained many of the natives with beefsteak, gingerbread and rum. They, in return, came with tapa cloth, rare shells, oranges and coconuts. One presented Lloyd with a rare gift, a carving done on the bone of one of his ancestors. The entire party of natives took a last walk through the vessel. Some of them were dressed in white shirts and trousers and had their finger nails polished. Then all shook hands and the guests departed. Hoka, the most beautiful and graceful dancer, sat staring at the floor, disconsolate, sighing heavily. After the Stevensons had shaken hands with him, he turned his head and never looked back. The others, led by Chief Moipu, stood on shore waving their hands in sorrowful farewell as long as they could see the schooner. The captain saluted; and as the ship sailed away, all men on board bared their heads.

CHAPTER III

GUESTS OF ORI

ON SEPTEMBER 4, 1888, the *Casco* left the Marquesas for Tahiti by way of the Paumotus. The Dangerous Low Archipelago was feared by navigators, for its numerous sharp reefs were poorly charted and dimly lighted by the French Government. Even adventurous Captain Otis long hesitated to risk his small over-rigged yacht in these dangerous waters with their many turbulent crosscurrents. Stevenson, however, who was insistent on visiting these out-of-the-way places, prevailed, and the captain grudgingly consented, though both realized that it was an extremely foolhardy venture.

During the voyage the *Casco* experienced calms, with splendid purple and gold sunsets, and terrifying squalls. Often, in the intense darkness, the lookout had to depend upon his hearing for the safety of the schooner. Frequently a member of the crew kept his ear to the mainmast for the sound of the surf. Even Stevenson joined the crew, eagerly spying the horizon for distant atolls.

At dawn, on September 8, the *Casco* began to approach the atoll zone. At 8:15 Tikei was sighted, "flat as a plate in the sea and spiked with palms of disproportioned altitude." A few hours later another atoll appeared, "lost in blue sea and sky: a ring of white beach, green underwood, and tossing palms, gem-like in color; of a fairy, of a heavenly prettiness. The surf ran all around it, white as snow, and broke at one point, far to seaward, on what seems an uncharted reef." A lonely white trader stood on shore gazing at the passing schooner, no doubt with mingled emotions. On the following day the *Casco* reached her destination, Fakarava, the main and central island of the Paumotus. It was a typical coral atoll, eighty miles in circumference, several hundred yards wide, and not more than twenty feet above the sea. The French Government chose this atoll as its headquarters for the entire archipelago.

The *Casco* was anchored in the horseshoe-shaped lagoon, some thirty miles long by ten miles broad. On atolls the villages and all life center on the shore of the lagoon, for the ocean beach is considered by the natives as accursed and haunted ground, scene of shipwrecks and murders. The Stevensons found the irregularly scattered houses of the village, nestled among the tall palms, deserted, for the natives had gone to neighboring atolls to gather pearl shells. The French Government unsuccessfully attempted to control the trade in order to derive revenue from it.

Two dreary weeks the Stevensons spent on this monotonous atoll where the crickets sang and clouds of mosquitos whirred and stung. At sunrise Stevenson bathed in the shallow waters of the lagoon. After lunch he walked across to windward to gather shells and strange fish, and to study the coral. Brown as a native he walked about and played tunes on his pipe. He was fascinated by the contrasts between the mood of the lagoon and the ocean shore: on one side the gentle wavelets on the shore; on the other side, the deep sturdy breakers pounding rhythmically on the coral reef. Being on this narrow flat-top of an atoll that might be washed away by the ocean waves gave him a sense of insecurity.

From ten in the morning until four in the afternoon, when the danger from sunstroke was greatest, the air was often extremely hot and stifling, as if the tiny atoll had been smothered by a down quilt. Everything was at a standstill, even the tallest palms stood motionless. Suddenly the weather would change; the trade winds would begin to stir the palm tops, to fan the baked dwellings and bring deliverance to ships lying becalmed. Life around the lagoon would then begin to stir and quicken.

The food supply, too, was monotonous: coconut beefsteak, coconut raw and coconut cooked; coconut hot and coconut cold. Stevenson was willing to concede that coconut, as salad or cooked pudding, and the milk were most tasty, but like the Israelites in the desert, he was ready to grumble about this eternal manna.

During his stay, he had an opportunity to study the natives: their habits, customs, and beliefs. He was pleased to find such unusual places and races. He made himself popular with the natives. They brought gifts and shouted *Yuranna!*, a word of salutation; he invited them to visit the *Casco* which they greatly admired. *Pahi Muni* (Silver Ship) they called it. When he served biscuits, jam and syrup-water, only one of the natives asked for "t-rum." The natives, who spoke French, appreciated the fact that Stevenson gave them plates and spoons for their jam. The French admiral, who had entertained them previously, served sardines but they had to eat them with their fingers in native style. Though they appreciated the honor, most of them took the jam in the spoon and then skilfully conveyed it to their mouths with their thumbs.

Though the Paumotuans were of Polynesian stock, Stevenson found them less attractive than the Marquesans, whom he considered the most handsome of the human race. The Paumotuans were darker, shorter, but better behaved than the Marquesans. The latter were self-indulgent, generous, and indifferent to religion; the Paumotuans, on the other hand, were greedy, hardy, ascetic, eager to be rich, and not averse to work. They seemed to be model family men. The husband was strongly devoted to his wife and children, by whom he was often ruled. The family would preserve the bones of their deceased children and even carry them along on their wanderings from one atoll to another.

It struck Stevenson as remarkable that he should be able to attend services, and listen to a sermon preached by a native pastor whose people had only so recently been redeemed from cannibalism. In fact, the islands had been considered "siren isles," and the people dangerous savages. In 1855 the schooner *Sarah Ann*, with some women and children on board, sailed from Papeete for the mainland. When no word came from the schooner and the passengers, it was presumed that they had perished in a squall. A year later, however, bodies of some of the passengers were discovered in a cave, including the head and golden hair of the captain's wife.

Now Stevenson found the Paumotuans greatly interested in religion. The two dominant sects were the Catholic and the Mormon, but there was also the Whistler cult, whose members sat about the room singing and whistling. The leader, wrapped in a sheet, would sit in silence in the center of the room. Then suddenly from above his head or from the roof, whistling would commence and pronouncement would be made. The Catholic services were performed by *Tainiera,* the native rendering of Daniel, who had been removed from his chiefdom and imprisoned for mishandling government funds. He sang in a splendid voice and preached a moving sermon with graphic gesticulations. When Stevenson showed him pictures in an encyclopedia, he was especially attracted to the cuts of an ape, candlesticks, cardinals and cathedrals. Though nominally Christian, the natives retained a good deal of paganism: the fear of ghosts, devils, and other superstitions.

On September 25, the *Casco* lifted anchor from the Paumotus for Tahiti. Before the departure the French Resident, Donat, said to Stevenson: "I am glad that the *Casco* came in just now, otherwise I should be forgotten: but now the people will always say this or that happened so long before—or so long after—the coming of the *Silver Ship,* when Donat represented the government." Many of the islanders stood on the pier waving till the *Casco* was well out of sight.

After a journey of 250 miles in forty-eight hours the *Casco* arrived at Papeete, the "Pearl" of the South Seas, capital and port of the French possessions in the Society group. At day-break everyone was on deck to witness the entrance into the harbor of this historic town. Here was a picture of sublimity and grandeur on a vast scale: in the background a blue sea melted into a blue sky; peaked Moorea Island in the far distance floated on a vast sea of blue; in the foreground a white line chalked the barrier reef; a silvery lagoon and green hills on every side were hemmed in by blue mountains, crags, pinnacles, leaping cascades and graceful palms. The quay was crowded with native boats filled with piles of green and red bananas, yellow mangoes and breadfruit wrapped in green leaves. There were other vessels in the harbor, including a French warship. The town of Papeete, peeping through tall palms and groves of breadfruit trees, sprawled around the bay.

For Stevenson, the adventurer, Tahiti and Papeete had a romantic ring. They recalled the explorations of Cook and Bougainville; the colorful romances of Melville's *Omoo,* Stoddard's *South Sea Idylls,* and Loti's *Marriage.* For several weeks Stevenson lived in a cottage surrounded by flowers and vines, within hearing distance of the eternal surf beating on the coral reef, and in sight of miles of the blue sea. The little dwelling was next to the prison in which Melville had been confined.

Papeete, however, was a disappointment to him. He resented the encroachment of western civilization; a street named *Rue des Beaux-Arts,* giving the sprawling town the title of "Paris of the South Seas." The people, too, disillusioned him. While he admired the size, muscular strength and bodily grace of the men, the undulating movement, the large, liquid, melting eyes of the women, he deplored this half-way house between western civilization and primitive simplicity. The large number of half-castes with their "white-brown or dirty-white" complexion suggested weakness and decay. Even the full-blooded natives, affected by the white man's civilization and religion, had an expression of listlessness and melancholy.

Before the advent of the white man each district matched its beautiful women with those of other districts; they displayed their graceful figures while riding the surf; they sang their old songs and danced their native dances. Their national ballads reflected their achievements in war and peace. Then came the French Government and the missionaries. The newcomers did not appreciate the colored man's civilization; his rights, his views, his customs. They did not realize that what may appear to the white man as savagery and superstition may be closely interwoven with the natives' fundamental reason for existence. Now forbidden to dance their national dances and to sing their old songs, they became bored with life. They were sunk in idleness, with idleness leading to vice. Excessive rum drinking became the main amusement. This promoted the decay of the race and the ruination of the plantations. Even their *himene*, a mixture of old songs and church music, lacked flavor and spontaneity. It was the same story as that of the Marquesas: where there had once been some 60,000, only a few thousands remained by 1890. A Papeetan chief quoted the death sentence upon his people pronounced by one of their own prophets: *e tupu te fau, et toro te farero, e mou te taata.* [The hibiscus shall grow, the coral spread, and man shall cease.]

At Papeete Stevenson began to suffer again from his old affliction, hemorrhages. Believing that this might mean his end, he began calmly to arrange his affairs. He did not seem to fear death when he bade goodbye to the captain and made arrangements about the yacht. When he recovered somewhat, he was rushed back to the *Casco* which left immediately for Taravao, the southern part of the island. Twice on this journey the schooner nearly perished. Once, when suddenly becalmed, the *Casco* began drifting toward the barrier reef of Tahiti; the pilot thought she would surely be wrecked. As a precautionary measure Captain Otis ordered a boat to be cleared. When Fanny heard the order she remarked to Mother Stevenson: "Isn't that nice? We shall soon be ashore!" Commenting on this episode Stevenson exclaimed: "Thus does the female mind unconsciously skirt along the verge of eternity." The second time was when the schooner arrived at the enclosed harbor of Taravao and it had to plunge through a heavy surf into the narrow opening of the reef. For a moment the ship stood on end and then she leaped over and into the smooth water inside. Even Stevenson was not unaffected by this stunt. Turning to the skipper he asked, with a smile on his lips, if Captain Otis did not think such yachting gymnastics were rather risky sport for invalid authors to indulge in!

The climate and the mosquitos at Taravao proved disagreeable and Stevenson was rushed in a wagon hired from a Chinaman to Tautira, some sixteen miles distant over a most difficult road, crossed by a number of streams. The journey turned out to be so trying to the invalid that he was in a state of collapse when he arrived at Tautira, a little paradise village in a charming setting of flowers, ferns, and palms on the wild side of Tahiti.

Crushed by this misfortune Fanny gazed at the village green, trying to collect her thoughts. Suddenly she saw a tall, graceful, noblewoman entering the house of the chief of the village, amidst a great ovation from the crowd. Since her visit had been expected for several days, the villagers had made great preparation for the reception of Princess Moë, ex-queen of Raiatea, daughter-in-law of Queen Pomare and familiar to the readers of Pierre Loti.

When this kindly and charming Tahitian of "mystical type of face with strange eyes half-shut, and an expression of introspection," heard that there was a sick white man in the village, she offered to do what she could for him. While the patient was lying half-dead, with a burning fever and lungs congested, the door opened and there stood Princess Moë with a plate of raw fish prepared with *miti* sauce. Speaking perfect English she said that she had heard there was a sick foreigner in the village who would not eat, so she had prepared the dish herself. Without opening his eyes the sick man turned his head to one side. On the advice of the Princess, Fanny slipped a few morsels of the food into the patient's mouth. The sick man opened his eyes and asked, "What's that?" Several times a day Princess Moë came with her fish plate, which was white meat of mullet cut into tiny pieces and covered with sauce made of milk of coconuts mixed with lime juice, red pepper and a little sea water. She fed him stewed fruit, cooked fowl and salads. Mother Stevenson was convinced that the brown angel had saved her son's life, for within a week Stevenson was able to walk. He took enthusiastically to the native fashion of eating raw fish with sauce.

Perhaps Moë's devotion to the invalid was influenced by her personal unhappiness, brought on by an invalid child and the brutalities of her husband, Tamatoa, eldest son of Queen Pomare. Tamatoa was a colossus in size, a hercules in strength and a heavy drinker. When drunk he cut throats and committed atrocities beyond imagining. Often he had to be kept confined.

The poor princess died in 1891. In a charming poem *To an Island Princess,* Stevenson expressed his gratitude.

I threw one look to either hand,
And knew I was in Fairyland.
And yet one point of being so,

I lacked. For, Lady (as you know),
Whoever by his might of hand
Won entrance into Fairyland,
Found always with admiring eyes
A Fairy princess kind and wise.

It was not long I waited; soon
Upon my threshold, in broad noon,
Fair and helpful, wise and good,
The Fairy Princess Moë stood.

To make things more pleasant for the white patient Princess Moë invited the Stevensons to take over the delightful home of a local sub-chief, Ori-a-Ori. This giant Tahitian, six feet three, broad and strong, looked like a Roman emperor in bronze. To the Stevensons he was "The Colonel," for he looked and acted like an English colonel of the Guards.

Stevenson and Ori soon became warm friends, a friendship that was destined to endure. Since both spoke French they were able to carry on long conversations. The two spent many an evening exchanging tales of adventure. Stevenson told of his Scottish Highland clansmen; Ori, of the legends of his Teva clan and of the South Sea islanders. Although he was a deacon of the church Ori dressed in ancient Tahitian costume and demonstrated the ritual of the old festivals.

To entertain Stevenson and to enable him to collect material for his book, Princess Moë and Ori staged exhibitions of native songs and dances. Sleek, bronzed men and women, decked out gorgeously with flowers, their hair smelling of sandalwood, stood around the magnificent Ori whose head was graced by feathers and neck adorned by a triple collar of sharks-teeth and shells. They sang and clapped their hands to the tomtom. They sang a secular *himene* in a "rattling chorus" that rose above the thunder of the surf on the coral reef. Then the circle broke up into a processional. To the rhythm of the drums they danced the passionate wildly suggestive and traditional *Upa-Upa.* At first the music and the steps were slow; then they gradually swelled to a delirium pace. Every limb and muscle vibrated and pulsated. Strait-laced Mother Stevenson, wife of the late Covenanter

Thomas Stevenson, looked askance at this backsliding of the natives.

Though Stevenson spent some time at Tautira collecting material for his South Sea book and to writing up this material, the most important project before him was the continuation of *The Master of Ballantrae.*

The genesis of this novel went back to his travels over the lonely moors at Perthshire in the Highlands. But it was not until his stay in Saranac, New York, several years later, that he finally plunged into the novel. Let Stevenson tell how he came to write *The Master:* "I was walking one night in the verandah of a small house in which I lived . . . For the making of a story here were fine conditions. I was besides moved with the spirit of emulation, for I had just finished my third or fourth perusal of *The Phantom Ship.* 'Come,' said I to my engine, 'let us make a tale, a story of many years and countries, of the sea and the land, savagery and civilization; a story that shall have the same large features and may be treated in the same summary elliptic method as the book you have been reading and admiring. . . .' There cropped up in my memory a singular case of a buried and resuscitated fakir. . . . I had to create a kind of evil genius to his friends and family, take him through many disappearances, and make this final restoration from the pit of death, in the icy American wilderness, the last and grimmest of the series. . . .

"And while I was groping for the fable and the characters required, behold, I found them lying ready and nine years old in my memory . . . conceived in the Highland rain, in the blend of the smell of heather and bog-plants, and with a mind full of the Athole correspondence and the memories of the Chevalier de Johnstone. So long ago, so far away it was, that I had first evoked the faces and the mutual tragic situation of the men of Durrisdeer."

How Stevenson happened to call the novel *The Master of Ballantrae* is partly explained by Fanny. Louis, she tells, was always fascinated by names which were "peculiarly euphonious" or expressing the atmosphere of a place or person. When he came across one he would make a mental note of it to be used later in his writings. "The mellifluous sound of *The Master of Ballantrae* he felt gave an impression of elegance and smooth duplicity that should suggest the character he meant to depict."

Stevenson felt inspired by his new project. Days and nights, "whether walking abroad or lying wakeful in my bed, were hours of unadulterated joy." To Colvin he wrote: "Have fallen head over heels into a new tale, *The Master of Ballantrae*. No thought have I now apart from it . . . It is to me a most seizing tale; there are some fantastic elements; the most is a dead genuine human problem—human tragedy, I should say rather." He considered it a potential masterpiece.

At Saranac Stevenson worked in a glow of enthusiasm and vivid imagination. His early chapters were powerfully conceived and brilliantly executed. The characters of the old lord, the Master, his brother and the rest were beautifully delineated. Some of the scenes, such as the duel, were graphically described. When he took up the novel at Tautira, he found it dragging. Somehow it was difficult for him to concentrate on it. He then laid it aside to write two South Sea ballads: *The Feast of Famine* and the *Song of Rahero*. These were Marquesan and Tahitian legends. Though the themes were of minor importance they were, nevertheless, well done, if not as poems, at least as narratives.

The two months that Stevenson spent in Tautira he considered among the happiest in his life. Tautira was really a fairyland, "an earthly heaven." There were the great rugged mountains, the valleys with their palms, ferns, the hibiscus hedges of pink, orange and red blossoms intermingled with yellow oleander; the houses seemed as if they were tossed down among the flowers and the clear, fresh, murmuring streams. Here he lived in a "bird-cage" house on friendly terms with the natives. He rode horseback; he played the flageolet; feasted on native food—raw fish, taro, roasted bananas with coconut milk. There were also coffee and wine and other products of civilization. The natives considered him "the rich one," the richest one who had ever visited their village.

Stevenson gloried in their high esteem. In gratitude for all the courtesies shown him he requested the chief to announce in the *farehau*, a large public "bird-cage" where all the Sunday announcements were made, that the "rich-man" would give a feast for all the villagers. The affair was on a grand scale, costing over eighty dollars. Four large, fat hogs were roasted whole in a pit, and four cases of ship's biscuits were brought from the *Casco.* The roasted hogs were placed on their stomachs in green baskets, each with a case of biscuits beside him. Early in the morning the people commenced bathing in preparation for the great occasion. Though the hour for the feast was set at four the guests began arriving at three, some even earlier. Stevenson, dressed in white clothes and shoes, and Mrs. Stevenson in a red and white muslin gown, but barefoot, stood on the verandah to receive the guests. An immense crowd assembled. They came in detachments: first the Protestants, headed by their clergymen; second the chief, council, and the irreligious, headed by one of their council; third the school children with their schoolmaster; then came the Catholics; and finally a small group of Mormons headed by the wittiest speaker of the assembly. Each group arrived carrying bamboo poles laden with fruit, pigs, fowls, etc. Even the children, who marched two abreast, carried bamboo poles and gifts across their shoulders. All were dressed in their gayest *pareus,* some decked with leaves and flowers.

When the offerings had been placed in five heaps and all the people had found their places, Stevenson addressed them in French. He thanked them for the generous gifts. He assured them that of all the countries he had visited he liked Tautira best; that he would always remember them and when in the future he would be sitting over a fire in the midst of snow and frost in his native land, he would look back nostalgically to their lovely village with its delightful climate. After an elderly chief had translated the address to the audience another old man arose and spoke in behalf of the entire village. He thanked Stevenson warmly for the gifts and assured him that his people were pleased to have his whole family with them as long as possible; the longer they stayed the better they would like them.

When the addresses were over the presentation of the gifts commenced. Each of the five detachments had its orator stand, describe the gifts of his group, and express the hope that the host would be good enough to accept them. At the conclusion of each speech the spokesman walked forward and presented one of the smaller of the gifts to Stevenson personally, shook hands with every member of the family and then retired.

Among the gifts were fishhooks carved from mother-of-pearl

shell. The witty and popular Mormon speaker humorously described the hens he presented as being descendants of the "cock that frightened Peter." He handed Stevenson two eggs, saying: "Carry these to Scotland with you, let them hatch into cocks and their song shall remind you of Tautira." The Stevensons thought the whole scene most touching, "like a story out of the Bible." They were so impressed with the beautiful procession of school children that they wept for joy. The Catholic Priest, Father Bruno, assured them that for the next fifty years Tautira would be talking of the great feast given by the "rich one."

At the time of the great feast Stevenson asked Princess Moë whether, in her opinion, Ori would be willing to exchange names with him. The Princess was delighted with the idea; she was confident that Ori would be most happy to accept this honor. The ceremony was properly held, Stevenson was adopted into Ori's clan, the Tevas, and his name now became Terriitera, which was Ori's Christian name. Ori now became Rui, which meant Louis, for there was no sound for "L" or "S" in the Tahitian language. During the ceremony Stevenson blushed "like a school girl." Princess Moë and Fanny also exchanged names, each taking the mother's name of the other.

Stevenson's stay in Tautira was prolonged on account of the timely discovery that the *Casco* was unfit for sailing in dangerous seas. According to one story, this fortunate discovery came in dramatic fashion. In appreciation of the hospitality she had received from the native women, especially the converts of the London Missionary Society, Mother Stevenson entertained a group of the ladies on board the yacht. When the entertainment was over an elderly woman prayed for the safety of the ship and passengers, and that any defects the ship might have should be discovered before she departed from Tahiti. "May God preserve you, and if any danger threatens, may you be warned in time," she prayed. Captain Otis, who overheard the prayer, expressed himself, in sailor-fashion, quite contemptuously about the "praying-psalm-singing natives." He was proud of his yacht and was quite confident that she was absolutely safe. "How can you stand those pious, snivelling natives," he exclaimed. With a sailor's oath he brought his clinched fist down on the mainmast, and to his great horror his fist sank into the wood. He discovered that the masts were actually crumbling of dry-rot. It was a miracle that they had not collapsed in the gales encountered on the journey. Mother Stevenson was convinced that the timely discovery was due to the direct intervention of Providence. She also felt a certain satisfaction at the discomfiture of the profane skipper.

Captain Otis placed the blame for the oversight of the defective masts on his predecessor, for the latter had assured Dr. Merrit that the schooner was in good condition. He also attributed the failure to overhaul the yacht to the hurried departure from San Francisco, necessitated by Stevenson's condition. Realizing that it would be impossible to proceed with the journey to Honolulu, for should the masts go overboard in a stormy sea the schooner might perish, he took the *Casco* to Papeete for refitting.

For five weeks the *Casco* was stranded in Papeete. In the first place, not a piece of proper mast timber could be found. When Captain Otis secured a good topmast from a wrecked French barque he discovered that the only mechanic competent to install the new spar was a stray beachcomber who had once worked as a ship's carpenter. Since time seemed unimportant and money no inducement to the beachcomber, he worked slowly and only if the spirit moved him. When days and weeks passed and no word came from the Captain of the *Casco,* the Stevensons became apprehensive. The schooner must have perished in the stormy sea on the way to Papeete. On account of bad weather and a rough sea communication between Tautira and Papeete was difficult. Every morning everyone, including the natives, scanned the horizon for a sign of the *Casco,* and always the disappointed cry was: *E itaphai!* (no ship!). One afternoon the "shipwrecked mariners" detected a schooner; they felt certain it was the *Casco,* but when morning came there was no sign of the vessel.

With provisions and money running low and the possibility that the *Casco* might have stranded or even perished, gloom reigned in the Stevenson house: Fanny and Princess Moë wept, and even Stevenson looked anxious. Listening to the sad story of the shipwrecked mariners Ori addressed Stevenson thus: "You are my brother: all that I have is yours. I know that your food is done, but I can give you plenty of fish and taro. We like you, and wish to have you here. Stay where you are till the *Casco* comes. Be happy—*et ne pleurez pas.*" Also Madam Ori, who, like a dutiful wife, sat on the floor silently listening to the words of her husband, now spoke, giving a number of reasons why their guests should stay as long as could be managed. Moved by the genuine hospitality of their hosts the Stevensons shook hands with Ori and his wife and thanked them for their kind offer.

Though the weather was still bad Ori and a crew of stout young men went in a whaleboat to Papeete to learn the fate of the *Casco.* Stevenson attempted to dissuade Ori from risking his life on such a dangerous mission, but was unsuccessful. When a week passed and Ori did not return the Stevensons became even more apprehensive. But Ori was enjoying his stay on the *Casco* while in Papeete. He thought the food on the yacht was so good that he had "to eat a great deal." Ah Fu remarked to Captain Otis: "Him must leave dam quick, or else bust um bank!"

Great was the joy when Ori finally returned with a letter from Captain Otis informing Stevenson that the *Casco* would soon return. Ori also brought with him money, provisions, and a basket of champagne from the yacht. Stevenson opened a few bottles and all "suddenly fell to drinking and clinking glasses quite merrily." Ori declared that the champagne was a "drink for chiefs." "I shall drink it continually," he remarked while pouring a fresh glass. "What is the cost of it by the bottle?" he inquired. When Stevenson informed him how expensive it was Ori's eyebrows rose; he set down his full glass, exclaiming: "It is not fit that even kings should drink a wine so expensive!" Nevertheless, when Mother Stevenson announced that it was St. Andrew's Day, the celebration continued.

At last a white speck appeared on the horizon; everyone was certain it was *Pahi.* Some time later the *Casco* cast anchor within the reef. Preparations were completed for the departure. On Christmas day, December 25, 1888 all Tautira assembled on the beach to bid *bon voyage* to their most favored guests. The parting with Ori and his wife was truly touching; they were in tears all day long. When the *Casco* weighed anchor and turned her prow northward the French officials fired a twenty-one-gun salute. The schooner returned thirteen shots and thrice dipped her flag in farewell. All stood on deck frantically waving their handkerchiefs until the people on the beach faded from sight. In less than an hour the peaks of Tahiti were a mere dark patch on a blue sea, and soon they completely vanished in mist and clouds.

On the beach Ori watched the ship as long as he could, until night fell. He believed he could hear Stevenson shouting: "Rui, farewell!" In his letter, written the following day, Ori expressed his great sorrow over the loss of his good friends. "If I had wings," he wrote, "I should fly to the ship to meet you, and to sleep amongst you." He rested badly that night. When morning came he wrote he could hear Stevenson calling: "Rui, here is the hour for *putter* and *tiro*" (cheese and syrup). "Afterwards I looked into your rooms; they did not please me as they used to do. I did not hear your voice crying, 'Hail Rui.' I thought that you had gone, and that you had left me. Rising up I went to the beach to see your ship, and I could not see it. I wept, then, till the night, telling myself continually, Teriitera returns into his own country and leaves his dear Rui in grief, so that I suffer from him and weep for him."

When Stevenson read this touching letter tears came to his eyes. He vowed never again to stay too long in a place. Parting from friends can be real sorrow. He hoped to re-visit Tahiti one day. Not only had Ori refused to forget Stevenson; all Tautira felt the same way. Some thirty-six years later an old native, when questioned about Stevenson, sadly remarked: "We shall never see his like again in Tahiti. He is dead and we are dying. None of the Europeans is as he was, whose body and soul and spirit were white as the moon and pure as the stars."

When the *Casco* departed from Tahiti almost half of her crew was new. Some of the old ones had to be dismissed because they could not resist the temptations of the port. It was a common experience. For that reason most ship captains disliked landing at Papeete. The new members of the crew consisted of a Dutchman, an Englishman, a Tahitian, and a Hawaiian.

In the thirty days that it took to reach Honolulu the only land sighted was an outlying island of the Paumotus. Not even a sail was seen the entire time. "We began to realize how vast and desolate was the ocean. It gives one an idea of the hopelessness of expecting help should anything go wrong," wrote Mother Stevenson.

During the journey the *Casco* experienced calms, squalls and heavy rain. The women fell back into their former routine: knitting and reading Gibbon's *Decline and Fall of the Roman Empire.* To relieve the monotony and tedium Fanny suggested that each member of the party, including the skipper, should in turn write and read on deck, after the dinner hours, a short story of the cruise. Stevenson drew the first chance, Fanny the second, and Captain Otis the last. When the skipper's hour came, he was unfortunately, on the sick-list.

During calms and squalls the *Casco* was able to make only about seventy miles a day. It was also discovered that the liberal consumption of food, and the delay in reaching port was reducing provisions to a dangerously low point. Stevenson remarked: "It seems, then, that we are between the devil and salt-horse, and the deep green sea." The question now was, should sail be reduced, to minimize the danger of accident. This would also mean the reduction of rations. The alternative was to crowd on all sail and risk the rising gale and suffer discomfort, in order to reach Honolulu sooner. Being adventurous, Captain Otis decided to follow the second course, which caused considerable anxiety among the passengers and which he admitted was fraught with some danger.

For days the schooner was running from the gale like a madman. During this period none but the crew dared come on deck, and they were continually soaked and swept by the severe squalls. The passengers were confined to the cabin, passing the time playing cards. Occasionally streams of water would come down into the cabins through the skylight, which of course occasioned screams from the women. Fanny was so seasick that she vowed never again to leave shore.

Stevenson, however, did not seem to mind it. In fact he appeared to enjoy the situation. Entering the captain's cabin and steadying himself against the walls to keep from falling, he said, with a twinkle in his eye, that this was "a new experience and a desirable one, which he would certainly find a place for." Although there is always some danger for a small craft in a stormy sea, Captain Otis knew his ship, and he proved that she was a seaworthy vessel. He doubted whether many small schooners could have kept up with his beloved *Casco.*

The last few days of the journey were most unpleasant. To clear the southern point of the island of Hawaii in safety the *Casco* was forced to lie to in an angry, tempestuous sea. For nearly a week she drifted about the Hawaiian islands. Three times the Stevensons celebrated with a farewell dinner, each meal with "diminishing splendor that finally struck bottom on salt horse." It was a frustrating experience to go to bed in sight of Honolulu with the expectations of fresh food and letters that were awaiting them there; then to rise in the morning and find themselves not nearer, but farther from their point of destination.

When the weather at last changed the yacht took advantage of the rousing trade winds and dashed into the harbor like a steamboat, flashing past the buoys and warships, to the great alarm of the pilot. It was a dramatic moment for Captain Otis and Stevenson when their famed overdue "Silver Ship," flying the Stars and Stripes and the Union Jack, raced triumphantly into the port of Honolulu, to the admiration of the crews and passengers on board the warships, steamers, and freighters. At three p. m. January 24, 1889, the *Casco* cast anchor in the harbor of Honolulu. The first part of Stevenson's Odyssey had come to a dramatic end.

CHAPTER IV

ALOHA

ON THEIR FIRST day in Honolulu the hungry seafarers greatly enjoyed the roast beef dinner at the beautiful Royal Hawaiian Hotel. Everyone was excited; everyone talked. The conversation was interspersed with references to Nukuhiva, Fakarava, Papeete, Tautira, cannibal Moipu, "Colonel" Ori, Princess Moë with her life-saving raw fish salad, and finally the prized leg of Queen Vaekehua. Fanny, with her exquisitely engraved big half-moon Marquesan earrings, looked like a South Sea princess.

With deep regret Stevenson paid off the *Casco* and sent her back to her owner in Oakland, California. During the following years the once glorious yacht had a rather checkered career.

She changed owners and was used at first for seal-hunting. She proved to be a great sealer, one of the best. Her deck was slippery with the blood of her many victims. Her hold became rotten from the constant drip of the countless pelts that she carried. After this sealing adventure, she was temporarily discarded and left to disintegrate on the mud flats of Victoria, B.C.

But she was destined to sail again, this time as a smuggler, an opium runner in the Orient, following which exciting interlude, she had her turn, in 1917, as a dredge and junk carrier between Victoria and Vancouver, B.C. Later, in 1919, she sailed in northern waters where she sank during a storm, forty miles from Nome, Alaska, on bleak King's Island in the Arctic. And there now lies the skeleton of the once-proud, glamorous yacht, the Silver Ship that carried Tusitala to the romantic South Seas.

Although Stevenson's first cruise in the South Seas was expensive, he felt it had paid off handsomely. His health had improved greatly. He no longer was tied to an invalid's couch. He was buoyant; he was alive, and a world of new material was opened up to this ever alert observer. "I never knew the world so amusing," he wrote. He was charmed with the islands he had visited; their scenery, their climate, their songs, and dances. He considered the men handsomest in the Marquesas and the women in Tahiti.

During its five months' stay in Hawaii, the Stevenson family lived on Waikiki Beach, about three miles from Honolulu but connected by telephone with the town shops and only a quarter of a mile from a streetcar. The house, called *Manuia* (welcome), was old and rambling; it was rather a collection of wooden cottages. The main bungalow contained a big sitting-room without walls on two sides, and overrun with flowers and creepers. Fanny enlivened this *lanai* with a collection of mats, flags, pennants from the *Casco*, shells, bracelets, shark's-teeth, necklaces from the South Seas, and arms. The surrounding environment was beautiful. On one side were the bay and the volcano; on the other, the hills.

For his writing-room Stevenson characteristically selected a shanty in the garden, sharing his quarters with spiders, scorpions, and a mouse. At dawn faithful Ah Fu would bring him tea and toast. It was Stevenson's practice to place on the shelf above his head a slice of toast to munch on later, during his work. Once he detected a mouse nibbling his toast. Considering the rodent to be the real inhabitant of the cottage and he merely the intruder, he remembered to place a slice of toast on the shelf every morning for the mouse to nibble. A visitor once found Stevenson lying on his cot, propped up with pillows, playing his flageolet while a mouse sat upon its haunches listening to the music.

In his little workshop at *Manui* Stevenson "toiled like a galley slave," working on *The Wrong Box* and writing and rewriting *The Master of Ballantrae*. The former was Lloyd Osbourne's idea, but Stevenson rewrote it, and it was published in 1889. Though it was not favorably received, Stevenson considered the story, "a real lark," full of exciting intrigue. "If it is not funny," he wrote, "I am sure I do not know what is. I have split over writing it." This was his first attempt at collaboration with Lloyd.

Far more important and more difficult was the continuation of his work on *The Master of Ballantrae*. Since the previous November it was appearing serially in *Scribner's Magazine*, and the editors were rushing him for more "copy." Unlike the beginning, which he wrote with ease and power, he found the going of "the damned ending" laborious, as if inspiration had forsaken him. "This cursed end of *The Master*," he complained, "hangs over me like a gallows . . . I cannot see my way clear." "It contains more human work than anything of mine but *Kidnapped*." "I shall breathe when done."

When he finally finished the novel in May, he felt as though freed from bondage: "I have at length finished *The Master*. It has been a sore cross to me; but now he is buried, his body's under hatches, his soul, if there is any hell to go to, gone to hell; and I forgive him: it is harder to forgive Burlingame for having induced me to begin the publication or myself for suffering the induction." "I am quite a wreck and do not care for literature." He considered this novel, however, as "first chop, sir, first chop," and was pleased to find that most of the reviews were favorable. Even the sales, though not exceedingly large, were encouraging.

It was not, however, all work and no play. At Honolulu Stevenson lived a full life. He, who for years had lived the life of an invalid, "shut in like a weevil in a biscuit," now was running, bathing, and "cutting about the world loose, like a grown-up person."

There was a great deal of social life. His arrival in Honolulu was an event of considerable interest to his large and growing number of readers and admirers. His home was the center of all celebrity chasers and would-be literati, who compared him with England's greatest writers. The host welcomed his visitors with a friendly handshake, a whiskey and soda, and cigarettes. But when a particular woman visitor annoyed him, he did not hesitate to tell her: "Please, madam, go; you bother me and I must write!"

Favorite visitors, especially officers of English and American men-of-war, he would invite to dinner and pleasant conversation. He formed a close acquaintance with the officers of the British *Cormorant,* with whom he frequently dined. Ah Fu, in his white suit and braided queue, waited at table and often would venture to offer unsolicited remarks. One evening at a formal dinner party the subject of conversation was "Bully" Hayes, a notorious South Sea character. Ah Fu overhearing it, shouted, "I know that fellow plenty!" When Stevenson unwittingly remarked: "I am afraid he was a very bad man," the bumptious Chinese blurted out, to the embarrassment of the host, "Him son-of-a-bitch!"

On reception days Stevenson welcomed the townsfolk in gracious fashion as part of what he frequently termed the *comedie humaine.* Among his white guests were some who did not approve of his close association with the dissipated Hawaiian King Kalakaua. They were, however, willing to disregard this indiscretion and attribute it to an artist's eccentricities.

Stevenson was introduced to King Kalakaua by his step-daughter, Isobel Strong, who belonged to the "Royal Club" in Honolulu and who had designed the Royal Order of the Star of Oceania. Isobel, who had come to Honolulu long before the arrival of the Stevenson family, had been introduced to the king and had designed the Hawaiian coat of arms. Kalakaua was so well pleased that he asked her to design a flag for Hawaii. Stevenson and the king immediately formed a strong friendship. The author found the handsome, dusky Kalakaua hospitable, cultured and stimulating. The king was an aristocrat and a believer in the theory of absolutism; he was also a lover of music, literature, and philosophy. He was especially interested in recording Polynesian legends.

Stevenson was impressed not only by the king's gracious manners and his intellectual interests, but also by his ability to remain presentable, and even dignified, after consuming a number of bottles of champagne. "O Charles!" he wrote Baxter, "what a crop for the drink! Why a bottle of fizz is like a glass of sherry to him; he thinks nothing of five or six in an afternoon as a whet for dinner. He carries it, too, like a mountain with a sparrow on its shoulders." One of those present on the *Casco* the afternoon Kalakaua went on a drinking spree, reported that, in addition to five bottles of champagne, His Majesty had taken in his stride also the better part of two bottles of brandy. Then, in the evening, as a dinner guest on board a visiting man-of-war, he embarked on a similar drinking bout. Few were surprised when Kalakaua died in January, 1891, possibly from excessive dissipation.

King Kalakaua, on his part, found in Stevenson a boon companion. The two spent many an evening at the king's bungalow, at the boathouse or on the *lanai* of the Royal Hawaiian Hotel. Often there were stag parties with exhibitions of singing and hula dancing. At a breakfast given by the king in his palace in honor of his friend, His Majesty turned to Mother Stevenson and asked her how she liked the music of the royal Hawaiian band. The good lady replied that it was nice and "didn't disturb her in the least."

At his *luau* where the king staged a feast honoring Stevenson, the guests sat on the floor around a large mat decorated with the fragrant foliage of wild ginger and fronds of the mountain fern. The aroma of the chickens, baked dogs cooked underground and perfumed with tropical plants, blended nicely with the soft Hawaiian music and hula dances by maidens in grass skirts waving feathered staves—*Kahilis*. For the benefit of his distinguished guests the king revived an ancient but repugnant court custom that had long been abandoned, when an aged member of the royal household was ordered to crawl on all fours towards His Majesty.

After the king's toasts had been acknowledged, Fanny presented Kalakaua with a beautiful golden pearl. Stevenson then read a poem:

> The Silver Ship, my King—that was her name
> In the bright islands whence your fathers came—
> The Silver Ship, at rest from winds and tides,
> Below your palace in your harbor rides:
> And the seafarers, sitting safe on shore,
> Like eager merchants count their treasures o'er.
> One gift they find, one strange and lovely thing,
> Now doubly precious since it pleased a king.

When Professor Scott of Tokyo University, then visiting Honolulu, called Stevenson's attention to the marked similarity of the above lines to Caedmon's Anglo-Saxon poetry, the latter leaned forward in surprise, then blurted out: "Why man, I never read a single line of Anglo-Saxon poetry in my life!"

King Kalakaua found in Stevenson not only an interested student of Hawaiian music and legends, but also a champion of the cause of the Polynesian race. Kalakaua told how, in response to the appeals of the Samoan king, Malietoa, the Hawaiian government dispatched a mission to Samoa to help prevent German encroachment on that country. The objective of this mission was to assist Samoa in organizing a stable government, patterned on that of such Christian and civilized countries as Hawaii, and to form a confederation among the Polynesian islands whose people were closely related by blood, by language, by historic traditions. The Samoan government, according to Kalakaua, received the Hawaiian embassy with open arms. But the German and American governments, fearing that the plan represented an expansionist policy on the part of Hawaii, in an area on which they themselves cast longing glances and toward which they harbored annexationist designs, forced the recall of the mission in disgrace. The United States government feared that expansionist designs by Hawaii would entangle the northern Pacific "pearl" in difficulties with Germany and England.

Kalakaua's story fired Stevenson's imagination. Being romantic, chivalrous and a sincere lover of fair play, he considered it his mission to champion the cause of the Polynesians, "God's best and sweetest," against the encroachment of white traders and diplomats, especially the Germans.

To rouse the conscience of the world against the injustices done to Samoans, he wrote the London *Times* a militant letter condemning the high-handed, outrageous conduct of the Germans who deposed and deported the native king, installed their puppet ruler, insulted British and American citizens, burned the American flag and shelled native villages. He deplored the weakness of the Anglo-American attitude and the aggressive, brazen policy of the Germans. "I have had through my hands," he wrote, "a file of consular proclamations, the most singular reading—a state of war declared, all other authority but that of the German representative suspended, punishment (and the punishment of death in particular) liberally threatened. It is enough to make a man rub his eyes when he reads Colonel de Coetlogon's protest and the highhanded rejoinder posted alongside of it the next day by Dr. Knappe. Who is Dr. Knappe, thus to make peace and war, deal in life and death, and close with a buffet the mouth of the English consuls? By what process known to diplomacy has he risen from his one-sixth part of municipal authority to be the Bismarck of a Polynesian island? And what spell has been cast on the cabinets of Washington and St. James's that Mr. Blacklock should have been so long left unsupported, and that Colonel de Coetlogon must bow his head under a public buffet? . . . Is it what the English people understand by the sovereignty of the seas?"

He felt that the poor natives were the only ones who came out with honor. "Violence has not been found to succeed with the Samoans; with the two Anglo-Saxon Powers it has been found to work like a charm," he concluded. He often wondered whether it was wise for him to meddle in political matters. He felt, however, that it was his duty to champion the cause of the underdog.

King Kalakaua even hoped to enlist Stevenson's sympathy and support for the Hawaiian royalist side against the aggressive elements of discontent, particularly the American. He boasted that the famous author had promised to publish a pamphlet against the "reform" party in Hawaii. There is some evidence that Stevenson did become a sympathiser of the royalist cause in Hawaii. To his friend, W. H. Low, he wrote from Honolulu: "If you want to cease to be a republican, see my little Kaiulani . . . You will die a red: I wear the colours of that little royal maiden . . . But, O Low, I love the Polynesian."

In the above letter he had reference to the sixteen-year-old Princess Kaiulani, daughter of a fellow Edinburgh Scot, A. S. Cleghorn, and the youngest sister of King Kalakaua. This young lady, heir presumptive to the Hawaiian throne, charmed Stevenson with her beauty and grace. He had such an affectionate regard for her that many an afternoon he would drive up to her father's secluded old mansion where the princess always eagerly hastened to welcome her friend. Together they would walk, sit under the great banyan tree and talk. She was fascinated with Stevenson's tales of adventure and plied him with questions about Scotland. Stevenson protested when he heard that she was to be sent to Edinburgh to study. He feared the harsh effects of the cold and rigorous climate upon this delicate girl. But it was too late; the plans had been made. Before her departure he wrote in her red plush album:

> Forth from her land to mine she goes,
> The island maid, the island rose,
> Light of heart and bright of face:
> The daughter of a double race . . .
> Her islands here, in Southern sun,
> Shall mourn their Kaiulani gone,
> And I, in her dear banyan shade,
> Look vainly for my little maid.
> But our Scots islands far away
> Shall glitter with unwonted day,
> And cast for once their tempests by
> To smile in Kaiulani's eye.

Sitting in the shady *lanais* Stevenson and Cleghorn spent many an hour discussing Hawaiian politics. When Stevenson visited Hawaii again in 1893, after the fall of the monarchy and the establishment of the republic, he was still a royalist and greatly regretted the shape of events.

"Stay and make your home with us, Hawaii needs you," Kalakaua begged Stevenson. Other friends urged him to make Honolulu his permanent home. Though he genuinely enjoyed the convivial gatherings, Stevenson maintained that neither the climate nor the civilization of Honolulu appealed to him. In fact, he was cruel enough to write: "In vile Honolulu, there are too many cesspools and beastly *haoles*." Nor had his health improved sufficiently for him to risk returning to the cold climate of his native land, even though he no longer suffered from coughs or hemorrhages.

To him the ideal place was a Polynesian village where one could "drink that warm light *vin du pays* of human affection and enjoy that simple dignity of all about you." The cruise of the *Casco* whetted his interest in the South Seas, and intensified his love for the islands and natives. He was willing to admit that sea traveling among strange islands had its perils; in fact it was the highest form of gamble, but it was worth while risking the chance when one considered the thrills of approaching a new island with its strange inhabitants. He even dreamed of discovering an island or two.

Fanny agreed that it would be unwise to return to England before Louis' health was "firmly reëstablished." Moreover, it would be a pity not to avail themselves of the opportunity to visit other interesting Pacific islands. She was aware of the difficulties—of meeting hostile natives, and of the inconveniences of traveling over that "horrible sea." She loved, however, tropical weather and welcomed the sight of new and strange peoples. But even more, she loved to see her "boys" happy. In case of danger she could shoot accurately. "By jingo if I must, I can," she boasted, though she really did not believe that there would be any occasion that called for shooting.

The plan was to visit the Marshalls, the Carolines, Fijis, Tonga, Samoa, Tahiti, the Marquesas, then to return to England. Their final home was to be the Madeira islands which were nearer Britain, yet blessed with a healthful climate and attractive scenery. Mother Stevenson was to return to England, for she could not endure the hardships encountered in wild Pacific islands.

The problem was to find means of transportation. There seemed to be only one vessel available, the *Morning Star*, an American missionary ship which was to sail for its annual inspection tour around the stations in the western Pacific on some of the most remote islands. Stevenson was not too pleased with the idea of having to spend four months in close contact with bible-reading, strait-laced Protestant missionaries who would frown on smoking, drinking, and the occasional use of profane language. There was even the possibility that the missionary society might refuse to welcome such an unconventional party as the Stevenson family. Nevertheless he did apply for passage and even resorted to wirepulling. He was accepted on conditions.

Fortunately for all concerned, Stevenson soon discovered a ship more suitable for his purpose. In a "tin" office in Honolulu he was able to charter a trading schooner, the *Equator*, for a four month's voyage. According to the terms, Stevenson was to pay down a lump sum for the four month's cruise, with the privilege of extending the time. For an additional payment the schooner was to stop, at his request, at any of the islands in the line of the trading cruise. So delighted was he with his find that he shouted excitedly, even before he jumped off his panting horse, when he arrived at his home in Waikiki: "Have chartered a schooner! Have arranged the details and signed the charter—party as she was casting off—tug tooting, and people pulling at the owner's coat tails, and the sweat running off our faces in a tin office! The *Equator*, sixty-eight tons, and due back from San Francisco in a month to pick us up for the Gilbert Islands. Finest little craft you ever saw in your life, and I have the right to take her anywhere at so much a day!"

The good news threw the family into jubilation. At luncheon, with foaming bumpers of champagne, they toasted the *Equator*. Everybody talked; each was happy that he would not have to be confined on the straight-laced *Morning Star*. "And we can smoke on that blessed ship!" shouted Stevenson with his glass uplifted. "And drink! Hurrah for the *Equator!*" joined in Lloyd. "And swear!" added Fanny. Soon all were startled when Ah Fu yelled, pointing to the seaward side where the *Equator* with her full spread of canvas was dipping her ensign in farewell as she sailed gracefully out of the harbor on her way to San Francisco. All exclaimed in unison: "*Our* ship!"

While waiting for the return of the *Equator* Stevenson spent a week in the leper colony on the island of Molokai. Here he played croquet with seven leper girls and yarned with leper beachcombers. While he refused to wear gloves, fearing that it might make the unfortunates conscious of their tragic condition, the deformities of the patients and the other abhorrent spectacles he was witnessing sickened him. To one newly landed Sister who was crying, he said: "Ladies, God Himself is here to give you welcome. I'm sure it is good for me to be beside you; I hope it will be blessed to me; I thank you for myself and the good you do me." The courage and cheerfulness and devotion of the priests and Sisters inspired him greatly and intensified his respect for these angels of mercy. Later, as we shall see, he penned a flaming open letter defending Father Damien against charges brought against him by a less godly Protestant missionary, Doctor Hyde.

When the *Equator* finally returned from San Francisco, June 20, the Stevensons began their feverish preparations. Ah Fu was busy stowing away barrels of sour kraut, salt onions, delicacies, an assortment of wines and liquors, tobacco, fish heads, strings of beads, wreaths of artificial flowers, and red calicoes for trading purposes. They also supplied themselves with photographic equipment and a hand organ. They loaded the schooner with packages of garden seeds, chests of carpenter's tools—anything that might be useful in event of shipwreck. Fanny had a sneaking suspicion that Stevenson would be disappointed if he were not shipwrecked and cast ashore on an island. She sincerely believed that Ah Fu would prefer to rely upon his own hands and ingenuity, for he could make fire by rubbing two sticks together, catch fish without a line, bring down birds with a mere stone, climb a tall coconut tree, and use a stone for a knife or hatchet. In fact Stevenson felt that Ah Fu was civilized only as much as they liked to have him and savage only as far as was useful.

This was to be Ah Fu's last cruise with the Stevensons, for he had fallen heir to rice lands, houses and bullocks in his native land, and his relatives were urging him to return. Ah Fu was sad, for he had forgotten his native tongue; he considered himself a Marquesan rather than a Chinese. He feared that his mother would not receive him well. However he was eager to visit China and "lick um my bludder," who was cheating the family. He finally decided to continue with this cruise, then go to China, make the necessary arrangements, and return to the Stevensons to attach himself to them for the remainder of his life.

Before departing on the *Equator* Stevenson shared with his friends his eager anticipation of the second cruise in the Gilbert Islands. "It is a singular thing," he wrote Colvin, "that as I was packing up old papers ere I left Skerryvore, I came on the prophecies of a drunken Highland sibyl, when I was seventeen. She said I was to be very happy, to visit America, and *to be much upon the sea.* It seems as if it were coming true with a vengeance. Also, do you remember my strong, old, rooted belief that I shall die by drowning? I don't want that to come true, though it is an easy death."

He warned his friends he might be shipwrecked cruising in the ill-charted seas of the Gilbert Islands and be forced to linger on some lonely island for years. But not until the lapse of considerable time should the party be given up as having "gone to Davie Jones in a squall, or graced the feast of some barbarian in the character of Long Pig."

On June 24, exactly six months after their arrival in Honolulu, the seafarers were again ready for an extensive cruise on the vast Pacific. Everything was in a hustle on the *Equator*. Ah Fu kept stowing away more baggage. Stevenson entertained friends from Honolulu who had dined and wined him. When the mainsail had been set and the host of visitors had gone ashore, there was a stir on the wharf: two carriages had driven up the pier at full speed bringing King Kalakaua and a part of his royal Hawaiian band. While the king drank several healths to his departing friends, the band struck up with *Aloha Oe*.

In the afternoon the lines were cast off and the *Equator* began to slip carefully out of her berth. Wreathed in Hawaiian *leis* the Stevensons stood on deck smiling and waving to the cheering crowd at the dock and on the surrounding warships. Without the services of a tug the tiny, trim-looking schooner picked her way through the many vessels anchored in the harbor, and turned her nose southwest, toward Micronesia. In the distance the *Equator* looked like a toy sailboat. In the setting sun the peaks of Oahu began to fade and finally vanish in the endless expanse of the sea. When evening came, the tiny schooner, a mere speck, glided gracefully over the silver-tipped waves, out of contact with civilization. Among the gifts on board was a model schooner whose silken sails bore the heartening legend: "May the winds and waves be favorable!"

CHAPTER V

ON THE EQUATOR

THE *EQUATOR* DEMONSTRATED her sailing qualities with flying colors the first day of her departure. By nightfall she overtook a small vessel also bound for the Gilberts which had left Honolulu earlier in the morning. When the crew of the ketch recognized the schooner, they waved *bon voyage*. The skipper toasted Fanny Stevenson in a glass of wine, which courtesy she and the other members of the family graciously acknowledged. As the craft pulled ahead the crew of the ketch called back that they would report her in the Gilberts.

The *Equator* rested low in the water. This gave Fanny an uncomfortable sensation, though at the same time it made her feel more intimately in touch with the sea, an emotion which passengers on large vessels do not experience.

The accommodations on the ship were entirely inadequate for the twenty persons on board. They had to dine in relays; and the sleeping quarters were even less satisfactory. Some slept on the counter and some on the floor where giant cockroaches gnawed at their nails and noses and tugged at their eyebrows. Sleep was made even more unpleasant when the vessel was loaded with green copra which filled the air with an acid odor and enveloping steam. The crew was cosmopolitan: Hawaiians, Prussians, Norwegians, and Scotsmen. Captain Denis Reid, a small, youthful, fiery, vain Ulster-Scot, had been a deep-water sailor from boyhood. He was extremely efficient and knew how to handle his ship and crew. He was also popular with island traders, for he had been in the trading service in the western Pacific for a number of years. When gay he loved to sing, especially *In the Gloaming* and *Annie Laurie.*

The youthful skipper was eccentric and ever eager for adventure. The crew and passengers, however, did not always appreciate his amusing antics. Fanny, once hearing a splash in the water, saw to her great amazement the skipper swimming, protected by a circle of the crew, to drive away lurking sharks. When she later remonstrated with him for his selfishness in endangering the lives of his men, he protested: "No, for if the captain should be lost think how much worse it would be for all on board than if it were a mere sailor!"

Anderson, the mate, a quiet man with a cleft palate, known as Sou'wegian, came from a family of sailors. He was older than the skipper and knew more about sailing, but he had never learned navigation. Affected by the literary atmosphere of the Stevenson party Captain Reid once announced that he too was writing a novel. Evening after evening he would read part of his writing and felt delighted when it was praised, and, when it was laughed at, he laughed with the others. There was also Murray Macallum, son of a Kirk minister who later wrote a book on the cruise of the *Equator.* The youngest member of the crew was the Hawaiian cabin boy, George Muggery Bowyer, "whose jacket shrunk almost to his nipples, his little breeches (once they were trousers) leaving bare his knees below and a part of his hips above." Every evening before bedtime he would be asked to sing *Shoo, Fly, Don't Bother Me,* be given a dose of a patent medicine, Kennedy's White Discovery, and, in solemn pretense, a spanking over the skipper's knee. Often all members of the crew would line up for their dose of Kennedy's Discovery or Mother Siegel's Syrup and each one had to answer a question from the skipper to prove that he had swallowed his medicine. Captain Reid was instructed by the owner of the *Equator* to make the cruise as pleasant as possible for the Stevenson party. The skipper responded most generously to his brother Scot.

Once back on the sea Stevenson's adventurous spirit lifted and he recovered his health. "I cannot say why I like the sea," he wrote. "No man is more cynically and constantly alive to its perils; I regard it as the highest form of gambling; and yet I love the sea as much as I hate gambling. Fine clean emotions; a world all and always beautiful; air better than wine; interest unflagging; there is upon the whole no better life. I think that it is only there that a Briton lives: my poor grandfather, it is from him I inherit the taste, I fancy, and he was round many islands in his day; but I, please God, shall beat him at that before the recall is sounded." He advised his friends "not to be in a hurry to think us dead, but rather to believe in our continued existence, as flesh and blood obscurely tossed in the Pacific, or walking coral shores."

It is understandable that eccentrics and adventurers such as Stevenson and Captain Reid would grow to enjoy each other's jolly company and yarns. Frequently their imagination toyed with the golden age of piracy and smuggling in the Pacific. It was during one of these glorious evenings that the idea struck them of establishing a South Sea trading company with dual headquarters: one on an island, the other on a schooner larger than the *Equator*. Since Stevenson had contemplated making his home in the South Seas, he planned that the vessel be half trader, half yacht. Captain Reid, in whom Stevenson had absolute confidence, was to command it.

In both Stevenson and Reid, familiar with the exploits of Elizabethan buccaneering, enthusiasm ran high for this project which was to bring them adventure and fortune. Even Fanny and Lloyd were intrigued by the scheme. They spent many an hour talking and planning. The enterprise called for a topmast schooner of about ninety tons, costing about $15,000. All details were complete, even to the library, rifle racks, patent davits and steam launch. Everybody on the *Equator* was encouraged to think of a suitable name for the trading vessel and for the company. When Murray Macallum suggested "Jekyll-Hyde and Company," he was applauded. Stevenson drank a toast to his loyalty. The name finally adopted was *The Northern Light,* a name with a British tang and a pleasant musical sound.

To his friend Colvin Stevenson confided in August, 1889: "Would you be surprised to learn that I contemplate becoming a shipowner? I do, but it is a secret. Life is far better fun than people dream who fall asleep among the chimney stacks and telegraph wires."

Nothing, however, came out of the elaborate design which seemed to promise high adventure and a full purse. During the cruise and the weeks of trading in the Pacific Stevenson had opportunity to reflect on the seamy side of the business: "the tricks, the false scales, the bamboozling and chicanery that were customary in dealing with the natives, who themselves were irritatingly dishonest." "Thus," wrote Lloyd, "our trim and rakish trading schooner, *The Northern Light,* melted away into a dream of the might-have-been; and with it her romantic headquarters—that 'island of our own'—with all the unforeseen inconveniences."

Yes, the carefully worked out plan of the trading schooner failed to shape into the business venture that Stevenson had hoped, but it, no doubt, played its part in a literary venture that was to add to the writer's growing fame and fortune.

Furthermore, shortly before the *Equator* departed from Honolulu there was excitement over the landing of a number of castaways picked up on Midway Island by a passing ship. The captain of the wrecked barge, the *Wandering Minstrel,* reported that he had left Hong Kong for the purpose of catching sharks for liver oil. But there were too many discrepancies and omissions in the captain's story. One suspected that catching sharks was not his sole objective. The wages of the crew exceeded the prevailing rates. The captain of the rescuing ship demanded and was paid several thousand dollars for his service.

The mystery of the *Wandering Minstrel* lurked in Stevenson's mind when he left Honolulu. During the cruise he and Lloyd frequently talked of the wrecked ship. As they sat on deck one moonlit night, near the Johnstone islands, the idea of collaborating on a novel occurred to them. Why not draw on the episode of the *Wandering Minstrel?* Till late in the night, fanned by the fresh trade wind, they sat hatching the plot of *The Wrecker.* "What a tangle it would make," suggested one, "if the wrong crew were aboard. But how to get the wrong crew there?" "I have it!" shouted the other; "the so-and-so affair!" Stevenson remembered how months ago and not far from the place where they had been cruising, English castaways had been asked to pay for their rescue by another British captain. Before Stevenson and Lloyd had retired that night, the scaffolding of *The Wrecker* had been erected. To make possible the publication of the novel in serial form, Stevenson decided to make Samoa his temporary home, for it provided satisfactory service of mail steamers.

The journey from Honolulu to the Gilberts was ideal and most pleasant. The passengers and crew celebrated the Fourth of July with generous servings of excellent wine from Stevenson's stock. They spent their evenings in song and story, for sea-dogs love to tell tales of ships wrecked on the coral beaches. Then came days when the sea was becalmed, and the *Equator* barely moved. There was not a speck on the entire horizon. The skipper paced the afterdeck nervously; the others lolled about vainly searching for a cool spot.

At four o'clock, July 12, a lookout from the mainsail detected a waving line along a glistening white beach. At dawn the island, though only about fifteen feet above the sea level, was clearly visible from deck. It was much wider than the atoll of Fakarava. The *Equator* anchored about a mile from the shore of Butaritari, the main town of Great Makin island, and was surrounded immediately by canoes carrying practically nude natives. In the olden days the women of the island wore no clothing at all until their marriage, and widows carried their dead husbands' skulls about with them.

The *Equator* reached Butaritari at an inopportune time: the natives, from the king down, were intoxicated. The island, which was under the influence of American missionaries and traders, had begun celebrating the Fourth of July on the Day of Independence and continued until the fourteenth. The white storekeepers were eager to sell all their liquor supplies, and the king, together with his subjects, was not averse to enjoying the ordinarily tabooed alcoholic spirits.

Disregarding any possible danger, Stevenson went ashore and

took up residence with a hospitable Hawaiian missionary. Before the *Equator* departed for other trading posts Captain Reid warned Stevenson against "taking sauce from d— niggers." The first evening Stevenson dodged two stones hurled at him as he sat on the verandah. For a while the situation looked quite serious. Then Stevenson went to the white storekeepers and urged them strongly to cease selling liquor to the natives. To this they finally agreed. Furthermore the king was informed that Stevenson was a personal friend of Queen Victoria and that, should he be molested, he would report to his queen who would send a warship to make reprisals. The threat worked; the king was much affected by it. He apologized; he had suspected that the newcomer was a man of importance, a friend of Queen Victoria. In fact some even whispered that he was a son of the Queen of England. Immediately the taboo on liquor was reimposed. The great personages were to be considered absolutely inviolable.

The remainder of their stay at Butaritari the Stevensons spent in comparative tranquility. They witnessed native dances and in turn entertained their hosts with exhibitions of their magic lantern pictures. When they visited the "palace," which resembled a movie lot, they found King Tebureimoa dressed in striped pyjamas and the queen in a purple *holoku*. The king carried a satchel in which he stored his pistols. When he was teased about having only one wife —monogamy had been imposed by the missionaries—while his rival, King Tembinoka of Apemama, enjoyed a whole harem, he felt envious of his bitter enemy. Patting his fat belly he exclaimed: "Me, I got power, me plenty. Tembinoka, I think I like fight him!"

After spending a month at Butaritari, the Stevensons were picked up by the *Equator*. Sunday, September 1, the schooner entered the lagoon of the atoll of Apemama, in the Gilberts, which was ruled with an iron hand by the despot Tembinoka, notorious in South Sea songs and gossip. He was a man about forty-five, of medium height, flabby and double chinned. His hooked, parrot-like nose; his mane of black, shaggy hair; his inquiring, haughty, arrogant eyes; the half sneer on his lips; his powerful, shrill, sea-bird-like voice, made him impressive and forbidding. His dress, too, was rather bizarre. Often he wore a woman's frock, a naval uniform, or a masquerade costume. His fat legs were covered by a pair of colorful trousers and his flabby body was draped in a coat of green or cardinal silk.

Tembinoka was unique in many ways. He was a great fighter who figured in the patriotic war songs of the Gilberts as the Napoleon of the group. Once when he attempted to seize some of the neighboring islands a British warship forced him to disgorge his prey and sank his "navy." Nevertheless fear and suspicion of his designs still prevailed among his neighbors. To all other Gilbert islands the white man could come, and there live, trade, and sell liquor. No tourists, no missionaries, no traders were allowed to enter Apemama without the consent of its despotic ruler. Though conservative and suspicious, Tembinoka was not averse to absorbing new ideas—of the practical kind, that is. When missionaries first came he welcomed them, attended their services and learned to read, write, and cipher, and to speak his unique English. He soon became suspicious of the sermons, however. "Here, in my island, I 'peak. My chieps no 'peak—do what I talk," he boasted. When he saw that the missionary "Kanaka 'peak in a big houtch" (house), and, what was worse, was encroaching on the king's copra monopoly, he unceremoniously deported him. This was the abrupt ending to the evangelist's attempt in Apemama.

Tembinoka had an absolute monopoly on the entire copra trade of his triple kingdom: Apemama, Aranuka and Kuria. Hence trading vessels arriving in Apemama would make strong efforts to cater to the autocrat. The skippers would greet him with broad smiles; the cooks would flatter his palate with dainties. When satisfied with the treatment he had received from the visiting traders, he would spend days on board the ship, part of the time in the cabin, consuming the strange food, and the rest of the time in the trade-room, shopping. During all this time his obsequious female bodyguards squatted by the door and down below in his boat. Often these women would be allowed to come on board to exchange their share of copra for hats, ribbons, dresses, scents, tins of salmon and, above all, tobacco, which was the island currency. "You got copra, King?" the trader would inquire. "I got two, three outches," His Majesty would reply.

In return for the copra he would choose all kinds of strange foreign products. His houses were stocked with clocks, musical boxes, blue spectacles, umbrellas, knitted waistcoats, tools, rifles, bolts of stuff, medicines, sewing machines, and European foods. Tembinoka was always ready to pay any price for anything which caught his fancy. Of course the traders knew his weaknesses and took advantage of him. Once he spotted scented soap in a trader's cabin. He pointed to the soap, asking: "How much you want? How much you got? I take him all." He thus acquired seventeen boxes of soap at two dollars a cake. Little wonder he classified skippers and supercargoes in three groups: first, "He cheat a litty;" second, "He cheat plenty;" third, "I think he cheat too much."

In order to impress Tembinoka the crew gave the *Equator* a good cleaning. The decks were scoured and, inside, the rooms were put into "apple-pie order." Fanny had not believed that the schooner "could be brought to such a pitch of cleanliness."

No sooner had the vessel anchored in the lagoon of Apemama than the king's barge approached. He sat in the stern surrounded by his favorite wives. One held a green umbrella over his head; another about fifteen years old, half lying in his lap, fanned his fat face. She wore a loose dress of light flowered material and a wreath of brigh red flowers on her head.

The king boarded the craft by using his own steps which had been made fast to its side. The Stevensons were eager to land and spend several months in Apemama, in order to study at first hand the amaz ing character of Tembinoka and his people. But in order to appea dignified and to impress the despot, they decided to remain in the cabin and to exhibit no undue curiosity. Their first impression of the king when he boarded the *Equator* was somewhat alarming. They feared he might refuse them permission to land.

His Majesty spent many hours on board the *Equator,* relishing the dinners, suppers and many drinks. He enjoyed, especially, flapjacks, of which he ate a large number. "I likum," he commented. He also spent considerable time in the trade-room where he purchased a thousand dollars' "worth" of goods. Captain Reid tactfully presented to His Majesty the wishes of the Stevensons to reside in Apemam for several months. He dwelt on Stevenson's virtues as "one of the old men of England," a man of great learning who wished to study His Majesty's kingdom and report to his Queen Victoria. The king, however, did not seem to be impressed. In fact he pretended that he di not hear or understand. He held his guests in suspense for twenty-four hours.

Actually Tembinoka was carefully observing his visitors as if he were studying characters for a portrait sketch. His objections to whites were based on the following counts: cheating; meddling with the copra trade; "peaking," and political intrigue. Finally Tembinoka turned to Stevenson: "I look your eye, you good man, you no lie . . . Tuppoti I see man. I no tavvy good man, bad man. I look eye, look mouth. Then I tavvy." The Stevensons were elated with the verdict: they could land and stay at Apemama as His Majesty's guests as long as they wished.

It was agreed that the king's men were to build a "town" for the Stevensons; he was to lend them his cook and supplies whenever needed. For this he was to be repaid upon the return of the *Equator*. Furthermore, the king was to be free to come and partake of meals with the Stevensons, or a dish was to be sent to him. The "Equator town" was to be declared taboo by the king, and no natives were to approach it.

Early the following morning Lloyd and the captain, who spent the night in the king's palace, were alarmed when Tembinoka, who always carried a pistol, fired a few shots into the village. He explained to his guests that this was to remind his lazy people to get to work. He was an excellent shot; nevertheless "accidents" were possible. At any rate this unusual method of "speeding" his subjects was effective, for immediately they set to work putting up the promised houses. The king sat on a mat directing the construction, and whenever a native passed His Majesty he had to crouch and crawl. He asked Fanny to sit near him and to give him a cigarette, for he was extremely fond of smoking.

From the very first the Stevensons found Tembinoka "the most magnificently royal personage they had ever met, a gentleman by nature and a king every inch of him," in fact, the unique character in the South Seas. His "palace" was guarded day and night by old women. In the daytime they were engaged in household occupations; at night they lay hidden or crouched along the palisade. All arms were under lock and key. The king also had a number of spies who would report to him every morning.

His relations with his thirty wives, the best looking women in the kingdom, were platonic. Thus lived Tembinoka, the absolute dictator amidst a bevy of women of varying ages and ranks, seldom using harsh words or expressing displeasure. Once, however, he shot one of his wives on board a schooner, for misconduct; another one he slew for a more serious offense and exposed her body in an open boat until it became putrified. "My chieps no 'peak, do what I talk.—I kill plenty men," he told Fanny. "Him 'fraid now. I no kill any more." He boasted his father had a head house where he displayed the heads of his enemies.

Although Stevenson was troubled by this despotic rule and absence of all liberty, he found, nevertheless, much to admire, and appreciated the beneficence of that stern rule. Together with al the traders visiting Apemama, he noticed the absence of violence theft, and drunkenness. The men of Apemama were noted for their politeness and gracious and courtly, though somewhat effeminate manners. Often there was gaiety in the palace. One evening Stevenson heard dancing, clapping, stamping and singing, which sounded as savage as the howling of a pack of dogs. Frequently Stevenson would find His Majesty in his palace lying on his belly, writing the history of his reign or songs to be put to music and sung in chorus When he was asked what his songs dealt with he replied: "Sweethearts and trees and the sea. Not all the same true, all the same lie." He related many tales connected with the history of Apemama for Stevenson to use in his book.

Quite often Tembinoka would arrive before meal time, take a chair, talk and dine with the Stevensons as though he were an old family friend. He was careful, however, not to drink or stay too long When ready to leave he would simply rise and in an appealing tone say: "I want to go home now." Eager to copy white man's etiquette he was careful to use his knife and fork at dinner. He also begged Stevenson to correct his English, though he was assured that his speech was beyond correction. Truly, said Stevenson, his language was ample and without many profane or gross expressions. Tembinoka was also interested in government, medicine, law, polic and a variety of other subjects. When told about Captain Cook, h ran to the Gilbert New Testament to read up on that famous navi gator. Once he took a fancy to Fanny's old dressing bag, and begged her to sell it to him. When he was assured that it was not for sale he offered twenty pounds. Stevenson then agreed to give it to him. Realizing that his persistence was not in accordance with white man's etiquette, he lowered his head and cried: "I 'shamed!"

When a rumor reached Tembinoka that his enemy, King Tebureimoa of Butaritari, had declared war on him, he was overjoyed; at last he had his opportunity to fight, an adventure that greatly appealed to him. It would be a fight sanctioned by the British who had forbidden him to engage in aggressive war. He held council meetings with his chiefs; his soldiers drilled with arms; plans of strategy were devised. The rumor, however, proved to be a false alarm. King Tebureimoa had a greater appetite for fishing and drinking than for war. Besides, he was in great fear of insurrection at home and had no stomach for trouble outside his kingdom. Needless to say Tembinoka was a disappointed man. His favorite expression was always: "I got power!"

Stevenson passed the time pleasantly at Apemama writing *The Wrecker,* playing on the flageolet, and studying the natives. He and his family suffered, however, from heat, flies, mosquitos, and the monotonous diet. "The excitement of wondering what was under the covers of the dishes was only exceeded by the disappointment in tasting it." "I think I could shed tears over a dish of turnips," he lamented. To offset the growing monotony of their diet Fanny attempted to plant onions and radishes and Ah Fu shot a number of wild chickens which, perhaps because of their rations of slimy slugs, were rather tasteless. More palatable were the turtles which Tembinoka's fishermen caught and Ah Fu turned into steak and soup. Ah Fu was the boy in the kitchen. His limited supplies only challenged his skill and ingenuity. Once he became ill but told no one. When Stevenson spoke to him somewhat sharply he cried: "Yes, Mr. Stevenson, I heard you. I very sick: more better you get a knife and come kill me now. I no can work." He offered Stevenson a large knife and bared his throat for the kill. He then retired to the kitchen and wept bitterly. In gratitude for Fanny's nursing he offered to shoot several men who disturbed her with Christmas carols, or break into a trader's house to steal some goods for her.

The *Equator* was long overdue. She was to have been gone for several weeks, but when she was absent over a month the anxiety of the Stevensons mounted. The supply of salt beef was exhausted and they were sick and tired of the wild chickens shot and grilled by Ah Fu. Often Ah Fu would announce: "I think welly soon be all finish," his way of saying they were scraping the bottom of the barrel. When Stevenson explained his embarrassing situation to the king and asked him whether he would be willing to spare some of the necessary food, Tembinoka smiled: he felt flattered. Graciously he opened his ample storehouse. There were large supplies of pork beer, flour, rice, sugar, coffee, tea and other staple commodities.

One day the king's messenger excitedly brought the news that a vessel was coming in, perhaps the *Equator.* Unfortunately the glass soon revealed that it was only a strange schooner. As Stevenson awaited her in a boat, the cry went up:

"Ship, ahoy!"

"Ahoy, there!"

"What's your name, and where from?"

"The *H. L. Tiernan,* Crawford & Co., Captain Sachs—from Jalui and Big Muggin. Who are you?"

"Stevenson of the *Equator,* three weeks overdue from the south Any news of her, Captain?"

"Not a thing. Come aboard."

The question confronting the Stevensons now was: should they charter the *Tiernan* for Samoa, or should they take a chance on the *Equator's* return. Of course that might mean being marooned on Apemama for some time. Fortunately for the Stevensons, as it turned out, the captain's price was too high. Some say that the image of Skipper Reid appeared to Fanny. "Louis," she whispered, "I don't want to go." Shortly after the *Tiernan* departed she was caught in a storm and capsized with the loss of a large number of her crew The members of the marooned Stevenson party had good reason to congratulate themselves.

Stevenson, who always enjoyed being host, had purchased beer and other supplies from the *Tiernan* which enabled him not only to repay the king but also to stage a feast amidst considerable song and conviviality. Finally the *Equator* returned for its passengers

There was general rejoicing as they boarded the vessel and happily shook hands with the crew. The next day everything was packed and all were ready to sail. When the time came for the departure Tembinoka became melancholy. He confessed to Fanny that the loss of the company of his dear guests was harder to bear than the loss of his father. He did not respond even to the kisses and caresses of one of his favorite wives. "Sit down," he said to Lloyd, "I feel bad, I like talk. You like some beer?" Then smoking his meerschaum pipe and sighing, he continued: "I very sorry you go. Miss Stlevens he good man, woman, he good man, boy he good man; all good man. Woman he smart all the same man. My woman he good woman, no very smart. I think Miss Stlevens he big chiep all the same cap'n man-o'-wa'. I think Miss Stlevens he rich man all the same me. All go schoona. I very sorry. My patha he go, my uncle he go, my cutcheons he go, Miss Stlevens he go; all go. You no see king cry before. King all the same man: feel bad, he cry. I very sorry." The following morning Tembinoka confessed to Stevenson that he was very depressed. "Last night I can no 'peak; too much here," he said, pointing to his bosom. In parting he gave Stevenson three corselettes of plaited fibre, family heirlooms. Both agreed to celebrate the occasion in verse.

When the time came for final parting the stern, savage Tembinoka, dressed in a naval uniform, took the Stevensons to the schooner in his private gig. He spoke little, refused refreshments. He merely shook hands and turned back to the island. When night came Apemama finally dropped from view behind the horizon, and Tembinoka and his island became memories.

When the Stevensons left Apemama they had decided to make Samoa their next stop. During the journey they experienced calms and squalls. Stevenson walked the deck in a pair of serge trousers, a sleeveless singlet of Oxford gauze, and a red sash about his waist. The exciting sport was fishing for shark, dolphins, albacores, and porpoises, many of which were frolicking around the schooner. One day while sitting on deck and reading her book, Fanny was alarmed by a large shark jumping out of the water within a few feet of the boat and then falling back with an enormous splash. By this time a whole colony of sharks was circling the schooner. Stevenson, ever alert for excitement, suggested catching one. The sailors, who hated sharks, enjoyed the pleasure of lassoing a large one which was later served for dinner. The teeth were saved as a souvenir for Fanny. In the evenings the group played cards, gambled for shells, played some musical instruments, and sang songs. Captain Reid was a good singer as well as an excellent storyteller.

During the squally days the cruise was full of hardships. At best the *Equator's* limited accommodations of two rooms some eight feet square were inadequate for the sixteen people on board. One room had a counter across it, and the other served as a galley in which crew and passengers dined in relays. The captain's tiny cabin could accommodate but one sleeper. The rest had to dispose themselves as best they could in the space that remained. The floor of the cabin was so hot that it was impossible to stand with feet bare. Sleep was difficult. Often Fanny used to go to bed dressed, with an open umbrella in hand as a protection against the water that came through the skylight.

Before reaching Samoa the *Equator* encountered a menacing gale. The schooner staggered at every forward pull; she buried her nose in the foam, and the spray almost smothered her hull. One night she lost her foretopmast. When Fanny was awakened by the crash, she aroused Ah Fu saying: "I think him got trouble on deck, more better you go and help." Thinking that they might be shipwrecked, she stood prepared to take to the boat with the schooner's cat in her arms. When Ah Fu came on deck he found the young inexperienced fellows who manned the *Equator* huddled together as though paralyzed. "Why don't you do what captain tell you?" shouted Ah Fu. "Do what?" the men asked. Ah Fu pressed a rope into their idle hands. "Pull!" he shouted, while he scampered to the top of the galley. The captain later commended him for his coolness and resourcefulness. He had helped save the schooner.

Stevenson's 39th birthday was celebrated on the *Equator* with champagne, toasts, and songs prepared for the occasion. Members of the crew came in to wish the host a happy life. In appreciation Stevenson assured them that he had never enjoyed a voyage as much as that on the *Equator;* he had never found a company more pleasant.

I'll sing you a tale of a tropical sea,
On board of the old Equator.

There never were passengers better than we,
On board the old Equator.

Chorus
Captain, darling, where has your topsail gone,
pray?
Captain, darling, where has your topsail gone,
On board the old Equator.

Later the Stevensons were sorry to hear of the fate of some of the crew of the *Equator*. On the return journey to San Francisco one member was swept overboard; several others including the native youngster died of influenza. Captain Reid was later convicted of a fraudulent sale of a vessel and clapped in a Fiji prison.

CHAPTER VI

TALOFA

AFTER TOSSING FOR weeks at sea the Stevensons were to "rise like whales, from this long dive," and again enjoy life on shore. Hence, when early in December, 1889, Captain Reid called from the deck, "Land ho! Come up and see Samoa!" everyone scurried "top-side" to get the long-awaited first glimpse of the islands.

As usual Stevenson was the first on deck to take in the magnificent panorama. It was a gorgeous tropical sunrise. To the west the sky was still wrapt in fading darkness, while to the east the horizon was tinged with pink and purple. The air was fresh and invigorating. The captain pointed westward, shouting "There is Upolu!" the central and principal island of the Samoan group, though only second in size to Savaii. On the distant horizon could be faintly detected a hazy cloud which soon marked the purplish outline of an island. As the sun began to rise and like a disk of fire flooded the entire sky with gold, the blue peaks of Upolu gradually emerged from the depth of the vast expanse of water, rising higher and higher on the horizon. Off to the starboard could be seen the dim outline of another island floating on the sea.

As the *Equator* gracefully threaded her way, rising and falling upon the ocean swells, Upolu slowly took shape. It appeared, like a lofty pyramid of green, rising to a high range of mountains. There was wooded Mount Vaea with glistening foamy waterfalls spilling down its deep sides. Through the otherwise unbroken line of the snowy-white breakers hurling themselves upon the coral reef that stretched across the Bay of Apia, there was a narrow, dark lane. Captain Reid pointed it out, right in the center of the white line. The eager watchers around him followed his finger as it picked out the break which marked the entrance into the smooth waters that formed Apia Bay.

The trade winds blew across the bay; the waves dashed fiercely and broke over the barrier reef with a thunderous roar, throwing up glittering fountains of spray. The *Equator* merrily slipped into the lagoon through the opening and soon was gliding by the tall masts of merchant ships and men-of-war, of which latter there were three. She dropped anchor abreast a large warehouse flying the Union Jack. This was the headquarters of the British in Apia.

The Bay of Apia, often compared to the Bay of Naples, is beautiful in its shape and its surroundings. The beach is fringed with lofty palms, their tops swaying over the blue water. Nestling at the foot of the mountain and around the crescent-shaped bay lay the town of Apia, the political and economic center of the archipelago. The island metropolis seemed to consist of a string of straggling European houses of all sorts and sizes, most of them painted white, with roofs of galvanized iron. The flags flying over some of the buildings indicated that the town was divided into three sections: the British to the east; the Americans in the center, and the Germans to the west. Smoke curled upward from the huts on the outskirts where the natives lived. Undulating plantations climbed the steep slope; intense green hills stretched away on both sides. Here was "the Ireland of the Pacific."

Stevenson, who stood in his customary position at the bow, was entranced with the beauty of the country and breathed deeply of the air laden with perfume and fragrance from the orange groves. The calms and squalls and the monotony of the daily routine on the *Equator*, had cured him of "salt brine" and filled him with a longing for "beef steak." Two features of the harbor caught his attention; close by was the jagged upturned hull of the German warship *Adler,* lying on her side with her keel exposed, flanked by the wrecks of the *Trenton* and other vessels. These were silent but eloquent reminders of the memorable and tragic hurricane that swept into the bay April 16 and 17, 1889 and took many American and German lives and caused the destruction of three American and three German warships. The second striking feature was lofty Mount Vaea, towering majestically above the entire land mass. Did he dream that he would spend the happiest five years of his life at the foot of this mountain and that his final resting place would be on its stately summit? Did he divine that this peak, some 3,000 feet above the eternal melancholy thunder of the surf, would some day become a shrine for his admirers?

No sooner was the *Equator* at anchor than it was surrounded by many long, slender outrigger canoes, each one propelled by a number of natives whose broad-bladed paddles moved in rhythm with their songs. Stevenson watched their approach with keen expectation. He admired these naked, bronzed Apollos with their tall, lean, well-developed, oiled bodies glistening in the sun. He was also fascinated by the fine tattooing of the men, resembling brilliant silken patterns, and by their beautiful loin cloths, or *lava lavas,* of native brown bark, resembling flesh-like skirts hanging from the waist down. He sensed the beauty of the young women with their breasts concealed by garlands and their glossy hair falling to their waists. Some of them wore a "smile and little else." All shouted *talofa! talofa!* in their soft, melodious, Italian-sounding language. They offered baskets, limes, and bananas for sale. Stevenson's first introduction to Samoa and its people impressed him favorably; he imagined himself in ancient Greece.

On board the *Equator* Stevenson was greeted by H. E. Moors an American South Sea trader of long standing and a great admirer of the author of *Treasure Island.* Moors had had advance information of the famous author's voyage and looked forward to his arrival. They immediately formed a friendship that lasted to the end.

As the canoe carried Stevenson toward the shore he delighted in watching the clear blue water and the tiny fishes sparkling like ewels. He found the beach ablaze with hibiscus and hyacinth. ndolent-looking natives and whites greeted the strangers with the ustomary *talofa! talofa!* One of the whites, Reverend W. E. Clarke of the London Missionary Society, became one of his staunchest riends and five years later was to conduct his funeral services.

Reverend Clarke recalled his first impressions of the Stevenson amily upon their arrival. It was a gorgeous, hot tropical morning vith the trade winds sweeping, when he beheld a schooner flutter-ng into port, skimming across Apia Bay, and dropping anchor in the nidst of the small flotilla already there. An hour later, walking along he sandy track along the sea front, he met a group of three whites, wo men and one woman. The lady, small, dark-complexioned, with et-black hair and sunburned face, wore a loose native gown, a bril-iant plaid shawl, a straw Gilbert Island hat with strings of shells round its crown, a necklace of scarlet berries, and large gold ear-ings. On her bare feet she had white canvas sandals. The older of he two men looked gaunt and shrunken in a pair of flannel trousers, brown velvet coat flung across his shoulders. He wore a white peaked achting cap, had a cigarette in his mouth and a kodak in his hand. he younger man, a tall, English-looking lad of twenty, was clad in striped pyjama suit, the garb of white traders in the South Seas, and broad-brimmed straw hat. He wore dark blue sun-glasses, carried banjo in one hand and a concertina in the other. Reverend Clarke nistook the strangers for poor vaudeville actors who might be travel-ng on a trading schooner to the United States or to Australia. He vas impressed with the penetrating eyes of the older man who in-roduced himself as Louis Stevenson.

One evening when the Reverend met Stevenson again on Moors' erandah they discussed various subjects and Clarke was charmed y the newcomer's fund of knowledge and quick repartee. Clarke alled attention to the strange appeal which the horrible in fiction ad for most people. Stevenson confessed that he, too, enjoyed the readful, and that Edgar Allan Poe had a "grim fascination" for him. he Reverend then remarked on how the "psychological and fear-ome climax" of the modern story of *The Strange Case of Dr. Jekyll nd Mr. Hyde* had so captivated him that he was unable to lay the ook down until he had finished it. "By the way," he added, "it was written by a namesake of yours; have you read it?" "Yes," replied Stevenson, "I have not only read it, but I wrote it before I read it, and dreamed it before I wrote it."

The whole white colony in Apia, especially the English-speaking residents, soon learned that the distinguished author of *Dr. Jekyll and Mr. Hyde* and of *Treasure Island,* "one of the foremost geniuses that Scotland had produced," as announced in the Samoa *Times,* was in their midst. From that day to his last, four years later, Stevenson was the most beloved and most romantic figure in the South Seas. To natives who looked upon him as their great champion, he was their *Tusitala,* teller of tales.

Before the *Equator* hoisted sail Stevenson celebrated with a dinner at the Tivoli hotel in honor of Captain Reid. It was a happy feast at which the author addressed the guests and read one of his poems. Since the accommodations in the only Apia hotel were unsatisfactory Moors invited the Stevensons to share his home. They accepted the invitation and lived in his house on the beach for several weeks. During this time Stevenson had an opportunity to get acquainted with the Apia community. He found the natives "very genteel, very songful, very agreeable, very good-looking, chronically spoiling for a fight." Of the white residents, often labeled "The Beach," there were including the foreign officials and half-castes, about three hundred. Two-thirds of them were British, the remainder mostly Germans with a sprinkling of Americans and other nationals. Most of the whites were traders, owners of saloons, of various "degrees of respectability and the reverse." Many of them were married to native women of the better class. It was unkindly remarked that it was not tactful to inquire into the antecedents of some of the whites on the beach, especially the unemployed hangers-on or the beachcombers who were looking for work, hoping not to find it. He found the three consuls American, British, and German, "all at loggerheads with one another or at the best in a clique of two against one; three different sects of missionaries, not upon the best of terms; and the Catholics and Protestants in a condition of unhealable ill-feeling over whether a wooden drum ought to or ought not to be beaten to announce the time of school." In the Samoa *Times,* the only town newspaper and often accused of being subsidized by the government, he found that a "dashing warfare of newspaper correspondence goes on between the various residents, who were rather fond of referring to one another's antecedents." Though a German captain referred to Apia as "the hell of the South Seas," and another characterized it as a "poisonous gossip hole," Stevenson believed that it was not worse than many a town he could name. He thought many of its residents exceedingly agreeable people and sturdy enough to act in times of emergency. A few years prior to his arrival a white man who had committed murder was lynched by the members of his community.

Stevenson made friends with natives and whites. He was congenial with both Protestant and Catholic missionaries. According to Moors he had an unpleasant experience with Colonel de Coetlogen, the British consul. One Sunday morning, while Moors and Stevenson were sitting barefooted and in pyjamas discussing local celebrities, Stevenson jumped up, saying that he had not yet called on Her Britannic Majesty's representative, something that every good Britisher of mark should attend to. "Come along, Moors, let's get it off our mind!" he exclaimed. Moors reminded him that the Colonel was an "exclusive, crusty old fellow, full of pomposity." Stevenson, however, was determined. He put on a clean shirt, a pair of trousers, and shoes, and off they marched.

Expecting that the Colonel would welcome him, Stevenson opened the gates and strode across the consular lawn. When the two approached the verandah where the tall, soldierly personage with "white mustachios and close cropped hair" was sitting and drinking whiskey and soda, Stevenson shouted, "Good morning, Sir!"

The old soldier, who made no attempt even to rise to welcome his visitors, looked upon them as if they were distressed prisoners and grunted: "Well, what do you want?"

"My name is Stevenson, I am well known in Britain by my works —in fact, I am a novelist. This is Mr. Moors."

"Well, what do you want?" was the gruff reply. Stevenson was appalled by the hard, unsympathetic face that confronted them. "We have come, Sir, to pay our respects," he said. "If you have business and desire to see me," snapped back the soldier-consul, "I will listen to you on week days and in my office at the proper time. Good *morning!*"

This was one of the rare occasions when Stevenson was so disconcerted that he was unable or unwilling to reply. Moors tried to assure the consul that his friend was an honest and prominent man. But the crusty old soldier snapped back: "I don't care who you are—either of you!"

Making their hasty retreat, Stevenson exclaimed: "By Heavens, Moors, you were right! What a beast! What a damned—well, I supposed he has a right to choose his own Sunday morning company. I had thought that I was one of the foremost men of letters of the day, but this fellow differs. What a situation for a man of my supposed eminence to find himself in!" Then he burst into laughter. This was, however, according to Moors, a blow to Stevenson's vanity. He never forgot it, though he bore the old soldier no grudge. He was on far better terms later with the new British Consul, Cussac Smith.

In happy contrast to this unhappy experience was Stevenson's first meeting with High-Chief Mataafa. Shortly after his arrival in Apia, as the author was walking along the street reading a magazine, he was startled by a soft *talofa, Alii!* It was Mataafa in his white shirt and linen kilt returning from church. At the outset Stevenson was favorably impressed with this chief and remained his friend and admirer throughout his life. "Mataafa is the nearest thing to a hero in my history, and really a fine fellow; plenty sense, and most dignified, quiet, gentle manners," he wrote later. The admiration was mutual. One may wonder whether, at their first meeting, Stevenson dreamed that he was destined to play the part of Mataafa's friend and champion.

CHAPTER VII

VIKINGS OF THE SUNRISE

STEVENSON HAD COME to Samoa to collect material for a "big" book on the South Seas and for a history of the recent conflict between the Germans and the natives. In the back of his mind was also the passionate urge to expose the evils of the imperialism of the world powers, especially Germany. For four years, from the day when he stepped upon Samoan soil until the last hour of his life, he battled for the cause of the natives. He enjoyed fully the role of a Robin Hood, a Lawrence of the Pacific. This knight-errantry satisfied his passion for adventure and for the dramatic and his equally strong passion for justice. The natives, affected greatly by his sympathetic interest in their cause, hailed him as their protector and defender, their hero and idol. His name and reputation spread throughout the South Seas; no other white man had ever been so popular in that part of the world. He left many friends but few enemies; the latter were among some of the whites who resented his pro-Polynesian sympathies.

Immediately upon his arrival in Samoa Stevenson embarked seriously upon the task of collecting material for his books. He worked diligently to learn the history of the natives and their customs. He spent much time interviewing British, Germans, Americans and natives—the latter through interpreters. He studied German and Samoan, "mugging with a dictionary from five to six hours a day." He interrogated everyone to whose testimony he could attach any value. Realizing the difficulty of trying to get at the facts in controversial issues from prejudiced and often irresponsible sources, he spent considerable time sifting and evaluating the information he secured. Though absolute objectivity in handling controversial problems was not altogether compatible with Stevenson's temperament, he, nevertheless, performed his task with a fair degree of detachment and a desire for accuracy.

The first few weeks in Samoa the Stevensons lived with the Moors. Even after he rented a cottage in the "bush" he was a frequent visitor at his friend's home. Often Moors would ask: "Well, Stevenson, will you stay for dinner?" He would reply: "No thanks, I'll get home." Then as an afterthought he would ask: "What have you for dinner, Moors?" If something that tempted him was mentioned he would weaken: "Yes, I'll stay for my stomach's sake!" Often when he was in the midst of an exciting discussion Fanny would come and drag him home, saying, "Too much talk is not good for Louis." Moors observed that Stevenson was very fond of his wife and was "easily led by her." Louis believed that his Fanny could do no wrong.

Barefooted and clad in white, Stevenson enjoyed lounging on Moors' verandah writing or listening to the rhythmic roar of the crashing breakers; to the muffled whisper of the feathery palms silhouetted against the sky; to the plaintive songs of native boys and girls sitting in the moonlight, or gazing languidly at the ocean, or fishing by torchlight. Here he was frequently joined by Moors and Reverend Clarke, both wide wanderers and veterans of the South Seas. They yarned and exchanged information about the South Pacific. Stevenson would listen to the recital of these tales with childlike delight till bedtime. Hoping to collect and translate native legends and poetry he plied his colleagues with countless questions about the past and present of Samoa.

The great story of Samoa gradually unfolded itself in these

nightly conversations: ethnologically the Polynesian type is a composite, physically, culturally and linguistically, of Indonesian and Europoid. The branches of the Polynesian race are the Hawaiians in the north; the Maori in the south; the Tongans, Samoans, Tahitians and the Marquesans in the center of the triangle. When, whence and how these people reached the Polynesian triangle are questions shrouded in mystery. No written records of early Samoan history can be found among the natives, but their sagas are helpful. Certain families in each district were appointed to act as depositories or keepers of national traditions. These traditions were transmitted orally from father to son for many generations. Since these record keepers had to depend upon their memory they developed this faculty to a high degree. Greater accuracy in preservation of these traditions was assured by their constant repetition by the recorders themselves and the public orators.

Through a study of these legends and scientific anthropological data Stevenson learned that in the very remote past the ancestors of the Polynesian race lived on the Asiatic mainland. Pressure of population and the lure of adventure prompted them to migrate southward, during the first century before the Christian era. For a time they sojourned in Indonesia; then they moved on. When they reached the sea, "salt entered into their blood;" they changed from landsmen to seamen.

Stevenson's own hunger for adventure and his love for the sea had their parallel in the romantic sagas of these mariners who in waves extending over generations traversed the Pacific Ocean. But, marveled the author, without the aid of the compass, guided during the day only by the sun, the flight of birds, and the shape of clouds, these courageous "Vikings of the Sunrise," made voyages of thousands of miles, actually dwarfing the exploits of the Vikings of the Atlantic. Some journeyed in single canoes; others traversed the ocean in outrigger and double-decked twin canoes placed side by side several feet apart, fastened together with wooden cross-pieces and paddled by men in each craft. Some of the boats might have been equipped with sails of pandanus.

Often about two hundred men, women and children traveled in this manner thousands of miles over the vast Pacific. What faith, what courage, what skill, mused Stevenson, guided these odysseys. Undoubtedly many perished from lack of food and water; many others were engulfed in the stormy seas. Some, however, succeeded in reaching islands and coral atolls, convenient stopping places. To these atolls and islands they brought non-indigenous fowl and plants: breadfruit, banana, taro, yam, and coconut. But limited natural resources on some of the islands forced a number to move ever onward. The big problems during these long migrations were cooking food and carrying drinking water, which was often stored in flasks made of gourds. It is quite possible that these mariners frequently chewed leaves to slacken their thirst.

What routes did these daring Vikings follow? This, too, was a moot question. There were two possible courses of travel: A northern route by way of the Micronesian islands, the small atolls of the Carolines, the Marshalls, thence to Samoa, to Hawaii and to the other islands; the possible southern route by way of Melanesia, New Guinea, Fiji, Solomons, and thence to Samoa, which was a center of distribution.

The Samoan islands were on the dividing line between Polynesia and Melanesia. To the west were the dark, frizzly-haired negrito Melanesians; to the north, the mixed Micronesians; to the west, the pure Polynesians. Among the Polynesians of Hawaii and the other islands there was a tradition that after death the spirits journeyed homeland to distant "Hawakiki," which is commonly identified with Savaii, the largest and westernmost of the Samoan group. When did the Polynesians come to Samoa? That question Stevenson sought to answer. At the opening of the Christian era they were already found in the Pacific. By the eighth and ninth centuries a large number of island groups on both sides of the Equator were occupied.

Stevenson liked the simple Samoan myth which offered several versions of the origin of the land. Tangaloa, the god of heaven, sent down his daughter, in the form of a bird, Turi, a species of snipe, to find a resting place. She flew over the surface of the ocean and, finding no resting place, she returned complaining to her father. Tangaloa then hurled a stone down from heaven which became Savaii; another stone became Upolu; and so with the rest of the group. When Tangaloa sent out Turi again in search of land, she found at first a spray of waters, then lumpy places, then land. On the next journey down she found plants on the land and the plants swarmed with maggots which finally turned into men and women.

Another legend of the creation of Samoa is that Tangaloa lifted stones from the bottom of the ocean with a fish-hook. When the rocks married the earth, the latter became pregnant. Salveo, the god of rocks, observed motion in the center of Moa, the earth; hence he named the child when born, Moa, and announced that everything that grew would be sacred to Moa or *sa ia Moa,* contracted later to Samoa.

Tangaloa then sent down his daughter Turi with a plant. The plant grew leaves which swarmed with maggots, which later became the men and women of Samoa. The gods met at Upolu to decide what was to be the end of the life of man. One god proposed that it be like the extinction of a coconut leaf-torch which when it goes out can be shaken into a blaze again. Thus, after sickness and death, men might be resurrected in full vigor of youth. Another god, called the Supa or Paralysis, proposed that the life of man be like the extinction of the candlenut torch, which when once out could not be revived. Other gods spoke. Some favored one idea; others, another. In the midst of the discussion came a downpour of rain, and the gods ran to the house for shelter. As they were dispersing they called out: "Let the proposal of Paralysis be carried and let man's life go out like the candlenut torch." This accounts for the proverb as given in George Turner's *Samoa: A Hundred Years Ago and Long Before:* "It is as Paralysis said, 'Man dies and does not return.'" (p. 9) Another version, however, stated that only man was to die—woman was to survive.

"How about these 'Godless Samoans,'" Stevenson would insist. Some of the early explorers who visited the islands and who believed that the natives were destitute of all forms of religion, dubbed them "Godless Samoans." A closer examination, however, proved that the natives believed in a number of deities. Though they did not possess idols and did not offer human sacrifices, they did propitiate their deities with food. Annual feasts were held in honor of the gods.

From birth on, every native was under the supervision of some god or spirit who might appear in a visible incarnation, such as an eel, an owl, or even a shark. The father of the household was the high priest. In addition you had village gods with the village chief as high priest. The spirits of dead chiefs were often deified. There were also national war gods. Rank existed among some of the deities; some were superior, others inferior.

It must have pleased Stevenson to learn that Samoan society was patriarchal and somewhat democratic. In every village, which usually consisted of from two hundred to five hundred people, all sons, daughters, uncles, and cousins constituted a family. The heads of the families were highly honored, and upon them fell the responsibility of selecting the chief of the village, who would assume the title of protector and defender. Though the chiefs were selected from a family of distinguished pedigree, the heads of families did not have to choose the son of the deceased chief; they could eliminate the one in direct line of succession in favor of another member, even an uncle. Chiefs married into families of chiefs and might marry a number of times.

Though the chief shared in the usual every-day occupations, such as planting, fishing, house building, and even cooking, he did, however, enjoy special courtesies. There was an express vocabulary used when speaking to a chief. According to Stevenson special words were set apart for his leg, his face, his hair, his belly, his eyelids; for his son, his daughter, his wife, his wife's pregnancy, his wife's adultery, adultery with his wife, his dwelling, his spear, his comb, his sleep, his dreams . . . his ulcers, his cough, his death.

"To address these demigods is quite a branch of knowledge," Stevenson discovered, "and he who goes to visit a high chief does well to make sure of the competence of his interpreter." To the chief went the first cup of *'ava;* to him was served the best joint of meat. When he was to marry, all the heads of the families had to provide for the needs of his household.

The unit of Samoa's political structure was the village, made up of closely related families. The total number of villages in Samoa was about 122: forty-four in Upolu, thirty-six in Savaii, thirty-six in Tutuilaa, and six in Manua. Every village considered itself practically autonomous in local matters; free to act as it pleased in its own affairs. The chiefs and the heads of the families constituted the legisature and judiciary, competent to settle disputes and punish any iolations of the laws which, though unwritten, were well understood y all. Among the punishable crimes were assault, adultery, rude anguage to a chief or to strangers. The village heads also controlled he disposition of the land, which was held communally.

For mutual protection eight, ten or more villages united to form district. Throughout the Samoan islands there were about ten districts of which Upolu comprised three: Aana, Tuamasanga and Atua. One of the villages in each district was considered the capital of the ntire political unit, where all weighty matters of the section, such s war and peace, were discussed at the *fono*. This parliament was eld at the public guest-house or in the public square—the *malae*—y the leading men whose decisions were respected by all the people f the district. In the event of a general Samoan war some districts ould decide to remain neutral. Each province or district enjoyed he privilege of conferring a name on one of the most distinguished igh chiefs. Samoan aristocracy consisted of three great families: Sa Mataafa, Sa Malietoa and Sa Muangututia. If one man received five of the famous names, he became king. Therein lay trouble for Samoa.

At a *fono* the chiefs rarely spoke; it was considered more dignified for them to remain comparatively silent and to leave to their *ulafale*, or speaking-man, the expression of their wishes. Each chief generally had his speaking-man, literally, his mouthpiece; the higher he chief, the more important his speaking-man. The *tulafale* of the district chief was the leading orator of the entire district. These *ulafales* constituted a powerful and influential class, generally large landholders and advisers to the chiefs. He was a bold chief, indeed, who dared oppose the counsel of his *tulafales*. Often these influential personages did not hesitate to criticize their chiefs, and even to remove obnoxious ones.

That was Samoa before the advent of the whites and the introduction of western civilization. That was the Samoa that Stevenson found upon his arrival, though vast changes had already taken place since the *papalangi* had invaded the islands.

CHAPTER VIII

PAPALANGI: SKY-BURSTERS

STEVENSON, NO DOUBT, pondered the question, as did others, as to how and when Samoa was opened to western civilization. Though it is possible that some of the navigators who crossed and recrossed the Pacific Ocean before the eighteenth century might have sighted the Samoan islands, there is no evidence of it. The credit for the discovery of the islands goes to Jacob Roggewein, who, in charge of a Dutch East India Company expedition, sighted Upolu in 1722. When the billowing sails hove in sight, the cry went up. *Papalangi! Papalangi!* (sky-bursters). Astonished and wondering crowds lined the shore; some of the natives climbed the coconut trees and watched with intense interest and excitement the mysterious giant ship with its tall masts whose sails billowed over the rim of the horizon like the clouds of the sky.

When some of the more curious and daring natives ventured in their canoes to approach the amazing ship, they were astonished to find below deck large "caves" filled with strange things. There they saw "colorless" people speaking a queer language, dressed in baggy clothes into which they put various articles, and with feet not divided into toes. These strangers must be man-eaters, the natives thought, for they mistook portions of a pig hanging in the kitchen for human flesh. Whence did these strangers come? What did they want? Believing that the ship came from the spirit land, the disturbed and superstitious natives placed food along the beach for the gods on board and prayed that the offerings be acceptable and that human sacrifices would not be demanded.

The astonishment was mutual, for the Dutch admired the tall, brown natives and their beautiful canoes, and were favorably impressed with their grace, humor, gaiety, and the tattooing on their bodies, which resembled silken trousers. The Dutch considered the Samoans the handsomest people they had seen in the South Seas.

The second explorer to visit the islands was the Frenchman, Louis Antoine de Bougainville, in May, 1768. From the skilful manner in which the natives handled their numerous well-constructed canoes, Bougainville named the islands *L'Archipel des Navigateurs.* The name Navigator Islands was used by the missionaries until 1840, and in the official foreign dispatches until 1875, when the native name Samoa was adopted.

The first westerners to land on the Samoan islands, however, were members of the ill-fated French La Pérouse expedition of two ships in 1787. La Pérouse was impressed with the beauty of the islands and the native houses built under fruit trees along creeks and by the seaside. Unfortunately he had a sad experience upon landing. Twelve of his men, including M. de Langlie, a scientist and second in command, were killed. Who was to blame for this unfortunate incident? There has been considerable controversy over what actually happened. The French naturally accused the natives of treachery and barbarism. The natives, however, insisted the French were partly responsible, for they started the shooting.

Stevenson accepted the contention of Reverend John B. Stair, who claimed he was familiar with the facts; and of Charles Wilkes, commander of the American exploring expedition, who visited the islands in 1839. Wilkes obtained his information from Reverend Murray, who in turn had it from an old native, an eyewitness to the affray. According to the latter's testimony, the quarrel started when a native was suspected of trying to steal an iron bolt from the French ship. He was shot and mortally wounded. This act outraged the natives. They immediately left for shore and there attacked and killed twelve of the Frenchmen who were on land gathering plants and talking to the native women. The Samoans maintained that they later collected the bodies of the slain Frenchmen and buried them on the beach with the honors given only to chiefs.

Stevenson was convinced that this tragic incident gave the Samoans an unmerited reputation for treachery and ferocity. The site of the conflict had become known as "Massacre Bay." "If the truth be known," wrote William B. Churchward, the British consul in Samoa, it "would be found to have been more of an outrage on the Samoans than one committed by them." La Pérouse, in the first part of his journal, gave his own version of the tragedy.

Other explorers and navigators, English and Russian, visited Samoa, and the islands were invaded by a backwash of renegade white sailors and convicts whose influence upon the natives was invariably harmful. Thus, until the coming of the missionaries, the contacts between the natives and the whites were unfortunate. It is understandable that the Samoans prayed: "Keep away from us sailing Gods, lest they come and cause disease and death." "Here is *ava* for you sailing Gods; do not come on shore at this place; but be pleased to depart along the ocean to some other land."

The coming of the missionaries, about 1830, Stevenson believed, opened up a new era for the Samoans; it marked the advent of real western civilization. Tongan converts of the Wesleyan Society were the first to introduce Christianity. However it was the undenominational Protestant London Missionary Society, founded in 1795, that became most influential in Samoa and gained the largest number of converts.

The pioneer worker sent out by the London Missionary Society was an adventuresome, courageous and energetic young man named John Williams. He plunged into the South Sea mission work in 1816, at the age of twenty, the year he was ordained. Williams was ambitious. "I cannot content myself within the narrow limits of a single reef," he cried out. In his sixty-ton ship, the *Messenger of Peace*, which he built, he sailed eighteen hundred miles to Tonga and to Samoa.

Williams was fortunate in having a talking-man with him when he arrived, an exiled Samoan who could speak the proper chief's language. A converted chief spoke thus: "I look at the wisdom of these worshippers of Jehovah, and see how superior they are to us in every respect. Their ships are like floating houses, so that they can traverse the tempest-driven ocean for months with perfect safety. . . . Their persons, also, are covered from head to foot in beautiful clothes, while we wear nothing but a girdle of leaves. Now I conclude that the God who has given to his white worshippers these valuable things must be wiser than our gods, for they have not given the like to us. We want all these articles and my proposition is, that the God who gave them should be our God."

"They all," says Williams, "appeared to understand and appreciate this reasoning, and gazed on us with interest and surprise." It seems, however, that the acceptance of the new faith was due to no experience of a deeply religious conviction on the part of the natives. The missionaries themselves often expressed doubt as to whether the "inhabitants had experienced a change of heart, or that their desire of instruction arose from a knowledge of the spiritual nature of the Gospel."

Whatever may have been their motives, the Samoans accepted the new religion eagerly. They "drank in the words of the missionary with outstretched necks and gaping mouths," says Williams. Every native soon owned a Bible, attended divine services at church on Sundays, and sang the hymns lustily. Sabbath was truly a day of rest and religious devotion. "It was impossible," says Wilkes, "to get a native to do anything whatsoever on that day, but perform his religious duties." No war was waged on Saturday; that day was used to forage and cook food for Sunday. Revival meetings were held at which emotionally aroused sinners wailed and fainted from excess of religious fervor. So strong was the hold of the London Missionary Society that the natives did not flock to the French Catholic priests when they arrived in 1845, despite the love of the Samoans for ceremony and pageantry such as the Catholic church offers. The London Missionary Society established a college at Malua to train native teachers and pastors for religious work in Samoa and the other islands in the South Seas.

The missionaries did much good by teaching useful arts and crafts and discouraging indolence and some of the least desirable primitive practices of the natives. They also frequently defended the latter against the injurious influence of the traders and beachcombers. There was much, however, observed Stevenson, that one can criticize in the so-called benefits of civilization which the missionaries introduced, especially their zealous determination to proscribe dancing and singing and to clothe the natives in "respectable European," or rather, garments such as shirts, trousers, stockings, and bonnets made in Britain. This change from grass loin cloths to cotton prints proved to be not only unsuitable to the climate, but positively unhygienic and ugly.

Wilkes witnessed the consort of Pomale, wife of the most influential native in Tutuila, arriving for church service in a "red calico gown, four or five petticoats of different colors, woolen socks, green slippers, cap and bonnet, a large plaid blanket shawl, and a pair of polar gloves, the whole surmounted by a flaming red silk umbrella —and this with the thermometer at 87!" Before long "all her finery became awry," added Wilkes. The natives generally had a natural desire to exhibit their new apparel in church. And to think that this mode of dress took the place of the gay, fragrant garlands of flowers! The missionary may have changed the native outwardly; at heart he remained as before; even in the Christian ritual he incorporated much of his former practices.

Western civilization, introduced to the Samoans by the missionaries, explorers, and "salt water vagrants," was not an unmixed blessing. The missionaries combated what they considered evil customs, encouraged industry, opened schools and preached the spiritual life; the explorer and "salt water vagrant" introduced firearms and spiritous liquor. At any rate these pioneers made Samoa known to the world and paved the way for the traders. Trade frequently follows the Bible. "Where the missionary goes, new channels are cut for the stream of commerce," wrote John Williams in 1837. Officials, particularly from Great Britain, Germany and the United States, followed the traders. Samoa entered the ken of the world powers and became a zone of international rivalry.

Because British missionaries were the first and the most active among the Samoans, many of whom were converted, Great Britain gained special advantages among them. Though the missionaries and traders often disagreed, and in their struggle for mastery were at times a "thorn in the side of the statesmen," they were above all British patriots and not uninterested in promoting trade and political relations between Samoa and the Empire. In his appeals for funds to purchase a missionary ship, John Williams turned to the "Honourable the Court of Common Council of the City of London, and so convincing was his statement of the advantages of missionary labour to British commerce . . . that the grant was made with scarcely a dissenting voice." The *Missionary Magazine* stressed the fact that "The Gospel not only supplies the means of a spiritual renovation, and opens the way to eternal happiness, but it is likewise eminently favourable to the cause of social improvement . . . numbers of natives display uncommon eagerness to obtain articles of British manufacture." The missionaries—patriotic Britishers—did not forget to impress the natives with the advantage of coming under the wise rule of Queen Victoria and British justice. Of course, the extension of British influence in the South Seas would benefit the poor natives! British missionaries and traders were the first to persuade Samoans to produce coconut oil for export to Europe, where it was in great demand for the manufacture of candles and soap. The trade proved extremely lucrative for the whites; conversely, the goods bartered to the natives were of little value.

On the heels of the traders came the consuls and men-of-war. *Die Flagge folgt dem Handel,* is a good German slogan. The French say similarly, *avant soldat le marchand.* In 1844 England established a consulate in Samoa, the first attempt to extend European political control in the islands. When Reverend George Pritchard, who had been expelled by the French from Tahiti, became consul in Samoa, he began to scheme for the annexation of the western Pacific islands, to forestall the "French Anti-Christ." He urged his government to hasten warships to Samoa to impress the natives with the power of the British Government, even if it were necessary to burn a village or two.

Prompted thereto by the British missionaries and consul, chiefs of Tutuila drew up a petition to Queen Victoria begging her to take them under her protection. But the British Government, whose appetite for colonies had slackened considerably between the period of the American Revolution and the fourth quarter of the nineteenth century, declined the honor and instructed Consul Pritchard not to encourage such movements.

The consuls and the missionaries, however, continued their agitation for a British protectorate. They were especially apprehensive of the designs of the French Roman Catholic missionaries. "It seems," said a writer in the *Samoan Reporter* of 1846, "a strange mongrel affair for his Holiness the Pope to be engaged in the buying of oil and in disposing of powder and shot." Pritchard wrote to the Foreign Office that the Society of the Virgin Mary was organized "for the purpose of supplying the whole of Polynesia with merchandise at a little more than cost prices in France, and to render facilities for opposing the Protestant missions, by placing amongst them Roman Catholic priests, and by these cheap goods to win over to the Roman Catholic faith all the isles of the Pacific."

Mindful that the Samoan group is only about 1,500 miles from Auckland and is on the main steamship route between the American and Australasian ports, the governors of New Zealand claimed to have superior interests in the commercial, cultural and military affairs of the archipelago. One of the early champions of the doctrine of "Monroeism" for Australasia was Sir George Grey, the imperialistic governor of New Zealand. He pointed out that the extension of British control in the South Seas would afford revenue and employment for young men who might lead in the effort to civilize the islanders. But Downing Street refused to assume such responsibility in Samoa, though fearful of seeing the islands fall into the hands of any other nation. Britain did not hesitate to dispatch warships occasionally to keep an "eye" on the general situation.

The British soon found that they had to worry more about the Germans than the French. The Germans, who came to Samoa merely as traders in the late fifties, established themselves there much later than the British. They pushed their interests, however, so energetically, and at times so unscrupulously, that by 1875 they controlled the trade of the islands. The German interests in Samoa centered largely around the activities of the trading and shipping firm of John Caesar Godeffroy of Hamburg, Germany. Its successor was *Die Deutsche-See Handels-Gesellschaft*, popularly known as the "Long Handle Firm."

These gigantic firms, "the Grab-alls of this side of the world," were managed efficiently by the strong Bismarckian Theodore Weber who came to Samoa in 1861 at the age of twenty-seven. For twenty-five years Weber was the dominant personality in the islands. His influence was doubly effective owing to his position as agent of the most powerful commercial company in the South Seas, and to his position as German Consul at Apia. This dual capacity can be explained by the fact that the German Government was controlled by large landowners and the industrial-commercial interests.

According to many no doubt biased British observers, Weber's methods were alternately those of a Machiavelli and a caveman. "He was of an artful and commanding character; in the smallest thing or the greatest, without fear or scruple." He and his firm "supplanted other traders and secured their own footing by artfully fostering the inter-tribal disputes, which were ever smoldering among the Samoans, and then liberally supplying the combatants with arms and ammunition from their own arsenal at Liège (Belgium). For these useful imports they accepted payment in broad tracts of the most fertile lands in Samoa."

The same accusing finger could be pointed to other nationals, English and Americans. One of the Samoan songs tells how "all things, land and food and property, pass progressively, as by a law of nature, into the hands of Misi Ueba, and soon nothing will be left for Samoans." This song had reference to Weber's shrewdness in acquiring for his firm some 134,000 acres of the best land in Samoa by taking advantage of the simple-minded natives who had no conception of the mortgage system and who in return for arms and ammunition relinquished their most fertile tracts. In 1889 the land claims were estimated as follows: British, about 1,250,270 acres; German, about 134,419 acres; American, about 302,746 acres. Thus the total area claimed was 1,700,000 acres, about 1,000,000 acres more than the total estimated land area in the entire Samoan archipelago! The German company chose its personnel carefully, and carried on its work secretly. Their people were instructed to keep their mouths shut and have a woman of their own for "a trader without a wife is in continual hot water."

International complications in Samoa were destined to become even more involved Stevenson learned, when American interests began to penetrate into the islands. The United States, like Germany, in the last quarter of the nineteenth century, was beginning to embark upon a career of industrial and territorial expansion. This expansionist spirit that resulted in the conquest of the western frontier, did not exhaust itself during the Civil War. It was to be expected that the impulse toward expansion would continue even after the nation's boundaries had been pushed to the Pacific coast. The Civil War, moreover, accelerated industrial development in the United States; it released the energy of the American people, particularly of the triumphant industrial North, for new commercial and industrial pursuits at home and abroad.

The increasing interest and growing activities of the Germans in the Pacific awakened naval and commercial groups in the United States to the advisability of action on their part in that region. The United States was determined to build up her power in the Pacific. Hence the Navy Department and American shipping interests began to look in that direction for coaling and repair stations. Also the American "Polynesian Land Company," which during the frequent civil wars had acquired large tracts of valuable land by trading arms and ammunition to the belligerents, was eager to see the United States extend control over the Samoan islands.

In 1839 the attention of the American Government was called to the Samoan islands for the first time when Commander Charles Wilkes made his famous expedition. Wilkes surveyed Tutuila and its harbor of Pago Pago which he considered "one of the most singular in all the Polynesian isles." At a meeting with the chiefs and the dignified, white-haired King Malietoa, who reminded him of General Andrew Jackson, Wilkes appointed an American consul for Samoa, an Englishman named John C. Williams, son of the martyred mission-

y. Wilkes also entered into an agreement, the first of its kind, with e Samoan Government for the protection of foreigners and the gulation of their relations with the Samoans.

Some thirty-two years later Captain E. Wakeman was dispatched ' an American steamship company to examine and report upon the mmercial value of Samoa and the suitability of Pago Pago as a aling station. Wakeman appraised Upolu as the "garden spot in e Pacific," and Pago Pago as "the most perfectly land-locked har-r that exists in the Pacific Ocean." He could see no reason why oolu should not "become a Java, a Borneo, a Mauritius, a Ceylon, iba, or a Barbadoes."

Captain Wakeman's warning that both Germany and New Zea-id were plotting to annex the Samoan islands was supported by e American agent in Apia. In response to this threat the Navy De-rtment dispatched Captain Richard Meade, commander of the *urragansett,* to Pago Pago to locate a coal depot for American eamers. In 1872 Captain Meade entered into a treaty with Magua, e principal chief of Pago Pago. The treaty granted to the United ates the exclusive right to establish in Pago Pago harbor a naval ition for the use of American vessels, in return for which the Sa-oans were to "gain the friendship and protection of the great Gov-nment of the United States of America."

Commander Meade appealed to the natives to unite under one ief and one flag, to form a simple government. He assured them at the United States did not seek an inch of territory and did not n to control their government. He promised them that the United ates would "from time to time send ships of war and wise persons assist in framing good laws."

Captain Meade impressed the natives favorably, for they agreed draw up a petition asking the American Government to annex their ands. President Grant, who was in favor of American expansion in e Caribbean and Pacific, submitted the treaty to the Senate for ap-oval. Some members of both houses, especially those members from e Pacific coast, were in sympathy with the design to extend Ameri-n control over Samoa. The Senate, however, took no action.

Influenced no doubt by the Meade report and agreement, Secre-ry of State Fish sent Colonel Albert Steinberger in 1873 as special agent to Samoa to investigate the situation, and to deliver kind messages and tokens to the chiefs. Steinberger arrived in Apia at a opportune moment; the natives, who had just terminated one of the civil wars, were assembled for the purpose of establishing a constit tion. By appointment Steinberger met the leading chiefs and aft an interchange of compliments told them that he was the rep sentative of a great nation "accredited to Samoa and the Samoa not the foreign residents," that he was interested in their welfare a advised them against selling land to foreigners.

The Colonel's charming personality, friendly interest and since advice endeared him immediately to the natives. "For the first ti they had met a white man, other than missionaries," who had th interest at heart, and who mingled with them without sinister m tives. Throughout the islands the "Alii America" came to be know as their friend and trusted adviser. At a large *fono* or council of pro inent chiefs the "talking men" reviewed the history of Samoa: t causes of the factional wars, the evils of the loss of their land foreigners, and the weakness of Samoa in the face of English a German warships. After the addresses Saga, a tall, grave, gray-hair chief of Upolu, presented Steinberger with a government "sta and "fly-flap" which symbolized the unity of the country. He assur him that these tokens were being sent to America as "pledges of th desire to be ruled by that great Government."

Steinberger had so ingratiated himself with the chiefs that th made him their adviser or prime minister, and for a few years was the controlling spirit of a rejuvenated Samoan government. I apparently sincere interest in the welfare of the country, his d gence, his obvious ability and tact endeared him to the natives a many whites, especially the missionaries and the Americans. Af a careful investigation a later American consul, G. W. Griffin, ported that Steinberger was "self-denying, earnest and enthusias in his efforts to ameliorate the condition of the people," and th they owed to him "their great national improvement, the peace a good order which had then recently prevailed among the people, a the comparative prosperity which began to be visible in the co try." He was held by the natives "in a degree of esteem amount most to veneration, and was considered by them as the wisest and est friend that Samoa ever had."

Unfortunately Steinberger incurred the disfavor of the British ıd Germans who feared that his position and influence foreshadowed oser relations between the United States and Samoa. As long as e remained in Samoa he was a threat to their own trade privileges ıd political aspirations. With the approval of the American Consul, oster, an impoverished land-speculator, and the wheedled and oaxed King Malietoa, Steinberger was deported on a British warıip, ending his career as premier. The deportation aroused severe iticism in the press of several countries. Captain Stevens, who legally deported Steinberger, was reprimanded and dismissed from ıe service. Also both the American and British consuls were removed om their offices by their respective governments.

Disorder in Samoa became again the order of the day. The chiefs, ıembers of the *Taimua* and *Faipule,* or parliament, were enraged ver the treachery of King Malietoa whom they accused of being an ccomplice in the removal of their beloved premier. Though Captain tevens addressed the chiefs, admonishing them that the action of ıe king was right, and should it not meet with their approval, "the ıore is the pity," they refused to be intimidated. That same evening ıe chiefs deposed Malietoa and removed him under guard to another island. Captain Stevens and the American and British consuls rought Malietoa back to reinstate him. The chiefs, however, would ave none of him whom they accused of treason. Meanwhile, in a lash between British bluejackets and Samoans, a number on both des were killed. The Samoans were ordered to surrender guns and mmunition. They, however, insisted that all they wanted was to be ft alone and not to be interfered with. The chiefs also dispatched a tter to President Grant, informing him of the misfortunes that had efallen Samoa through the aggression of Captain Stevens, Consul oster, and the London Missionary Society. They assured the President all the chiefs of Samoa were behind their premier and in favor f the United States.

The deposition of the king and the deportation of the premier, vho had been the mainspring of the Samoan government, dealt a

severe blow to the political stability of the islands. Even under th
most favorable conditions, without the encroachment and meddlin
of foreign traders and officials, the Samoan political system containe
elements of weakness. Unlike Tahiti, Tonga, and Hawaii, where
centralized monarchical government prevailed and the king coul
legislate for all the provinces of his realm, decentralized Samoa
kingship carried no power of legislation or supreme authority ov
all the districts. In Samoa each district was more or less autonomou
There was much rivalry among the jealous chiefs. If one or tw
districts bestowed the honor of kingship on one chief, others coul
refuse to go along; in fact it could be the signal for them to conf
the honor on a rival high chief. Frequent struggles between riva
for the kingship were not uncommon. Such conflicts took place b
fore the advent of the missionaries in 1830 and again in 1845 an
1869. These wars were not very destructive and often were looke
upon as a pleasant diversion, a sort of game, with the prospect
gaining military distinction for the number of heads taken. Man
a young Samoan was actually spoiling for a fight.

The injection of intrigue and domination by the white man i
creased the susceptibility of the native Samoan to the disease
war. First, there was the land question. The natives bitterly resente
the loss of their best lands to the foreigners, especially the German
whom they accused of acquiring their plantation land through tric
ery. Hence to communistically-minded natives, stealing fruit from th
German plantations, from lands which had once belonged to the
ancestors, was no crime. In fact it was considered a legitimate spor
and native Robin Hoods were not unpopular.

The German plantation owners naturally complained agains
these thefts, demanding that the authorities seize and punish th
offenders. But among Samoans it was the duty of the judge to fav
his kinsmen, and of the chief to protect his subjects. Under such co
ditions it was not easy to apprehend the thief, and even more diff
cult to convict and punish him. On one occasion when the prisone
pleaded guilty, the good native judge embraced him crying: "The
I, too, will forgive you!" The Germans, accusing the native author
ties of shirking their duties, often retaliated by shelling and burnin
native villages.

The situation in Samoa was made more critical by the presence nd meddling of traders, consuls, and naval commanders of the ıree world powers. The nationals of each country competed in the ale of ammunition to rival native districts and, together with their espective consuls and naval commanders, played the canny game f power politics. Each national group, suspicious of the others, eared that unless it took the initiative, its opponents might gain ıe upper hand. In the absence of telegraphic communication with ıeir home governments, where usually a broader outlook prevailed, ıe vainglorious German, British, and American consuls, and particurly the blustering, impetuous naval commanders stationed on the isınds, tried constantly to acquire greater power and authority, and ere inclined to embark upon extraordinary and unauthorized action nder the impulse of personal jealousies and sudden hysteria. Alıough most of these usurpations of authority were later disavowed by ıe home governments, much mischief had been done. Even Bismarck eplored the *furor consularis et navalis,* and Salisbury complained, "I on't know which are worse for a peacefully minded Foreign Office—Colonies or Consuls."

All this led to turbulence and increased interference in the affairs f Samoa by the three powers. However, even the foreign offices of ıe powers involved in the controversy could not be cleared of the uspicion that they were using the islands as pawns on the interational chess board. Certainly neither the commercial value nor the trategic position of the islands would explain what was happening.

This international farce that was staged at home and on the isınds was a comedy that often bordered on tragedy. Many of the raders, however, welcomed turmoil in the islands because it brought attleships with a fresh supply of spending money. "I never saw o good a place as that of Apia. You can be in a new conspiracy every ay," remarked a visitor.

For a time, after the deposition of King Malietoa, the *Taimua* and *'aipule* attempted to rule without a king. But the government did ot have the full support of all of the natives or of the missionaries. ome jealous chiefs joined the deposed king's party. Moreover British nd German commanders embarrassed the helpless government by emanding large indemnities. The British could not forgive the insult they had suffered in the clash between the natives and their sailor Some zealous Britishers inveigled the government into sending petition to Downing Street asking for protection. Fearing that th application might be successful, or that the Germans might tak aggressive action, the American consul hastened to hoist the Sta and Stripes.

When the natives failed to get British protection they sent on of their leading and ablest chiefs, Mamea, to Washington in 187 to petition for a United States protectorate. The outcome was th American-Samoan treaty of 1878 by which the United States gaine rights over Pago Pago harbor and promised in return "her goo offices" in the event of a dispute between Samoa with another powe

The Germans and British were determined not to be left out the feast of special privileges. The captain of a newly arrived wa ship announced that henceforth his government would station warship in Apia harbor for the protection and welfare of both th Germans and the natives. Native villages were shelled in the ba gain, and arms and ammunition were provided to the rebel party. Th outcome of all this bullying was the granting of special harbor priv leges to both Germany and England.

To prevent further civil war both sides were invited in 1881 o board the American warship *Lackawanna* where an agreement wa reached. Malietoa Laupepa was to be recognized as king, his riva Tamasese as vice-king. The strongest native chief, Mataafa, was le out altogether, presumably because he was considered too stron and too independent of mind to be trusted by the foreign powers. A any rate the peace now established continued unbroken for ove three years. New native houses were being built, the usual sign peace expectations.

This agreement of 1881 was merely a temporary lull. Since eac of the three powers had acquired special privileges and freedom fro any import and export duties, it became increasingly more difficu to maintain a strong government in Samoa. Additional foreign in trigue soon unleashed new dogs of war.

New Zealanders, headed by the old imperialist, Sir George Gre brought to reality an old dream: namely, the formation of a federa tion under New Zealand to include all the islands of the Pacific sti

›t annexed by a foreign power. The intrigues of New Zealand ush-ed in counter intrigues by the Germans, especially after 1884 when essure by army and commercial interests induced Prince Bismarck encourage a policy of colonialism in the Pacific and elsewhere. ıe Germans resented the preference of the natives for an American British protectorate. They bitterly resented the remarks made by few Samoan chiefs in a private home to the effect that the Germans ere land robbers and had no religion. To impress the natives with e superiority of the Germans over the British, the former displayed cartoon of Bismarck sitting with his feet on the Union Jack.

King Malietoa, Vice-King Tamasese, and a number of high chiefs ere summoned by the German officials who read them an agree-ent providing that control of Samoan affairs be handed over to ermany. When the king asked for a copy, his request was refused. he Samoan government was ordered to sign the agreement by the ening of the second day from the day of delivery of the ultimatum; the event of a refusal the German warships in the harbor would ke action.

"Is it the practice among white nations to make one another sign eaties without first reading and discussing the terms?" asked King alietoa of the British consul to whom he turned for help. Some of e chiefs favored resisting the unjust demands of the Germans. Better fight them," was their advice. "We know well we are in bond-ge to the great government," moaned the king, and realizing what ıe German warships could do to his helpless people, he and his vice-ng agreed to sign the paper.

In its distress the Samoan government prepared a letter to the ritish government appealing for help. A copy of the letter fell into ıe hands of the Germans, either sold by a scribe for thirty dollars, as some suspected, betrayed by Vice-King Tamasese himself, an nbitious but weak, amorous, ponderous high chief of Aana district. he Germans were enraged and accused King Malietoa of double-ossing them. With arms furnished by Weber, Tamasese organized rebellion against Malietoa, and the Germans appointed him king. ome whispered that this was a reward for his treachery. The Ger-ıans laid claim to Mulinuu, the capital of the Samoan government, nd leveled serious charges against the deposed king.

Malietoa pleaded for an extension of time to enable him to co sult his chiefs before replying to the serious charges and the heav demands. His request was rejected. The Germans declared war upc Malietoa and hoisted their flag over the government house. Th British and American consuls issued proclamations protesting th action, declaring that they would continue to recognize Malietc as king, not the German puppet Tamasese.

To ward off German encroachment King Malietoa turned t Hawaii, a country very popular among Polynesians. In response t Malietoa's appeals, King Kalakaua of Hawaii, "viewed with solic tude the internal difficulties that have encompassed the Gover ment of Samoa and the possibility of foreign intervention affectin its independence." Kalakaua dispatched a mission to Samoa to assi in the organization of a stable government, framed on a Christia and civilized pattern similar to that of Hawaii herself, and to form confederation among the Polynesian islands. King Malietoa wa given the "Grand Cross of His Royal Order of the Star of Oceania an order instituted for the decoration of kings and chiefs of Poly nesia "and those who may in any way contribute to any advancemer of Polynesian communities."

The Hawaiian embassy was well received by the Malietoa part though a drinking bout which resulted in many of the high chie carpeting the floor with unconscious bodies was greatly disapprove by the good, missionary-trained Malietoa. The king, however, a serted that: "It is true that the Hawaiians and Samoans are relate by blood and other ties. I have in my possession genealogical recor which prove that your kings and people and myself are related." Th Hawaiian-Samoan episode went beyond pretty and eloquent speeche Both governments signed a treaty uniting the two countries into a p litical confederation. However in the face of American and Germa opposition, the whole Hawaiian-Samoan episode was ineffective an ended in failure.

The three powers made an attempt to solve the Samoan proble at a convention that met in Washington in 1877, but without succes It was doomed to failure because the American insistence on mai taining native autonomy and the German demand for a mandate ov the islands were irreconcilable. After the Washington Conferen ended in disappointment German intervention in Samoan affairs became even more serious. An adventurous, spectacular, ex-Bavarian artillery officer named Brandeis, became prime minister of the Tamasese Government and drilled his warriors in preparation for war upon Malietoa and his chiefs.

Brandeis's activities in Samoa remind one of the Steinberger episode. But while the latter was opposed by foreign officials, including the American, Brandeis could count on the support of the German consul and German warships. As soon as the monthly steamer from Sydney had departed from Apia and Samoa was cut off from any means of communication for weeks, the Germans felt that the time for action had come and took sterner measures against the Malietoa faction.

Malietoa was summoned to explain his conduct; to pay an indemnity amounting to $13,000, of which $12,000 was asked for fruit alleged to have been stolen from the German plantations during the preceding years, and $1,000 as fine for a supposed insult to the German Emperor on his Majesty's birthday during a clash in a bar-room between drunken Germans and Samoans.

To fill his cup of bitterness Malietoa was to undergo an *ifu,* the most degrading and humiliating form of abasement known to Samoans—the penitent was required to crawl toward the injured party on his stomach in the most abject manner. It is an interesting commentary on the behavior of the "civilized" whites that while they demanded respect from the natives, they showed very little for the Samoans.

Martial law was declared, seven hundred marines with six guns landed and hoisted the German flag over the government building. Malietoa was officially declared dethroned; Tamasese replaced him. German warships sailed up and down the coast in search of Malietoa who had taken to the bush.

The Malietoa faction blamed the American and British consuls for having advised the deposed king's adherents to remain inactive when they could easily, at the beginning, have stamped out the rebellion. Seven-eighths of the natives were on Malietoa's side, and many of the chiefs were straining at the leash to fight the despised Tamasese faction. All that the American and British consuls did was to protest against the action of the Germans, insisting that they woul continue to recognize the kingship of Malietoa and not the puppe Tamasese. The American consul regretted having restrained th Malietoa party. The British consul was in sympathy with the Amer can consul, but his government instructed him to cooperate with th Germans.

Though still supported by the great majority of the chiefs and pec ple, Malietoa finally decided to surrender. Before he capitulated h wrote a pathetic letter to the American consul, reminding him tha he had yielded to his advice and that of the British consul, not to figh Tamasese when the rebellion had started. Now the Germans ha joined the Tamasese forces in making war upon his party. "I do no know what wrongful act I have done, and do hereby protest agains the action done by Germany. But the German Government is stron and I indeed am weak, therefore I yield to their strength that m people may live and not be slaughtered." Malietoa issued a mos heartbroken appeal and farewell address to his helpless people wh wept when their king was forced to board the German ship, *Bismarck* to be taken into exile, destination unknown.

The four thousand warriors of the Malietoa party, highly incense against the aggressive Germans, turned for leadership to Mataafa high chief of Atua, an admirable leader, possessing great courag and capacity.

Mataafa warned the Germans that the great majority of Samoan would resist to the end any attempt to force on them Tamasese wh had no right to the kingship. Both sides now began to arm fran tically. Even among the white traders a strong party feeling pre vailed, and they would ask the purchasers of arms upon which sid they were going to fight.

In the name of his Majesty, King Tamasese, Brandeis publishe a letter to the chiefs ordering them to return to their houses or thei villages would be burned. "These instructions," he said, "were mad in truth in the sight of God in Heaven." The threat was carried ou and native villages were shelled and fired. The Germans would hav gone further in their policy of frightfulness had they not been re strained by the American naval captain, Leary, whose sympathy was entirely with the Mataafa-Malietoa faction. Attired in full uni form and attended by his staff, Commander Leary visited the German warship to protest, in the name of the United States and civilization, the German bombardment of native villages. He warned Captain Fritze that if he attempted to fire again he would have to do it through the American warship, the *Adams,* and that he, Leary, would resist even if this led to the sinking of the *Adams* by the more powerful German *Adler.* When the Germans made their night signals Leary sat on the poopdeck of the *Adams* and confused them with his own rockets. The frank, fighting language and actions of Captain Leary infuriated Fritze.

Apia then witnessed the comedy-tragedy of the battle of flags and proclamations. All sides hoisted their respective flags and issued proclamations and counter-proclamations. All consuls hastened on board their respective warships, which got up steam ready for action. When at sunrise, on November 15 the German warship with its consul on board steamed from the harbor, the British and American warships with their respective consuls followed suit. Though no one wanted war, with the possible exception of fighting Leary, peace and war "trembled in the balance." When the German *Adler* lowered her gun ports, a clash appeared imminent. Fortunately it was averted, and the ships returned to Apia harbor.

The natives, too, were itching for a fight. Hostage chiefs fled the Tamasese ranks and joined the rebel Mataafa forces as a protest against harsh German rule. Both sides used rallying signs: the Tamasese men wore white handkerchiefs, the Mataafa braves used red handkerchiefs and blackened their faces to counterfeit full beards. When the long expected clash finally came, the Mataafa forces routed the Tamasese faction and warriors began to exchange their white handkerchiefs for red ones.

The excitement of battle was exhilarating to many ardent young braves. One young warrior, shot in the arm, wanted to fight on while the pain was not yet severe. Another one, a mere boy, with the end of his nose shot off, asked for a pain-killer so he could continue. The Mataafa forces, flushed with victory, crowned Mataafa king under the name of Malietoa t'oa Mataafa. Then they paraded in the streets of Apia and besieged the Tamasese forces huddled on Mulinuu, a mere finger of land, an inglorious position for his "majesty's" army.

The whites in Apia expressed their partisanship openly and flagrantly. British, Americans, and Germans supplied their respective sides with arms and provisions. The British doctors cared for the Mataafa wounded; the Germans aided the Tamasese injured. A German from the consulate, passing by, asked an amateur British surgeon, "Why don't you let the dogs die?" "Go to Hell!" was the laconic reply. Such were the amenities among the whites in Apia.

Smarting from the defeat of their Tamasese forces, the Germans decided on another ill-judged and disastrous venture. On December 18, 1888 a detachment of German bluejackets was landed in the night to disarm the alert Mataafa men. Each side accused the other of opening fire. The Germans, fighting under adverse conditions, were repulsed at Fangalii with the loss of twenty dead and thirty wounded. Like school boys the Samoans were elated with the great victory against the supposedly invincible men of the German warships. The Fangalii victory bolstered their self-esteem and confidence enormously. The Germans, however, were enraged by their defeat and the display of the heads of their slain by the native braves. They vowed vengeance.

CHAPTER IX

THE HURRICANE

TO THE SAMOANS, Fangalii was a great moral victory; to the Germans, it was a minor but a humiliating defeat. While the natives and their Anglo-American partisans were openly rejoicing, the Germans were mourning their dead and wounded. They raged at the audacity of this horde of "savages" who dared defy and resist the sons of the Fatherland. They accused the Americans and the British of supplying arms to the natives with which to murder German bluejackets.

Now began the climactic scene of the *furor consularis* and the battle of proclamations. Blustering, menacing, Consul Knappe announced that the Germans must now take matters in their own hands. He summoned Mataafa to appear on a German warship; he ordered the shelling and burning of native villages; and with an ultimate stroke of authority, he proclaimed martial law for all the Samoan islands, including the British and American subjects. The Germans suppressed the Samoa *Times,* an intelligently edited weekly; they boarded a British vessel and removed a British subject to a German warship; they fired on the British and American flags!

Already at daggers with his German colleague, bluff Colonel de Coetlogen, the British Consul, accepted the gauntlet thrown to him by Knappe. In a vigorous counter proclamation he challenged the right of the Germans to declare martial law for British subjects. The Americans likewise protested.

The clash in Samoa was soon echoed in Washington, Berlin, and London. Bismarck admitted that the German officials in Samoa had "gone too far." Consul Knappe was told by the Chancellor: "You had no right to take foreigners from the jurisdiction of their consuls. The protest of your English colleague is grounded. . . . The demand formulated by you, as to the assumption of the government of Samoa by Germany, lay outside of your instructions and of our design. Take it immediately back." On February 27th Captain Fritze formally announced the suspension of martial law in Samoa.

The German Reichstag and press screamed: "The Samoan Islands must be German!" To test the American temper crafty Iron Chancellor Bismarck sent out a feeler, a report of a battle between the American and German warships stationed in Apia Harbor. As the account appeared in the "official" German newspapers it read: "The *Olga* has bombarded Mataafa's camp. The captain of the American man-of-war protested, but seeing his protest unheeded, he opened fire on the *Olga.* The shell burst between decks doing much damage. The *Olga* directed a torpedo at the American ship blowing her up with all hands."

These "shots," though never fired, were heard round the world. In America the response was unmistakable. In the Senate it was asserted that Americans would not permit themselves to be "brickbatted" from the Samoan islands. Editorials in magazines and newspapers from the *Independent* on the Atlantic coast and the Portland *Oregonian* on the Pacific coast criticized the pusillanimous policy of the Administration. They reminded Washington how Presidents John Adams and Andrew Jackson and Secretary of State Daniel Webster refused to be bamboozled by empty apologies, and made France and Austria "gasp for breath!" They insisted that the United States could not allow a strong Germany to crush helpless Samoa, not merely because it was our duty to stand behind the treaty of 1878, but also as a matter of far-reaching policy of the future. We must not lose our foothold and influence in Samoa which must some day be to the South Seas what Hawaii is to the north Pacific. Congress unanimously voted money to execute our obligations to protect our interests in Samoa. Three warships were dispatched to the troubled zone.

In Apia the atmosphere was tense. Samoans under arms looked with awe and amazement at the gathering of the formidable armada: one British, three American and three German warships. Americans and Germans glared at each other; Bismarck's premature report could have become a reality had not one of the most violent hurricanes ever experienced in the South Seas intervened, destroying six of the warships with the loss of many lives.

Across the wide extent of the semi-circular Apia Bay a coral reef stretches like the string of a bow for a distance of several miles. At low tide much of it is exposed. The only gateway for ships entering the bay is a funnel-shaped break in the center of the reef. A large sand bar on the eastern side further restricts the space within the harbor. Another coral reef on the western side extends from about 200 yards off shore to the middle of the bay. Rapid currents shoot in all directions; when the wind blows from the north the running sea sweeps violently through the funnel-shaped passage. The deep water and the lack of holding ground, force ships to drag their anchors during a stiff breeze from the north.

In this diminutive, exposed harbor seven warships had crowded by March 15, 1889. The German *Eber* lay nearest to the shore; ahead of her were the German *Olga* and the British *Calliope*. The American *Nipsic* was berthed about 200 yards from shore, with the German *Adler* just ahead. About a mile off shore, stationed beyond the *Calliope,* was the American *Vandalia.* The largest and last to arrive, the American flagship *Trenton,* was forced to drop anchor just within the outer reef, the most dangerous berth in the bay.

Several days before the hurricane the barometer began to fall; clearly a storm was imminent. Yet, instead of escaping into the open sea, the warships clung to their dangerous berths, hoping to outride the storm. Only the usual precautionary measures were taken: the upper spars were lowered and tied to the decks; the big guns were securely fastened; steam was raised in the boilers; anchors were dropped with sufficient cable to afford the ships ample play in a heavy sea.

Friday, 4 p. m. the storm broke. At midnight the gale became a raging, howling tempest of hurricane proportions. Mountainous waves rolled in from the open sea; the helpless, ponderous ships pitched wildly. There was no sleep for those on board that dreadful night. Every hand was needed to batten down the hatches, to work the pumps, to fire the boilers. By 3 a. m. all the warships were dragging their anchors and faced collisions. The crews, though panicky, kept their posts.

The howling storm and the crashing trees and roofs shook Apia. On shore people huddled, trying to protect themselves against the driving rain, wind and sand. In the blackness of the night the anxious watchers could see the riding lights of the warships, crossing and re-crossing, rising and dipping. Above the roar of gale and wave they could hear the shouting of officers and men on board the helpless ships. Fearfully they watched the tossing vessels which might crash at any moment, sending their crews to destruction.

When dawn broke upon the bay the spectacle was terrifying, yet awe-inspiring. The rain fell in sheets; the gale howled and lashed the sea into a seething foam. Black smoke poured from the funnels of the wallowing ships. The once proud, ponderous warships were now pitching helplessly like so many corks caught in the vortex of a whirl-pool. One moment they perched upon their beam-ends; the next in-stant their sterns rose exposing their rudders and revolving propellers. Soon they plunged into the trough and were buried in a torrent of water, which threatened to engulf them. Collisions were numerous that terrifying night and morning.

The first victim to succumb to this fury was the *Eber*. For hours she fought desperately, but it was a losing battle. Nearer and nearer she was drawn to the threatening reef, to relentless doom. As if to make a final effort to avoid destruction, she shot forward. The current veered her to the right where her prow struck the port-quarter of the *Nipsic* and the *Olga*. Crazily she swung around and drifted toward the reef. Then a wave lifted her high, carried her broadside, and hurled her upon the reef with such terrifying force that she was completely crushed. She was washed in the direction of the sea, then vanished from view. The terrified crowd on the beach cried out in horror. Even the natives forgot that these were their enemies who had warred on them. All were ready to give what aid they could in this tragic moment. They plunged into the deadly surf, where no white man could survive, in order to rescue any victims who might come to the surface. At first it appeared as if everyone on the *Eber* had perished. Not a hand, not a head was in sight. The breakers engulfed several struggling men who came to the surface for a moment. Soon, however, a few who were seen still clutching the piling were dragged to shore. These fortunate survivors had been on the bridge of the *Eber* during the last scene and had been hurled into the water. The rest of the crew were either dashed to death on the coral prongs or drowned.

At six in the morning the *Adler* found herself in distress. She had been swept across the bay, had collided with the *Olga,* and drifted broadside toward the reef. Breathlessly the grim crowd on shore saw a gigantic wave sweep toward her, lift her bodily on its crest and cast her upon the reef with a thunderous concussion. Her back was broken. She was left lying on her beam-ends, facing the beach. However only twenty men were drowned; the rest, including Fritze, swam back, grasped the rigging and gained shelter behind the deck which shielded them from wave and storm. The natives succeeded in getting a rope to the *Adler* and pulled a number of the crew to shore. When the rope broke, the remaining survivors had to spend the long weary hours of the day and night clinging to the wreckage. They were utterly exhausted when removed the following day.

At seven those on shore noticed that the *Nipsic* was moving toward the place where the *Eber* had struck. She succeeded, however, in clearing the reef by putting on full steam. To avoid being rammed by the *Olga* which was bearing down on her, she hit and sank a schooner. When the *Olga* finally did strike her amidships, smashing her smokestack which cracked with a thunderous roar, the crew began to run up the rigging for safety. For a moment excitement was at a fever pitch. Realizing that it would be difficult to steam off the reef, Captain Mullan beached his vessel in front of the American consulate.

An attempt was made to lower a lifeboat, but the falls failed to work; one end dropped and the men inside were dumped into the water and drowned. Another boat capsized; but its occupants were rescued by natives who stood waist-deep in the surf, risking their own lives. Some who plunged into the water were unable to swim through the swift current. The rest of the crew crowded on the forecastle, waiting for rescue. Double hawsers from the deck to the beach were fastened to a tree, and the rescue work began. At times, however, the ship was in danger of being shattered by the powerful squalls that broke upon her stem. The waves rolled so high and the undertow was so powerful that the skilled native rescuers were in danger of being washed away. Above the roar of the storm could be heard the shouting of the *Nipsic* crew and the singing of the native rescuers battling against the surf. By grasping the perilous life lines, often completely submerged and in danger of being washed away, the *Nipsic* crew succeeded in reaching shore where they were caught by stalwart natives and carried to the American consulate.

At 10 a. m. there remained in the harbor the *Trenton,* the *Vandalia,* the *Calliope,* and the *Olga.* Their hour had now struck. The *Vandalia,* the most unfortunate of the American squadron, and the *Calliope* were drifting toward the reef; a collision was certain. Suddenly a gigantic wave lifted the powerful iron prow of the *Calliope* high in the air, dropping her with a thunderous roar on the port quarter of the *Vandalia,* whose heavy timbers shivered and creaked. Every man was thrown by the shock.

Realizing that to remain in the harbor was suicide, Captain Kane decided to make a last effort to steam out to sea. With her anchors released, her boilers steaming, and her powerful engines roaring, the *Calliope* swung her head to windward. It was a perilous venture; without anchors she was forced to depend on her engines to clear the threatening reef. The crew worked madly feeding the red-hot furnaces. It was a desperate struggle, but slowly the ship began to plow through the powerful waves which were breaking over her bow and flooding her decks. Inch by inch she crept toward the fairway where she barely escaped collision with the *Trenton* and the reef. "My anchors are gone, and I am going to try to force my way out to sea!" shouted Captain Kane. "Good luck to you!" waved Admiral Kimberley. Despite the critical situation, facing death at any moment, Admiral Kimberley and the 450 officers and bluejackets on deck and in the rigging, roared "cheer and Godspeed!" to the gallant *Calliope.* "Three cheers for the *Trenton* and the American flag!" was the answer that came from the British tars across the menacing waves. The *Calliope* passed out of the harbor into the sea, out of immediate danger.

The *Vandalia* was less fortunate. The collision with the *Calliope* had torn a hole in her stern; water was gushing in furiously. Realizing that her engines were less powerful than those of the *Calliope*, Captain Schoonmaker decided to beach his ship. He gave orders to slip the anchor chains and to stoke the fires. Then for a quarter of a mile the *Vandalia* ran along the edge of the reef until she struck a soft sandbar.

As the stricken ship lay broadside to the wind, the waves pounded her mercilessly, breaking over her and flooding her hatches. By noon water had covered her gun-deck; the torrent had swept over the rails, knocked down the men. Most of the crew clung to the rigging until every inch of space on the ratlines and yards was filled. Only a few of them had life preservers. Lower and lower the hull of the *Vandalia* sank into the water. When the waves broke across the stem of the ship, the breathless crowd on the beach shuddered, fearing that the men would lose their grip and be devoured by the raging sea. Expert native swimmers ventured into the surf to carry a line to the *Vandalia*, but despite the shouts of encouragement by those on shore and on the sinking ship, these stout men were helpless against the powerful current. Some on the *Vandalia*, too weak to cling to the ropes, fell into the surging sea and were swept away. Captain Schoonmaker, with one ear almost torn off, still remained on deck. Suddenly he was struck by a hurtling machine-gun which had been torn from its base. Another wave hoisted the captain overboard. Skilled natives clasping hands stood at the edge of the current forming a human chain, hoping to grasp any victim afloat.

The *Trenton* was in a happier condition until her rudder and propeller, fouled by wreckage, snapped with a thunderous crack. It was impossible to keep water out of the berth-decks, hatches, and engine room. Cooped up below, in water to their waists, the firemen worked feverishly and gallantly. Any moment a sudden collision might fling them into a watery grave. About 9:30 the fires flickered out and only the superb skill of her officers saved the ship from destruction. When she came broadside toward the reef, something had to be done quickly. As a last expedient all hands were ordered into the port-rigging. This man-made sail, this compact sheet of humanity, might keep the weight of the vessel on the side of the storm. The panting crew seemed to hesitate. But this was no time to falter. Cadet Jackson swung into the rigging and shouted: "Follow me, boys!" Up the mast-head climbed all who managed to get a foothold on the ratlines. It was a unique experiment; it saved the ship. The wind lashed against the men in the rigging; the giant sail forced the ship from the reef. A roar of voices that could be heard above the storm assured the people on shore that the *Trenton* had been saved!

Soon the *Trenton* began to drift back against the *Olga;* it seemed as if both ships would be smashed. Fearing that this was her last hour, the flagship hoisted the Stars and Stripes. She would go down with her flag flying! The *Olga* attempted to escape by releasing her anchors, but it was too late; her bow crunched against the starboard quarter of the *Trenton.* Both ships suffered irreparable damage. After the ships drifted apart, the captain of the *Olga* beached his ship.

When the *Trenton* began drifting toward the sunken *Vandalia* there was fear that the shock might shatter both ships. At 4 p. m. the crew of the *Trenton* was called to the deck to be prepared for the final scene. When an old sail maker, with his flowing white beard, appeared on deck with his satchel of precious diamonds, the crew, though it faced death, greeted him with a shout of merriment. The chaplain admonished a profane bluejacket to pray rather than swear. "Ah, chaplain," spoke the weatherbitten seadog, "I've been a bad egg all my life, and if I was to pray now, the Lord would think I was codding him, and it would not be any use."

The situation on the *Vandalia* was even more critical, sunk against the reef with the surf reaching her masthead, her rigging and fore-masts filled with hungry, exhausted, bleeding men, desperately cling-ing to life. They trembled as they watched the hull of the *Trenton* about to crush them and the dark, angry sea ready to swallow them. Suddenly a roar: "Three cheers for the *Vandalia!*" was heard from the 450 voices on the *Trenton.* This tribute from their flagship warmed the hearts of the desperate men in the rigging of the *Vandalia* who looked death in the face. Though exhausted, they mustered enough strength to respond feebly.

"God help them!" murmured Americans on shore. Some kneeled and prayed; some wept. Suddenly the hundreds of forlorn men on the ships and the fearful crowd on shore heard the strains of *The Star Spangled Banner* rising faintly above the howling, raging storm. The band of the flagship was playing the national anthem! Americans on shore cried in despair but were unable to help.

Fortunately the collision was mild and even proved the salvation of the *Vandalia* crew. As soon as the two ships met, the men in the mainstay and mizzenmasts leaped to the deck of the *Trenton*. Lifelines fired from rockets on the *Trenton* and attached to the rigging rescued the men in the foremasts. The rescue was timely; no sooner had the last man reached the *Trenton* than the main mizzenmasts of the *Vandalia* went by the board.

All night Saturday the *Trenton* continued to beat against the *Vandalia*. Filled with water to her gun deck, with her back broken, the gallant flagship had made her last cruise. At dawn Sunday, when the wind calmed, the exhausted crews were brought to safety with lines carried by the natives. The frightful hurricane had ended but the memory of it was a horrible nightmare. Examining his wrecked warships, Admiral Kimberley remarked sadly: "Is it not awful? In all my experience on the sea I have never been in a storm equal to this one." The *Trenton* and the *Vandalia* were completely wrecked; nothing could be done to salvage them. The *Nipsic*, however, was convoyed to Auckland for repairs.

When the battered and damaged *Calliope* reappeared in Apia harbor on March 19, she beheld a spectacle of desolation. The *Olga* and the *Nipsic* were beached, the *Trenton* and the *Vandalia* were wrecked; the *Adler* was a broken shell on the reef; the *Eber* had vanished. Captain Kane expressed his heartfelt thanks to Admiral Kimberley and his men for their friendly sentiments toward the *Calliope*. He assured the Admiral that his crew were greatly heartened by this proof of good will. "When they saw the noble conduct of the *Trenton* crew and heard them, in the face of a fate even more certain than our own, cheer us on in our perilous path, all traces of listlessness and insubordination vanished." Admiral Kimberley replied: "We felt from our hearts for you, and our cheers came with sincerity and admiration. We could not have been gladder if it had been one of our ships, for in times like that I can say truly with old Tattnall that 'blood is thicker than water.' "

The survivors of the disaster were dazed; many of them severely injured. They had faced death; they had seen their friends drown. The American and German survivors were wisely kept apart in different sections of Apia. To lift the morale of his men, Admiral Kimberley marched his bedraggled surviving forces behind the band which enlivened the beach-road with the strains of *The Star Spangled Banner* and *Hail Columbia.*

The news of the disaster which reached the United States by cable from Auckland, produced a profound sensation. Americans read the tragic account of this gallant struggle of men against the sea with mixed emotions of sympathy and pride. The most thrilling passages in fiction seemed artificial and prosaic by comparison.

This Samoa incident led not only to extensive naval building in both the United States and Germany; it also accentuated the bad feeling already existing between the two countries. On the other hand, the good sportsmanship between the two English-speaking fleets in Apia helped to usher in the new era of Anglo-American friendship. In 1898, during the Spanish-American War, Londoners displayed and cheered the Stars and Stripes; on the other hand, they hissed *Die Wacht am Rhein.* In 1899 American and British warships in Apia became allies in a common front against the Germans.

CHAPTER X

FAA SAMOA

TO STUDY THE mode of life of the natives and to confer with their chiefs, Stevenson visited villages around Upolu and on other islands of the Samoan group. To the native the interior, or the "bush," was filled with mystery and *aitus* (spirits); his villages hugged the shore. To reach them one had to travel by boat along the coast which is often a stormy journey or follow obscure foot tracks. At times the wayfarer could pass through village after village along the coast with little break between them. Every village looked like an exact duplicate of its neighbor. Each stood on fresh green lawns, studded with trees and foliage, as though in a lovely park. Most of them faced the sea, enjoying the advantages of light and air.

At the end of December, 1889 Stevenson and Reverend Clarke visited a village a dozen miles to the east of Apia. In order to catch the tide on landing, and to avoid the heat, the party left about four o'clock in the morning. The pleasantest time in the tropics is just before sunrise, and again after sunset. In Samoa there is a difference of only one hour and twenty minutes between the shortest and the longest days. On the shortest day the sun rises at 6:20 a. m. and sets at 5:40 p. m., while on the longest day it rises at 5:40 a. m. and sets at 6:20 p. m. The air is fresh and exhilarating after the cooling dew of the tropical night, perhaps nature's reward for the approaching heat of the day.

Inside the lagoon the water was tranquil and of a brilliant green color; outside, the long blue rolling waves of the Pacific dashed and boomed against the barrier reef, rising many feet above the surface, then bending over, forming a graceful liquid arch and finally dissipating in a foamy white. The dark hillsides grew brighter and the clouds hovering over the hills became flecked and spangled with pale gold and pink. The coastline, a succession of inviting green bays, was fringed with graceful coconut palms, whose erect heads were crowned with wavy plumes of lace-like leaves. Here and there one could spy native huts, like bee-hives, hidden in green foliage of breadfruit trees.

When the boat passed Falefa, where the reef left off and the coast faced the open sea, the sheltered part of the voyage ended. Here the hills became loftier and marked by naked crags. A heavy surf pounded the bluffs and the boat, passing the broken water, twisted and turned like a drunkard. The panorama of water, sky and cliff was majestic and inspiring. On the blue crest of the swells a native boat appeared, probably on a visit to a neighboring village for a *malanga,* an excursion.

At the end of the bay the boat reached its destination. The village stood under a rocky promontory, hidden in a palm grove and sprayed by waterfalls. Fishing boats were idling on the water or resting up on the beach. When the Stevenson party disembarked their arrival was announced by vigorous drum-beating and the cry went up, *Papalangi! Papalangi!* Like the Pied Piper, Stevenson was followed by a group of children who pestered him with questions. Two of the urchins attempted to take hold of his hand and pull the rings off his fingers. Another one proudly carried the white man's shoes and stockings. Stevenson thought them "unpleasant, cheeky, ugly urchins."

The whole village was now astir. Life in a Samoan village commences with the sign of dawn when faint light begins to fall on the roofs and on the slender palm trees. Young lovers emerge from their trysts; children wander to the beach; men go to work around the taro, yam, and breadfruit patches, shouting lustily: "Whither goest?" "To the sea, and thee?" "To the mountain." "May you live." Women prepare food; others saunter to the pool back in the bush for the morning dip, gossip, and flirtation.

Everyone greeted the strangers with a warm smile and *talofa Alii!* (greetings O Chief!) Stevenson admired the young men whose wide shoulders, strong, smooth arms, long backs, and muscles shining like red bronze made them resemble statues of the ancient Greek gods. He admired the dexterity with which the natives draped themselves when they came out of the pool, especially the women. These latter, also, when entering the water with their *lava lavas* knotted around their hips, removed them with a single swing and held them in one hand as they reached deep water.

The village, like all Samoan villages, consisted of a cluster of oval mushroom-shaped huts placed without regard to order or line, but just to suit the fancy of their owners. According to tradition the Samoan ancestors were housed by the heavens; then a chief conceived the idea of building dwellings to serve as a shelter against rain and wind. These huts, which looked like giant beehives, some thirty feet in diameter and one hundred feet in circumference, were built of hard, durable breadfruit trees. The turtle-backed thatched roofs, much cooler than those of shingles, were of strips of sugar cane sewed together by women and laid with great care.

The houses were raised from the ground on a number of short posts four to five feet apart. The spaces between the posts were open; they were the doors and the windows. During the day all blinds were rolled up and the interior was exposed to light and air. There were no dark spots in the home; but when the weather was inclement, or at night, the rough, plaited coconut leaf blinds were pulled down. The remarkable thing about these huts was that not a nail was used in their entire construction; every part was fastened by sinnets of fiber. It took some seven or ten specialists to construct such a house, which was expected to last some fifty years and was admirably adapted to the needs of the people. The Samoan dwellings were considered among the best in the South Seas.

The visitors were escorted to the *faele-tele* or guest-house, situated in the most prominent part of the village. It was a sort of free hotel in which to entertain strangers. When a party of visitors arrived it took up quarters in the guest-house without inquiring where and how it was to be entertained. Hospitality and courteous treatment were expected and received. Of course, the villagers knew that such treatment would be reciprocated when they themselves visited another village on a *malanga*.

Except for size the guest-house was an exact replica of any private house in the village. The *malae* or lawn around the guest-house was soft and clean of weeds, for the women of the village spent much time and extreme care weeding. It was so soft that no sound was heard from the bare feet of the natives when stepping on it. In the interior of the guest-house Stevenson observed that the pillars were placed at considerable distances from each other in the shape of an ellipse and were wrapped in huge leaves, studded with white gardenias and scarlet hibiscus. Palm branches entwined with flower garlands decorated the entire building. The pebbly floor was covered with layers of thick mats, the finer and more elegant ones on the top.

A festive atmosphere prevailed in the *faele-tele;* the air was heavy with the musky fragrance of the ceremonial oil and flowers. As the guest of honor and as a token of friendship, Stevenson was seated in the center. The chiefs lined up according to rank, each seated against a post of the house. They sat cross-legged, without changing their position. When a chief wished to stretch his legs, he pulled a mat over them in accordance with native etiquette, for sitting with outstretched legs was considered indecorous.

Stevenson was favorably impressed with the appearance and dignified behavior of the chiefs. Many of them were distinguished by their great size, strength, haughty bearing, their upright position in sitting and dignified manner of walking. Like ancient Greek and Roman heroes they were born to counsel and to guide.

At the proper moment the leading *tulafale* of the assembly arose to make the customary speech of welcome without which no Samoan gathering was complete. There was absolute silence; all eyes were focused on the talking-man. The elderly gentleman spread his legs and deliberately laid his fly-flapper, the insignia of his office, on his shoulder. He leaned forward gracefully, with both hands gripping his six-foot orator's staff; leaning his head upon his hands as if in meditation, he paused for inspiration. No inspiration was really necessary, for most of the welcoming speeches were of the conventional type.

The pauses were merely a part of Samoan etiquette. In language sacred to his rank he spoke in short sentences; the cadence rose with the last words so that the effect was an emphatic assertion. It was the usual flowery, courtesy speech, abounding in phrases appropriate to the occasion. He welcomed the *alii* or chief from across the waters; he thanked God for having brought him safely; he offered him his humble hospitality and expressed the sincere wish that he would make his stay in Samoa long and that everything would prosper. "The love will last till the walls of the house shall crumble away in dust." When he finished, he said, "This is all," and sat down. Stevenson, through his interpreter, thanked them all for their courtesy and hospitality. He assured them that he was a great friend of their race and would do everything in his power to assist them.

When the speeches were over the assembly was ready to relax and enjoy the indispensable *kava* ceremony. No social event took place without *kava* drinking; it was the national tipple of the Polynesians, especially the Samoans. It was served on all occasions, even to working gangs in the bush. To the Samoan epicure it tasted better and was more satisfying than the finest of wines. If he could help it, he was never without a bowl of *kava,* and he wanted the brew as strong as possible. Women and boys were not to take it in public.

This national drink consisted of a mixture of water and the grated or chewed substance of a root of the pepper family, the *Piper Methysticum.* This plant of narcotic power grew luxuriantly all over Samoa as well as in the other South Sea Islands. In fact, according to Samoan tradition, the plant was introduced from Fiji by a Samoan girl who had married a Fiji chief. In the home the drink is prepared by the wife, but for special occasions young, dainty maidens are preferred for this task. Even strangers may be pressed into service, for no one can refuse to make *kava.* At important assemblies the chief *kava* maker was the *Taupo,* or village virgin—"Perpetual Queen of May," as Stevenson called her—assisted by her attendants.

Much ceremony accompanied the preparation of *kava.* The *Taupo* and her attendants, dressed in their best, properly oiled and bedecked with flowers, took their places at one end of the guest-house. The ancient and orthodox way, still preferred by epicures, required that the *Taupo* and her assistants chew the root into a mass of woody pulp instead of grating it in the more modern "degenerate" manner.

Young girls of considerable personal daintiness would first take a mouthful of water and then with their fingers clean their teeth. Thereupon they would stuff their mouths with pieces of the root which young men sliced and handed them. Slowly they would grind and chew and from time to time take a sip of water to moisten the mass until their cheeks would almost burst. When thoroughly masticated, the root was dropped into the palm of the hand where it was pressed into a flattened ball and deposited in the *kava* bowl. The entire operation was repeated until a sufficient amount was accumulated.

In deference to the sophisticated and effete whites the *kava* root was not chewed but grated in a beautifully carved, oval bowl of red-colored wood supported on four short legs. When a sufficient amount had been grated, water was poured over it into the bowl. One of the girls then would plunge her hands into the mixture and stir it thoroughly. Then, taking a bundle of vegetable fiber or tree bark, she would spread it out on the surface of the brew, push it like a screen to the bottom, collect the thick fluid, gracefully squeeze it out until all fibrous portions of the root were removed, and the juice was clear. The finished product was a greenish-yellow. All the steps were performed efficiently, gracefully and charmingly; every movement was carried on in keeping with proper etiquette. The drink was now ready to be passed to the host and to the guests. The ceremonious serving of the *kava* commenced.

A loud clapping of hands by the makers of the *kava* announced the good news that the popular drink was ready. The assembly responded in like manner. The most elaborate part of the ceremony now began: namely, serving the *kava* according to rank. The *tulafale* in charge of the ceremony had to be a consummate diplomat and be fully familiar with the social customs and rank of the assembled chiefs in order to avoid giving offense by any neglect of rights and precedence. An error in this respect often caused much heartbreak, even led to quarrels and war.

As soon as the clapping of hands ceased, the *tulafale,* appointed to act as toastmaster and in charge of correctly distributing the *kava,* called out aloud in a singsong tone: "Here is *kava,* let it be shared out!" One of the girls rose, took the cup, or *hipu,* and presented it to the girl in charge of the bowl, to be filled. The one at the bowl dipped the *fou,* or strainer, into the liquid and squeezed the contents into the cup held over the bowl. Several times the bearer of the cup swung it away gracefully and then in a similar fashion returned it to receive the next squeeze, and so until the cup was filled. She then faced about, and with the cup held delicately at a level with her chin and with her arm raised, stood in a charming position awaiting the crier's directions.

The toastmaster then chanted loudly, *O lau 'ava lena, Matagi fauna!* and uttered a somewhat prolonged: "Oh!! a cup of *kava* for Chief Tamasese" who was the highest individual in rank. The cup bearer crossed the room in dignified fashion, holding the cup level with her shoulders. With a graceful sweep of her outstretched arm, moving her head to distinctly timed rhythm, she bent down elegantly, lowered the cup with a grand sweeping motion until it reached the hand of the dignitary whose name had been called out. She then returned to the other end of the room, respectfully waiting until the illustrious personage had gulped down the drink at one draught. The chief, before swallowing the drink, however, poured a few drops on the floor as an offering to God, saying *Manuia! Soifua! Alii ma tulafale ma faipule!* [Prosperity to you! May you live! Chiefs, orators, and rulers.]

And thus the distribution of the *kava* went on until all were served in the proper order, with the strictest regard for precedent. The taste of the beverage was acrid, pungent, sweetish and like soapy water, leaving a sense of smoothness in the mouth. Though it is non-alcoholic, it can be intoxicating when taken in large quantities. It seems to affect the legs of the excessive drinker. However when taken in moderation it is harmless. Stevenson soon began to like it and indulged in it frequently.

After the *kava* ceremony there was the usual native feast. Stevenson and the chiefs, garlanded with gardenias and lilies, seated themselves on the ground before an array of food spread upon banana leaves, the national tablecloth. The food which had been wrapped in banana leaves and cooked on hot stones, consisted of fish, pigeons, pig, taros and palusami. The last-named dish, considered a delicious preparation, consisted of the taro leaf cooked in salt-water. Copious supplies of coconut milk, cool and refreshing, helped to wash down the food.

After dinner Stevenson had a chance to chat through an interpreter with some of the chiefs and even the ladies who dropped in to take a look at the *papalangi.* They asked him about the countries and cities across the sea. It was difficult for them to visualize the city of London, bigger than Apia, with many streets and blocks of houses. "But there must be room for trees to grow around each house," asked one. When informed that there were few trees along the streets he exclaimed in complete bewilderment, "No trees! What do people do for food; they cannot live without breadfruit and coconuts." When told that breadfruit and coconuts were not the staple diet of the people in those countries, the chief shook his head; he could not understand it and did not care to live in such a country.

Another chief asked why towns in the far countries were not built along the seashore to enable their people to catch fish. When he was assured that fish was sent to every town by rail he was happily amazed. "How, fresh fish every day, and the sea so far away! Oh, I must go to see that."

The feast was followed by the *siva,* the most popular form of recreation and entertainment in Samoa. So fond of dancing were the natives that they were ready actively to participate or merely to look on for hours, any time, any day. Unlike the Hawaiian *hula hula* danced only by women, the *siva* was danced by men as well.

The house was full of spectators, sitting cross-legged, looking forward to the ceremony with great expectation. The performers, too, were straining to start. Finally the long awaited *siva* commenced. The music opened with a rhythmic clapping of hands. This was augmented by the beating of mats with sticks. On a stage appeared a half-dozen men whose bodies, naked to the waist, glistened; green wreaths crowned their heads; scarlet leaves of hibiscus were gummed to their cheeks, chins and noses; the red berries and the fruit of the pandanus encircled their necks. The entire room was filled with the aroma of flowers and strongly scented oil.

Seated cross-legged on the floor these bacchi went through various energetic posturings descriptive of a battle in which they were the victors. When exhausted they retired to the orchestral ranks making way for a half-dozen lovely maidens, the pride of the village. The girls came onto the stage, looking demure but fully conscious of the role they were about to play. The upper part of their bodies, down to the waist, was decorated with garlands of flowers and leaves of all colors; around their necks were strands of scarlet berries. Their lower garments were merely *lava lavas* of exquisite mats, reaching to the knees and fastened with girdles of native cloth entwined with garlands. Anklets of green leaves completed the dance costume. Their bronzed, healthy looking, satin-like skins glistened from a liberal coating of perfumed oil.

As they sat in a row with their legs curled up they looked like Oriental sculptures. The dances were a great display of pantomime, describing various events and activities: fishing, washing, bathing, and love. They clapped their hands and sang their songs and swayed their bodies, their arms, and their thighs in various directions: they stretched their arms to one side, crossed them, passed them under their armpits, pressing each other's shoulders, rising upon their thighs. It was a complicated dance; yet no dancer missed a "step," and at all times the movements of the body were graceful, even elegant. Though it was strenuous exercise, they seemed to enjoy it and looked gay.

At the opportune moment, when the tempo of the dance quickened, and the performers and spectators were fully stirred, there leaped onto the stage the majestic form of the village *Taupo*. Even more than her group of dancers she typified love of adornment and feminine physical perfection, a vision of delight. Her figure was full, round and firm; her movements showed strength and agility. Nude to the waist, she was crowned with flowers, leaves, and berries; a necklace of red berries touched her rounded breasts; the finest mats covered the lower part of her body and an impressive looking grenadier's headdress of human hair and shells was bound tightly to her head. Like the others she glistened with the aromatic oil. She performed a heroic dance opposite her companion. She danced against her young lover chief who also was draped in garlands and shining from an ample coating of oil. As a reward for his few whispering remarks she gave him an affectionate whack. The *Taupo* danced with fire and excitement; she brought her entire body into play. Not a single movement of the body, head, arms, or even fingers failed to express grace and elegance.

Often when swept into delirium by the vigorous clapping and shouts of "malie" (bravo) of the excited spectators, these demure and graceful dancers would work themselves up into a veritable frenzy and throw themselves into weird postures, occasionally disrobing completely—although only for a moment. This delighted many of the older women who were living again the days of their youth when they, also, were daring and naughty.

Little wonder the missionaries, especially the native ones, disapproved of all dancing, Samoan or European, and even threatened church members with excommunication. Stevenson, however, was delighted with the performance; he believed that Westerners should not condemn these dances which in the eyes of the natives were performed in all innocence. Besides, in a country where the people have few occupations, dancing supplies a compensatory outlet. Stevenson felt he had witnessed a scene of ancient Greece; a display of form and beauty of movement that would have delighted a classic artist.

After the dance the *Taupo* spent a little time speaking to Stevenson, asking him all sorts of questions about the distant world from which he had come; the kind of dances they had, and whether they too had *Taupos*. She hoped that he was not a "missionali" who might condemn the *siva* he had seen. She was relieved when he assured her that he was not one of those strict ones. *Aloha oi* (I like you), she said and in parting she pressed two long fingers against her lips and spat through them: an expression of affection.

Stevenson learned that every village was proud of its *Taupo*. She was chosen by the leaders of the village from a family of good descent; usually she was the daughter of the chief. She had to be beautiful and above all a lady. She held the post of honor from the day she was crowned to the day of her marriage or her displacement because of misbehavior. Mothers of other eligible maidens were not averse to discovering something to the disadvantage of the *Taupo*, or even daring to contrive something, hoping thereby to disqualify her. Her life was, therefore, not altogether a happy one; she always had to be on her good behavior. She was constantly surrounded by a number of duennas. It was quite a lark when she could manage to slip away from her solicitous guardians.

She was not even allowed freedom in adorning her person for special occasions. While some of her attendants briskly rubbed her body with sweet-scented oil until her skin shone, others vigorously ushed her glossy hair. The attendants also decided what finery e should wear. The *Taupo* had to accept all this regimentation with- t protest. When finally she stood forth in complete attire—mats, rdles, flowers, and leaves—she was conscious of her beauty and portance, so much so, indeed, that she even disdained speaking anyone. Her elaborate costume had its disadvantages. It was im- ssible for her to sit down for fear of disarranging the exquisite rfection of her finery.

The main function of the *Taupo* was to direct all social amenities activities in which women could take part: to receive guests, ex- nd courtesies, provide lodging, food, to arrange picnics. In time of r the *Taupo* led warriors to combat, danced gracefully and twirled r war club at the head of the victorious braves. Often she was in e thick of the skirmish; her person was, however, respected by th sides. She could pass through the ranks of belligerent armies th perfect impunity, especially in daylight. Great horror would eep the ranks of both armies when they discovered that a *Taupo* d accidentally been killed or wounded.

The counterpart of the *Taupo* was the *Manaia,* the "beauty man," the "magnificent one." He was generally the son of a chief or opted by him and given a poetical name, such as Taivale (Low ater), Afiola (Living Fire). One was even called Setevani, which embled the name of Stevenson. The main qualifications for this norable position were physical beauty, strength, and a magnetic rsonality, a combination of a prince charming and a Greek Apollo. had to be a master in the art of commanding, appealing, com- menting and even flirting. He was to lead in the many peacetime ivities, captain the cricket team, head fishing parties, lead in dance, d in song; in time of war he led the younger braves to battle.

When a party of women from another village arrived on a *ma- ga,* the *Manaia* and his assistants would arrange for the feasts, rts, and dances. When the *malanga* party was composed of men, *Taupo* and her assistants would do the honors.

The *Manaia's* dress was exotic and charming. His light brown n, well-rubbed with scented coconut oil, glistened like polished nze. From waist to knee he wore an exquisitely woven pandanus ncloth. A twisted wreath circled one ankle. His already imposing stature was increased by a towering headdress of plumes, yello dyed hair adorned with scarlet feathers and sea shells. Around l sturdy, athletic neck hung a necklace of whale's teeth; about t powerful biceps of his well developed arm a polished tusk of a wi boar was tied with strands of hair intertwined with shells. His he knife flashed in the brilliant sun as he brandished it aloft.

The Samoans, like the ancient Greeks, had a deep appreciati of beauty. A pretty face without a handsome body was not enoug Mrs. Isobel Strong once saw a group of girls jeering at a young wa rior who had lost his arm in battle. "He would not be like that," s remonstrated, "if it were not for his bravery." "Oh, yes," the gi replied, "but he looks so funny." "He fought in your defense, y ungrateful creatures!" cried Isobel. "True enough," they admitt "but a man without beauty is contemptible."

Impelled by his desire to become better acquainted with t life of the natives, Stevenson continued his visits to other islan Early in January, 1890 he arrived at Malua where the London M sionary Society was conducting a training school for the native s dents. In his address, which was translated into Samoan, Stevens assured the students that they were the hope of their race and t their position was one of privilege and responsibility; that th carried in their hands the hope and future of their people. He urg them to learn to protect their race and their country and their la from exploitation by foreigners; to help make good laws and to ol them; to teach the people to be more industrious and not to depe upon the fruit of the toil of their neighbors or relatives, a system t breeds laziness and injustice to the earnest and hard-working. "M the beggars ashamed of their idleness and wish to labor and produc he urged.

Since in the Samoan language there is only one consonant each syllable and every syllable ends with a vowel, the name Stev son in Samoan would be Se-te-vi-ni-so-ni. Reverend J. Newell, t one of the instructors at the Malua College, suggested the na *Tusitala* (the writer of tales, from *Tusia,* to write, and *Tala,* tal The title, Tusitala, was acclaimed by all, including the great wr himself. And as Tusitala he was known throughout the South Seas

CHAPTER XI

VAILIMA

TEVENSON'S ORIGINAL PLAN was to stay in Samoa only long
nough to enable him to collect material for his book on the recent
erman-Samoan conflict, and then return to England. His first im-
ressions of Samoa and the natives were not too favorable. The is-
ands, he thought, were "less beautiful than the Marquesas or Ta-
iti; a more gentle scene, gentler activities, a tamer face of nature."
anny believed that the Marquesans and Tahitians were more amica-
le than were the Samoans. "I am assured," she wrote, "I shall like
he natives very much when I really know them. Perhaps I may, but
have my doubts."

Gradually, however, the spell of Samoa and its people fell upon
oth Stevenson and Fanny. They began to admire the physical and
piritual attributes of the natives: their handsome athletic bodies,
heir noble gait, their sense of humor, gaiety, gracious manner of
ddress, courtesy and hospitality. In the eyes of the natives any one
who did not practice the little courtesies was nothing less than a boor.
tevenson called them "God's best—his sweetest work," the gentle-

men of the Pacific, speaking a language, consisting principally of vowels, the Italian of the Pacific.

The Samoans reminded him of the ancient rustic, Boeotian Greeks: the same love of physical perfection, of beauty, of pageantry, of song, and of good form. Even their dress suggested that of the ancient Athenians and Romans: men and women bareheaded, naked to the waistline; their single garments, the *lava lava,* a form of kilt draped and folded like a Greek mantle. The women who were often garlanded with flowers and anointed with fragrant oil, or just "clad in a mere smile," charmed Stevenson. The young men resembled bronzed Apollos, and the young women graceful fauns. Perhaps Stevenson's own physical weakness greatly intensified his admiration for the physique of the Samoans. He envied them their powerful limbs which gave roundness to their bodies. He delighted in their stage-like stance, with feet and knees turned outward like those of Greek statues. The Samoans were passionately fond of decorating themselves with flowers about their waists, necks, in their hair, even behind their ears. A flower behind the ear signified "a going on courting."

The country and the climate, too, soon began to grow on Stevenson. He was charmed by the beautiful rivers, waterfalls, overhanging verdure, the dreamy tropical atmosphere with the enchanting sunrises and glorious moonlight nights. The climate with 95 degrees at the hottest and never cold except in the very early morning, he found pleasant and health-restoring. It agreed with him so well that the erstwhile semi-invalid, accustomed to lying on his back, was now living a normal life, free from hemorrhages, coughs, fever, and night sweats. He and health had long been strangers, but he was now able to walk up and down Apia's main street in a lively, eccentric manner, and ride five miles so rapidly that he was once arrested and fined for speeding. The arrest and fine made his blood boil, for the wife of the manager of the German firm had twice almost ridden him down and yet there "seemed none to say to her nay!" He wrote his friends inviting them to come to Samoa to see the most beautiful and healthful place in the world. Bragging about his restored vigor he wrote "Remember the pallid brute that lived in Skerryvore like a weevil in a biscuit?"

"Moors," exclaimed Stevenson one day, "island life has charms not to be found elsewhere! Half of the ills of mankind might be shaken off without doctor or medicine by mere residence in this lovely portion of the world. How little our friends in Europe know of the ease they might find here in Samoa." He then confided to Moors that he would like to make his home in Samoa permanently. "I like this place better than any I have seen in the Pacific," he stated. Then he added that Tahiti and the Marquesas pleased him but not so much as Samoa. "Honolulu's good—very good, but this seems more savage!"

"Then," replied Moors, "as you can't live in Scotland, in France, or in the States, and as there's more of the savage in you than Honolulu can satisfy, why not pitch your camp near the capital of Samoa?" Stevenson promised to give the subject serious consideration.

Shortly afterward Stevenson informed Moors that "Barkis (Fanny) is willing," that both of them had made up their minds to settle in Samoa. An additional incentive for choosing Apia as his home was its good mail connections with England, the United States, and Sydney. A German steamer ran regularly between Apia and Sydney; a New Zealand vessel called at Apia on her trip from Auckland and Tahiti. He was only fourteen days from San Francisco, only one month from England, and seven or eight days from Auckland, from where he could communicate by telegraph. In fact Samoa has been called "the half-way inn of the Pacific." The question of adequate mail connection was very important to Stevenson, the author and letter-writer. True, Tahiti had tugged at him strongly, but the mail service there was less regular, and he was not enthusiastic about living under the control of the French Colonial Government.

Stevenson asked Moors to purchase a large and attractive piece of land on which he could build a suitable house, one that would compare somewhat with Abbotsford, the home of his famous countryman, Sir Walter Scott, though, of course, not so large or ruinous to its owner. He warned Moors to purchase sufficient land so that he, Stevenson, could have "elbow-room." Possibly the years he had spent in crowded cities and within the confines of sick-rooms inclined him to be a bit of a claustrophobe. He longed for space, open space, for unobstructed views. The prospect of owning an estate cared for by native servants was extremely appealing.

The rumor that the celebrated novelist was arranging for the purchase of land on which to settle permanently in Apia spread immediately throughout the white colony in Samoa and was received with real pleasure. "We feel proud," wrote the Samoa *Times*, "that after examining many places in the South Seas, Mr. Stevenson, who gained such a world-wide fame as an author, selected as his future abode Samoa. He will be an immense acquisition to Samoa."

The new law forbidding natives to sell their land to whites made it difficult for Stevenson to buy a desirable tract. After examining several places, he purchased from a blind Scotch blacksmith a strip of some three hundred acres three miles from Apia up on a shelf at the foot of the green slope of Mount Vaea with an elevation of six hundred feet. Though the place had once been partly under cultivation, it was now covered with a tangle of tropical forest plants. It had rich, deep virgin soil, with one of the most picturesque views in Samoa, of great cliffs, ravines, waterfalls—one with a two-hundred foot drop—and gigantic trees of different species. To the east the land sloped abruptly into the deep valley of the Vaisaigano, the main river of Upolu; to the west a stream formed by four tributaries plunged over a rock into a pool some twelve feet below. This stream with its four tributaries suggested to Stevenson the name *Vailima,* in Samoan "the five waters" (*vai*-water, *lima*-five), a name that was soon to become renowned throughout the South Seas. To the north was a splendid view of the ocean.

Stevenson was proud of his estate. "It would be worth a good deal more (than $4,000) if it were beside a railway terminus," he wrote to a friend of his. In a speech to chiefs he said: "I love Samoa and her people. I love the land. I have chosen it to be my home while I live and my grave after I am dead." In answer to an inquiry by Sydney reporters whether he considered conditions in Samoa sufficiently stable to warrant his settling there, he replied that he would have to take his chances. He hoped that in time the affairs of the islands would improve.

When the land purchase had been completed Stevenson entrusted the supervision of clearing it, and the construction of a temporary building, to his friend Moors, while he and the family left for Sydney. There they were to meet Isobel Strong who had arrived rom Hawaii and also to receive anticipated letters from England nd America. From Sydney the Stevensons planned to run over to ngland on a visit, before settling in Samoa. The thought of returnng "home" thrilled Louis. He pictured himself arriving there: "Some me in the month of June a stalwart, weather-beaten man, evidently f seafaring antecedents, shall be observed wending his way between ne Athenaeum Club and Waterloo Place. Arrived off No. 17, he hall be observed to bring his head sharply to the wind, and tack into ne outer haven. 'Captain Payn in the harbour?' 'Ay, ay, sir. What hip?' 'Barquentin R.L.S., nine hundred and odd days out from ne port of Bournemouth, homeward bound, with yarns and curiosies.' "

In Sydney Stevenson received a great ovation; he was now at the eight of his fame and his *Dr. Jekyll and Mr. Hyde* was among the nost popular books. Photographers clamored for pictures and reorters for interviews. All the newspapers carried his photograph nd articles about him and his work. Invitations came from town lubs, fraternal brotherhoods, church organizations and literary soieties. Australian authors welcomed him to their country. Stevenon seemed to enjoy being lionized, though he was embarrassed hen some of his visitors acclaimed him the greatest living author, hose "insight into human nature was the marvel of the age." When ome of the local intellectuals asked him what he had been reading, e mischievously blurted out "Lynch, of course." He was referring the shilling shocker, *Dashing Kate the Female Detective*, which mused him greatly. The inquirers were puzzled, for they had never eard of Lynch. On another occasion when a young author asked the reat master to explain a poem by Browning, Stevenson read it and onchalantly remarked: "I'm damned if I know what it means. It eads like cat's meat to me."

There were also many dinners and luncheons. One evening at a inner, someone asked Stevenson whether he had read in a religious ewspaper a letter written by Dr. Hyde, a Presbyterian missionary, everely condemning Father Damien. In this letter Dr. Hyde accused ather Damien of having died from illicit relations with the female epers on the island of Molokai, in Hawaii. Stevenson, who had visited ne leper colony and conceived a great admiration for the Belgian

priest, became enraged when he read this scurrilous attack. His ange
prompted him to reply to the traducer of the dead Father.

Fearing that his fiery reply might lead to a libel suit, possibl
with ruinous financial results, he decided to summon the whole fam
ily for consultation. When all the members were assembled and th
doors locked, Stevenson, serious and excited, read aloud the lette
in which he defended Father Damien. He was willing to conced
that the former Belgian peasant was, perhaps, a pigheaded, obstinat
and bigoted man; but his courage, self-sacrifice and generosity, h
insisted, earned him the title of hero and saint. "Well, the man wh
tried to do what Damien did, is my father, and the father of the ma
in the Apia bar, and the father of all who love goodness; and he wa
your father too, if God had given you grace to see it," he wrote. H
asked Dr. Hyde why he preferred to live in a clean house with goo
food instead of living with leper outcasts, ministering to their needs.

He read the letter in his deep vibrant voice; his eyes blazed wit
indignation and deep emotion. When he finished he turned to Fanny
with tears in his eyes, asking for her opinion. Should he publish i
and risk a libel suit? Fanny rose, holding out both hands to him
exclaiming enthusiastically, "Print it! Publish it!" The other member
agreed. The family spent many hours drawing up a list of the name
of those to whom copies of the letter were to be sent. Among then
were the Pope, Queen Victoria, and the President of the Unite
States. The London newspapers did not print the letter. Scot's *Ob
server* did. When it was published in pamphlet form Stevenson de
cided to contribute the royalties to the leper colony. "I am not a can
nibal, I would not eat the flesh of Dr. Hyde," he wrote to his mothe

Sometime later, when Stevenson discovered that Dr. Hyde did no
intend to bring any action against him and that the clergyman's offend
ing letter had been published without its author's sanction and eve
knowledge, he regretted the harsh tone of his pamphlet. He wrote
"It is always harshness that one regrets. . . . I regret also my lette
to Dr. Hyde. Yes, I do; I think it was barbarously harsh; if I di
it now, I would defend Damien no less well, and give less pain t
those who are alive." He was greatly relieved that the good Dr. Hyd
contented himself with "the (truly innocuous) vengeance of callin
me a 'Bohemian Crank.'" This episode well illustrates Stevenson'

character: the impetuous, chivalrous Don Quixote always ready to defend to the limit the helpless, the injured, but always ready also to admit, upon further reflection, that often his impetuosity was unjustified and regrettable.

The cold Sydney climate brought back his former enemy, and after eighteen months of comparative health, he again suffered from his old malady, colds, fever, and hemorrhages. The recurrence of his former sickness confirmed him in his decision to make Samoa his home for good. According to Reverend Clarke Stevenson's original intention had been to make his permanent home in Sydney, but to take frequent journeys to Samoa for rest and enjoyment. To his friend Charles Baxter he wrote: "I am sure I shall never come back home except to die; I may do it, but shall always think of the move as suicidal, unless a great change comes over me, of which as yet I see no symptom." It was his great regret not to be able to "hail the white cliffs of Albion," to go up the channel, and to listen to the merry bands on the Thames, and to "thrill to the music of the Scotch pipers as the 'Black Watch' went gaily past to the quick-step of the *Highland Laddie* or *The Campbells Are Coming.*" Alas, he must lie like a prisoner, in his bedroom at the Union Club in Sydney, restricted to a diet of eggnog and medicine. Why, he was not even permitted to play on his beloved flageolet, lest he disturb the sacred quiet of the Club.

When Stevenson failed to improve, the doctors' verdict was: "The Pacific or death." But how? For unfortunately there was a seamen's strike in Sydney and all shipping was at a stand-still. Fanny, however, with her usual resourcefulness, discovered that a six-hundred-ton trading steamer, the *Janet Nicoll,* with a crew of Solomon Islanders, was about to sail for the Micronesian Islands. The owners of the vessel at first refused to take on passengers, especially a woman accompanying a sick man, who might, in case of trouble on the high seas, frighten the superstitious black crew. But Fanny persisted, pointing out that it was a question of life or death for her husband. Finally Messrs. Henderson and Macfarlane, the owners of the vessel, took pity on a brother Scot and reluctantly agreed to take them. "Rolled like a mummy in a blanket," Stevenson was carried to the quayside and rowed to the steamer.

In some respects the black-painted *Janet Nicoll* was quite an improvement over the *Equator*. "Think of two bathrooms," wrote Fanny, "and only one other passenger besides ourselves, a nice long wide deck to walk on, steam to run away from squalls with, and no flopping about in calms." The ship was, nonetheless, grimy with coal dust, manned by a black crew, and the "worst roller I have ever been aboard of," in Stevenson's opinion. Not in vain was she called "lively Jane." The food was good and the company excellent. To the jovial company of the owner, Henderson, and supercargo, Ben Hurd, was added the handsome, adventurous Jack "Tin," a nick-name for Mr Buckland, a South Sea trader to whom Stevenson later dedicated his *Island Night's Entertainments.*

The journey from Sydney to Auckland was most unpleasant. The sea was rough; there was rain and heavy wind; the vessel rolled; eating was a trying experience. Stevenson was nearly pitched out of his bunk by the wild antics of the *Janet Nicoll.* On arriving in Auckland he was bitterly disappointed because he was not able to meet Sir George Grey, a meeting that he had been looking forward to for many years. Grey, ex-Premier and ex-Governor of New Zealand was fully familiar with the islands, peoples, and problems of the South Seas. Unfortunately when the *Janet Nicoll* reached Auckland Stevenson was too ill to visit the great statesman. He sent him his regard with a copy of one of his books. Sir George Grey, who was himself house bound by illness at the time, expressed his sorrow at being unable to visit Stevenson, but sent him his heartiest sympathy, best wishes, copies of his most important works, and a photograph. Stevenson had a great admiration for the veteran statesman.

When the steamer left Auckland Stevenson's health improved considerably. This further convinced him that only in the healing climate of Samoa could he live in comparative physical comfort. A tragedy almost took place on shipboard when Buckland's fireworks exploded and threatened to destroy the cabin. In the nick of time Fanny prevented the crew from throwing a blazing trunk containing her husband's manuscripts over the side into the sea.

The rest of the four-months' journey was uneventful. Though the heat on the steamer was trying, nevertheless Stevenson found time and energy to put in many hours on his writings. The numerous stopovers which the *Janet Nicoll* made enabled him to visit about thirty five Micronesian Islands. He found that there was greater variety among "Hackney cabs," than among the Micronesian atolls. At Savage Island the entire population turned out to greet and gape at the *Janet Nicoll.* "The path up the cliffs," he wrote, "was crowded with gay island dresses . . . who wrapped me in their embraces, and picked my pockets of all my tobacco, with a manner which a touch would have made revolting, but as it was, was simply charming, like the Golden Age." The men were dressed in red and blue and garlanded with green leaves.

At Apemama the Stevensons had a reunion with King Tembinoka. The despot, looking older and thinner, received his old friends in a most friendly fashion. He clasped Stevenson with one arm and Fanny with the other; kissed them and wept for joy. He related how often, day after day, he looked through the glass over the sea and pretended to himself that he could see his good companions returning; often he imagined he could actually see their friendly faces. He recognized the dress Fanny wore. Pressing his hand against his chest he exclaimed with a dramatic gesture, "I want see you!" The old despot deplored the fact that the Stevensons had taken with them the pandanus box which held the secret of healing. The islands had suffered from measles during their absence; he himself had almost died of the disease. He was delighted when Fanny unfolded the flag which she had made for him.

Some time later, after their departure, the Stevensons were grieved to learn that an abscess on his leg, which a native doctor had lanced with an unclean fishbone, had caused blood poisoning and the painful death of their friend, the great Tembinoka. With his death ended the independence of Apemama; England finally annexed the entire archipelago.

After another visit to Sydney Lloyd was dispatched to England to bring out the furniture from Skerryvore for the house in Vailima. This meant that Stevenson had definitely given up all plans for a return to his native land. In August, 1890, he wrote to Henry James: "I must tell you plainly—I can't tell Colvin—I do not think I shall come to England more than once, and then it'll be to die . . . Health I enjoy in the tropics; even here, which they call sub- or even semi-tropics, I come only to catch cold. How should I do in England? I fear not at all. Am I very sorry? I am sorry about seven or eight people in England, and one or two in the States. And outside of that, I simply prefer Samoa. These are the words of honesty and soberness . . . I was never fond of towns, houses, society, or (it seems) civilisation . . . The sea, islands, the islanders, the island life and climate, make and keep me truly happier. These last two years I have been much at sea, and I have *never wearied;* sometimes I have indeed grown impatient for some destination; more often I was sorry that the voyage drew so early to an end: and never once did I lose my fidelity to blue water and a ship. It is plain, then, that for me exile to the place of schooners and islands can be in no sense regarded as a calamity."

On their return to Samoa Stevenson and Fanny lived gypsy style in a two-room wooden bungalow while the large house was being constructed. In January, 1891, Louis went to Sydney to meet his mother who had arrived from Scotland.

Upon his return to Samoa he decided to accompany Harold Sewall, the American Consul General, on a visit to Tutuila, the easternmost island of the Samoan group. Here he spent three weeks studying the country and the natives. The harbor of Pago Pago often reminded him of a Scottish loch. When one night he heard the rain falling on the tin roof above his head, he imagined he heard the ringing of a bell and tried to recall which of the bells of Edinburgh had the same tone. The Samoan with his *lava lava* recalled the Highlander with his belted plaid.

After spending three weeks he returned to Apia in an open boat, a twenty-eight hour voyage of 65 miles during which he was subjected to exposure and hardships; but there were no ill effects. "It is like a fairy story that I should have recovered liberty and strength and should go round again among my fellow-men, boating, riding, bathing, toiling hard with a wood-knife in the forest."

There was a great deal to do in connection with the planning of Stevenson's mansion in Vailima. "I must have a fine large room," he insisted, to serve as a reception and banquet hall. "Elbow-room! Elbow-room! Let's have elbow-room!" he implored. He insisted also on a wide balcony and fireplace. Most of the plans, however, prepared by him in cooperation with Moors and a Sydney architect, were far too liberal and would have been far too expensive. Pointing to a plan he had brought from Sydney he exclaimed: "It suits me exactly, it's simply wonderful!" "How about the expense?" asked Moors. "Oh, I never thought of that. It will have to be gone into, won't it? I wish you'd try to figure it out for me," replied Stevenson, somewhat discouraged.

When Moors reported that a house according to the Sydney plan would cost over $20,000, Stevenson decided, regretfully, that it would be far beyond his means and would have to be given up as impractical. The final plan, prepared by Stevenson and Fanny, provided for a house on a more modest scale, but it was to include a brick chimney running up through both floors. Moors pointed out that, since bricks were so expensive in Samoa, the chimney would cost over $1,000 and would be entirely unnecessary in a tropical climate. Stevenson snapped back: "Well, I don't know that we will ever light a fire, but it's good to know that if you want to light one you have a chimney to carry the smoke away. Moors, a fireplace makes a house look home-like." Stevenson had his way. The fireplace was built, though, according to Moors, it was seldom used and did not draw well anyway. Henry Simele, one of Vailima's leading native servants, was delighted with the hearth fire, for it was the first time in his life that he had seen anything of the kind. He enjoyed looking at it and was always eager to put on another stick.

While the great "mansion" was being built the Stevensons lived in a two-room wooden shanty, devoid of any furniture, and often of food. During the hurricane season the Stevensons feared that their rustic cottage might be crushed and blown away. "Yesterday," wrote Fanny in her diary, Christmas 1890, "we had a terrific storm, quite alarming to people living in such a vulnerable abode . . . From that time the gale increased, lashing the branches of the trees together and sometimes twisting their trunks and throwing them to the ground. We could see the rain through the windows driving in layers one sheet above another." All day the storm raged; the ships lying in the bay vanished in sheer rain. Stevenson considered this was more dangerous than being on ship where the worst that might happen was to drown; in the "shanty" they could be crushed by metal beams. Fearing for the safety of his papers, he locked them up in an iron box.

Henry Adams, the eminent American author, and his friend, John La Farge, the well known American painter, visited the Stevensons in their temporary and unattractive abode. Adams was not at all favorably impressed, and in his characteristically snobbish style gave the following account of his visit. "We mounted some gawky horses and rode up the hills about an hour on the native road or path which leads across the island. The forest is not especially exciting . . . we came on some little touch of tropical effect that had charm, especially a party of three girls in their dress of green leaves, or *titi*, which La Farge became glowing about . . . At last we came out on a clearing dotted with burned stumps exactly like the clearing in our backwoods. In the middle stood a two-story Irish shanty . . . A pervasive atmosphere of dirt seemed to hang around it, and the squalor like a railroad navvy's board hut. As we reached the steps, a figure came out that I cannot do justice to. Imagine a man so thin and emaciated that he looked like a bundle of sticks in a bag, with a head and eyes morbidly intelligent and restless. He was costumed in dirty striped cotton pyjamas, the baggy legs tucked into coarse knit woolen stockings, one of which was bright brown in color, the other a purplish dark tone."

Adams found Fanny wearing a missionary nightgown, "which was no cleaner than her husband's shirt and drawers, but she omitted the stockings." Nor was the Yankee Brahmin impressed with the landscape of Vailima or the mode of life of its owners. "His place," wrote Adams, "is as he says, 'full of Rousseaus,' meaning picturesque landscapes. I saw no Rousseaus, the day being unfavorable, but I saw a very dirty board cabin, with a still dirtier man and woman in it . . . To me the place seemed oppressively shut in by forest and mountain, but the weather may have caused that impression."

But Adams and La Farge had to admit that both Stevenson and his wife were interesting, amusing and lively. They were impressed with Stevenson's wide experiences of the South Seas. He had seen more of this part of the world than "any other literary or scientific man ever did before." They were amazed at his knowledge of the geology, sociology, laws, politics and ethnology of the Pacific region.

Stevenson seemed to gloat over his discomforts on his travels and cruises. He thought that every traveler should sail for months in small schooners, rancid with copra, mouldy and damp from the constant rain; he should live in atolls and eat poisonous fish. But Mrs. Stevenson complained that the Pacific cruises had caused her rheumatism and dyspepsia. Adams thought only "a Scotchman with consumption can defy every fatigue and danger."

Adams and La Farge visited the Stevensons again some time later; they found them in the same outfit. The lady wore no slippers and her nightgown costume had "apparently not been washed since our visit." Stevenson wore a brown knit woolen sock without heels on one foot and a greyish purple one on the other. Adams speculated whether these were the same old socks he had worn at the previous meeting. The sleeves of his flannel shirt were rolled up to his shoulders, "displaying a pair of the thinnest white arms I ever beheld, which he brandished in the air habitually as though he wanted to throw them away."

Stevenson entertained his visitors brilliantly for over four hours. He was extremely restless, jumping up and down, darting off and flying back. "His eyes and features gleamed with the hectic glow." Adams expected him to "drop with a hemorrhage at any moment," or to break in two. He was amazed at his endurance. "His fragility passes description, but his endurance passes his fragility!"

The fastidious Adams obviously did not appreciate Stevenson. "Their mode of existence here," he wrote, "is far less human than that of the natives, and compared with their shanty a native house is a palace; but this squalor must be somehow due to his education. All through him, the education shows. His early associates were all second-rate; he never seems by any chance to have come in contact with first-rate people, either men, women or artists. He does not know the difference between people, and mixes them up in a fashion as grotesque as if they were characters in his *New Arabian Nights*. Of course he must have found me out at once, for my Bostonianism, and finikin clinging to what I think the best, must rub him raw all over."

On his return to the United States Adams reported that the Stevensons lived in squalor and poverty, subsisting on bits of fruit and crackers; that the Stevensons' cabin had only two chairs; that Fanny and her husband were perched on boxes. This story when circulated in Europe and America caused many of Stevenson's friends real concern. As a matter of fact the story was a gross misrepresentation of the actual situation. To a friend Stevenson wrote that he was very happy in the company of Henry Adams and La Farge, and if it were not for the fact that his commissariat department was at that time empty, with only an avocado and onions and a few biscuits in the house, he would have invited them to dinner. "What would you do with a guest at such narrow seasons," he jestingly remarked, "eat him? or serve up a labor boy fricasseed?"

As planter and settler Stevenson supervised the building of his "mansion." He helped Fanny, who was a genuine pioneer, to clear the jungle and to plant and manage the land. He enjoyed the outdoor labor. "My hands," he wrote, "are often covered with blisters and full of thorns. Often we come late for dinner and when we go to bed at night I would cry for weariness of my loin and thigh." But he enjoyed it all. "Beer and skittles are fine things," he wrote, "but give me farming in the tropics for real interest." In fact he found it enchanting. "I wish someone would pay me ten pounds a day for taking care of cacao," he wrote, "and I could leave literature to others. Certainly, if I have plenty of exercise, and no work, I feel much better; but there is Biles the butcher! Him we have always with us." It was a source of pleasure to him and his wife to think that the erstwhile prisoner of Skerryvore was now strong enough to labor with ax and hoe, to slash the jungle brush or to catch and thrust squealing young pigs into their pens.

Fanny enjoyed farming even more than did her husband. "Ill or well, rain or shine," wrote Stevenson, "a little blue indefatigable figure is to be observed hawking about certain patches of garden. She comes in heated and bemired up to the eyebrows, late for every meal." In her blue overalls, slouch hat, tucked up skirts, barefooted, she planted, weeded, raised flowers, experimented with cacao and other seeds. She constantly complained that whenever she planted anything new, the servants weeded it up; that whenever she kept anything for seed, they destroyed it. From Fiji she brought various plants: jasmine, gardenia, custard apples, an Indian rubber tree. There were so many bananas that they were fed to the cows. Luscious oranges and pineapples luxuriated at Vailima. There were also enormous eggplants and cabbages, "the size of a German head," said one of the native servants.

The job of building the Vailima mansion was not an easy one. There was only a foot-track up the mountain side and all the timber and other materials had to be transported laboriously on pack horses. Stevenson imported some excellent horses to supplement the poor Samoan specimens. Undoubtedly such a house could have been built in any civilized country for half of what it cost him here. Stevenson, however, was enthusiastic about the venture. Daily he would ride down on his gray horse, "Jack," to relate to his friends in Apia the latest developments. Even the most boring details he related with such gusto and humor that his listeners fully enjoyed them.

At last the great house was completed and the family moved into its new, spacious quarters. "Villa Vailima," or the "Flash House," as it was called by people throughout the South Seas, or "Marble Halls" by the Stevensons because of the great expense, was, in the opinion of Moors, "ill-arranged and inconvenient." Photographs seem to give the impression of a rustic, barn-like house, "disappointingly lacking in picturesqueness." Some one described Vailima as an "Irish castle of 1820 minus 'the dirt.' " Lloyd Osbourne and his cousin Graham Balfour, however, insisted that the photographs did not do justice to the structure. Moreover, in relation to the superb site it was quite attractive. When, in deference to Mother Stevenson, a new wing, adjoining and in communication with the older one, was added late in 1892, the family found its quarters spacious and entirely adequate to its needs.

It was a large, rambling set of buildings, consisting of two wooden blocks of equal size, two stories high. Upstairs and on the ground floor along the front and on one side of the house ran spacious verandahs, some twelve feet deep. Outside, the house was painted dark green, almost a peacock blue, rather than green, contrasting with the corrugated iron roof which was painted red. The main interior feature was the large reception or banquet hall, which occupied the whole of the ground floor, some fifty feet long and thirty-five feet wide. Large sliding doors opened on the verandah overlooking Apia harbor. More than one hundred people could dine and dance in this spacious room. The walls were of varnished California redwood, and great redwood stairs ascended from the hall to the second floor. The villa contained in all three living rooms, a bath, a storeroom and a cellar on the first floor, and five bedrooms and a library upstairs. All rooms were accessible from the verandahs through sliding doors. Onto the verandah opened Stevenson's green library, which was lined and overrun with books. There was no semblance of order here nor anywhere in the Stevenson household. Stevenson's bedroom contained a bedstead, books, a table, chairs, etchings, a rack with six Colts and rifles. The large guest chamber, decorated with tapa and a number of curios which the Stevensons had collected on their travels in the South Seas, was also on the second floor.

The walls of the banquet hall were decorated with tapa and flags: on one side the red ensign of the Union Jack; on the other, the Stars and Stripes with Kalakaua's royal standard in the center. Above these was an exquisite piece of tapa from Savage Island which was painted in an elaborate pattern, centered with the words *Soi fua* (welcome). The floors were covered with many soft, white native mats. Leather-covered chairs, a Chippendale sideboard and a corner cupboard with old china had been brought from the Stevensons' residences at Bournemouth and Edinburgh. When the thirty-seven cases, some fifteen feet square, weighing two tons, arrived in Apia, the population gathered around to watch and cheer, for the like had never been seen in this Samoan town. These boxes had to be delivered to Vailima on bullock carts belonging to a German firm, and on the backs of islanders. The piano was slung on ropes supported by poles and carried upon the shoulders of natives. The journey took from 8 a. m. to 2 p. m. Excitedly Stevenson watched the romantic procession. "It cheered our hearts to see the home things," he wrote. Among the previous articles brought over and placed in the great hall were marble busts of old Robert Stevenson, the lighthouse builder, with his mighty forehead and strong jaw. There were, also, portraits of Father Thomas Stevenson and of Robert Louis Stevenson and Fanny. In addition there were a few Hogarths and a plaster group of Rodins, and pictures of bonny Scotland. The big wonder to the natives was the huge fireplace in the corner, unique in Samoa.

The site and view of the estate were most impressive. Like a medieval castle the great house dominated the entire countryside for miles around. Behind it Mount Vaea rose to a height of 1,500 feet, covered to its peak with virgin forest. From one side the blue mountains of Atua were visible in the distance. To the south there were undulating woods. In front was a lawn for tennis courts. Beyond, was a green paddock stretching for about a quarter of a mile. Here and everywhere around the house were magnificent trees, eight or ten yards in circumference at the base, and 150 feet in height, with splendid creepers winding about their trunks. There were dense, symmetrical mangoes; fragrant orange and lemon trees; glossy-leaved breadfruit, limes, citrons, pineapples, cacao and avocados. Some of the pineapples weighed as much as eighteen pounds. There were hedges of magnificent flowers: double, crimson hibiscus, perpetually in bloom; scented moso'oi trees, jasmine, gardenias and tuberoses. The place was like a perfumed garden. A stream that fell in a series of cascades, terminating in a sparkling clear pool, was suitable for bathing. The small cabin, called pineapple cottage, which the Stevensons occupied while the big house was being built, was now converted into a guest-house. At some distance, behind the mansion, were grouped the servant quarters.

Then there was the marvelous vista of fifty miles of the Pacific, brilliant as sapphire, shading into turquoise at the horizon. At dawn, when the morning light crept over mountain and forest, Stevenson often stood on the upper verandah, his excellent vantage point, and watched the ships as they sailed out of or into the roadstead of Apia. He could see the topmasts of those that were anchored far out. The quietness was often pierced by the plaintive cry of a bird, the dull thud of a falling tree, the raucous salutes from warships, the clear ringing of the bells of the Catholic Church at Apia, or the low of the conch shell calling labor boys on the German plantation. He could always hear the incessant, soothing murmur of the ocean surf, some three miles away and 600 feet below. About the house all went barefooted, nothing broke the silence. Later, when the sun's rays brushed the dew-moist flowers, Stevenson could hear the clear, melodious note of the *jao*, or honey-eater, and the *tuia*, a dark-plumaged bird, and various species of doves. The forest was filled with the homey cooings of pigeons.

The three-mile approach from Apia to Vailima was difficult but picturesque. The first mile from Apia to the native village of Tanugamanono was good and pleasant. The road, shaded by palms and banana trees, passed a few native huts on the outskirts of Apia. Then it ran along in front of the German plantation where one could meet Solomon Islanders with packs on their backs and a cringing look on their faces. At the village of Tanugamanono the rider would find himself amidst a cluster of native cottages and breadfruit trees. In the daytime he would be greeted with *talofas* by the women weeding the neatly kept village green, or by the brown children playing cricket. In the evening the traveler could see the natives sitting at dinner or lying in their beds.

Beyond the village the road shrunk to a mere path, narrowing in some places to two or three feet and zigzagging through forest and dense jungle. The great trees, with blossoms like red hawthorn, met overhead and formed a vast, thick, green canopy. On rainy days the steamy atmosphere was trying and quite oppressive. All kinds of curious noises broke the great stillness; one could hear the shrill call of a bird, the gushing water of a stream, the cracking of trees and brush. In the daytime the rider could glimpse the Apia harbor far below. On a dark night he would find the phosphorus on the decayed wood giving the appearance of streaks of light, of fire twinkling and flickering like the footsteps of native *aitus* (spirits). Stevenson drank in the grandeur of the ever changing scene around him. "What's the use of having eyes if we can't see the world we pass through," he would say. He complained, however, that his horse Jack could not calculate the height of his rider when passing underneath the trees.

As the trail emerged from the forests and turned to the right, the traveler suddenly found himself in a light, open space fanned by a breeze from the sea. Mount Vaea, majestic and verdure-clad, stood there—the eternal sentinel. Another turn of the road, and Vailima appeared in sight. The colorfully painted two-story buildings with their verandahs made a brilliant picture. The path ended at a large wooden gate which was opened by a friendly native servant, welcoming the visitor with a cordial *talofa.* The Stevensons usually received guests on the verandah. When the master returned from Apia on his reliable Jack, he would give his war whoop and Fanny and Henry Simele, Stevenson's native head-servant, would appear on the balcony. If the laird was kept in town too late and had to return to Vailima in the evening, he ordered that the house was to be entirely lit up, so that when he emerged from the dark woods it would serve as beacon and he could behold the glow from its many windows; then he would exclaim: "My beautiful forest, O my beautiful shining windy house. What a joy it was to behold them again!"

The laird of Vailima enjoyed the stroll around his estate, for there was much to explore. Often he carried a knife to slash a path through the jungle. In conversations with King Malietoa he learned of the historic events that had taken place around Vailima. It had been the scene of a great battle and the place was full of dead bodies. Several years later Stevenson found a human skeleton in his bush. Near it he found a second skull with a bullet hole. The explanation of this mystery was that a brave native must have taken the much coveted head of his wounded or slain opponent, but, being mortally wounded himself, did not have the strength to escape. He had crept into the bush where he died with his war trophy by his side. The Stevensons felt great sympathy for their brave, unfortunate neighbor, and decided to give him a worthy funeral. They deposited the bones in a coffin and buried them with honors. Tusitala gave out with a short speech; all bid the stranger farewell and "rest in peace"; Lloyd fired seven shots from his revolver and all shouted *tofa!*

Frequently Fanny would accompany her husband on a stroll along their estate. "Our prettiest walk," he wrote, "an alley of really beautiful greensward which leads through Fanny's garden to the river and the bridge and the beginning of the high woods on the mountain-side, where the *Tapua fafine* (or spirit of the land) has her dwelling, and the work boys fear to go alone." One day when Stevenson ventured to climb Mount Vaea he was startled by curious noises: nuts falling, shrill cries of birds that sounded strangely human. The natives feared these desolate spots, for, according to their legends, here dwelt *aitus fafine,* that is the female spirits of the woods. This particular *aitu fafine* was once a living woman; then she became an *aitu* and resided in a stream and her presence was heralded by a "gust of wind."

Stevenson roamed extensively, exploring the neighboring country. Once he reached the mysterious, circular Lake Lauto, some twenty-five-hundred feet above sea level. Alluding to the perpetual verdure around the banks of the lake, the natives sang of it: *Lau-touto'oe le toi ae lau mea.* A Samoan legend tells that the lake was formed long ago during a war between Upoluans and Savaiians. Two brothers, To'a and Ata offered resistance to invading Savaiians. Ata was overpowered and slain; To'a barely escaped. Overwhelmed by sorrow at the loss of his devoted brother, To'a retired into the mountain forest. At the summit he scooped out a hollow and leaning over its brink suffered his tears to drop into the hollow until it was filled. The lake thus formed has been known as Lau-tou-to'o. This lake was regarded with dread by natives, for they believed it to be the abode of eel-like spirits.

Stevenson was filled with the pride and joy of ownership. But often, when he stopped to think of the money he had lavished on it, he wondered whether his "Subpriorsford" justified the great expense. He was confident, however, that it "would support life with few external expenses." And should he die, the estate would be an endowment for his family. He invited his friends to come and see a most beautiful place and learn to know a most delightful people. "I never lived in such a heaven," he wrote. "This place is beautiful beyond dreams, real stars and moon overhead instead of the imitations that preside over London."

CHAPTER XII

THE LAIRD AND HIS CLAN

ALII VAILIMA, as was fitting, presided over a number of devoted native retainers who were always picked for their sturdy physique, pleasing manners, and loyalty.

In general the natives were averse to working regularly for hire. They could see no good reason for exerting themselves too much, since their demands were so few and nature was so generous in providing food and drink. There was always an ample supply of breadfruit, bananas, coconuts and oranges. Sea-food was available, and it was good sport fishing for it in the lagoon. For clothing they needed only a *lava lava* made of tree bark which the old women pounded into a fabric called *tapa,* painted and prepared for wear. Moreover, under their communal system, everyone was cared for; nobody starved as long as there was a sufficient supply of taro, pigs and other kinds of food. Stevenson tells of one of his servants who always returned from a visit to her "communistic" relatives with fewer of her good garments than she had started out with. If a Samoan was lighting a cigar someone had given him, and a passer-by asked for it, he would hand it over as a matter of course. "Why did you give that?" a white man standing nearby inquired. "Because he asked," was the reply. "But is there no further reason?" "Yes; I might some day want a cigar, and if he had one, I should ask him for it." Under such conditions money meant little or nothing to the natives. Then, too, the average Samoan considered himself "gentlefolk," entitled to lead a simple, happy-go-lucky life with an abundance of leisure for songs, dances, and games.

While the natives were not eager to work with any regularity for other whites, they flocked to their beloved Tusitala. Stevenson's popularity with the native workers was not due to the high wages he paid or the indulgent way he treated them. "It may surprise you to learn," wrote Stevenson, "that I pay lower wages than anybody in Samoa, and it is my boast that I get better served; visitors have frequently said Vailima is the only place where you can see Samoans run. People always tell you that Samoans will not work, or even if they do, never stay with you beyond a few months. Such seems to be the general experience; it is not mine." In fact he believed that the natives actually enjoyed discipline. Hence he always demanded unquestioning obedience; every man had his job laid out for him in advance, and an order given was seldom rescinded.

The Samoans were happy to serve the generous, beloved, High-Chief Tusitala, the friend and champion of the natives against the greedy, meddling whites. They were proud to wear the Vailima uniform, the colorful Stuart tartan. Being accustomed to a patriarchal form of society and considering themselves gentlefolk, they appreciated being treated as members of the family and included in all the household festivals. The master, on the other hand, took delight in governing his servants. He was proud to see his boys coming to him to seek his advice on all matters, even marriage. He truly felt himself the laird of his estate with his servants, members of his clan. And they, in turn, found this semi-feudal regime quite congenial.

The number of native servants varied. Usually there were two in the kitchen, two or three for house and table service; one was Fanny's special helper, another was in charge of the livestock. In addition to these there were the outside boys, ranging in number from a half-dozen to twenty or thirty, working under a native overseer. With the booming sound of the conch shell, heard over the entire estate, all began and ended their work.

The Vailima estate was a well managed affair. Every member of the household, from top to bottom, knew his position and duties. Lloyd was the bookkeeper, general manager and overseer of the gang of outside boys. Isobel Strong was in charge of the household and house and kitchen servants. Fanny served as the Vailima "doctor" and was in complete charge of the experimental gardens. She corresponded with Kew Gardens at Honolulu, Brisbane, Florida, and other places. She was the special supervisor of all the additions and improvements, "working with her hands when her tongue failed her." When, because of rheumatism and injuries received in chasing pigs, she was no longer able to move about actively, she shouted orders from her chair on the verandah: "Paul, you take a spade to that—dig a hole first. If you do that, you'll cut your foot off! Here, you boy, what you do there? You not get work? You go find Simele; suppose Simele no give him work, you tell him go 'way. I no want him here. That boy no good!" Her husband wrote: "She runs the show . . . hellish energy; relieved by fortnights of entire hibernation."

Fanny was most enterprising. She tried to make beer out of bananas. The results were, however, a great disappointment. The bottles blew up and the fermented fruit produced a most offensive odor. She was more successful with her experiment in making perfume from the *moso'oi* flower. Supplied by the young garlanded native girls, the flowers were boiled and distilled and the oil was removed carefully with a medicine dropper. Colgate Company in New York pronounced a sample of the perfume as excellent.

Stevenson was the great chief, the laird of his clan. He appeared on the scene when some one among his retainers misbehaved. Serious misdemeanors were rare, for the Vailima boys were as good as "a set of well behaved young ladies." They were also thoroughly honest. They had been warned by Stevenson that the old silver was his totem mark and anything so engraved must be kept in good condition; if lost or neglected, it jeopardized the prestige of the entire household. The servants appreciated this warning, for nothing of value was ever lost though the doors and windows were always left open and unguarded.

For all cases of misconduct and all breaches of discipline, such as absence without permission or going to Apia at night, Stevenson imposed some form of punishment. On one occasion he felt that the house boys were not behaving well. He immediately announced that a *fono* would be held. With Talolo as interpreter and Lloyd as his assistant, they went to the boys' quarters. The guilty ones he reprimanded; the meritorious ones he praised.

When serious offenses were committed he would hold a court-martial, or a bed of justice, in the grand manner, with interpreters and oaths. "When it comes to the judicial, I play dignity," he said. It used to be an impressive spectacle to behold the Alii Vailima sitting on his bed and the Samoan retainers sprawled on the floor around him, listening to his speech and awaiting the verdict. One day a pig was stolen. Suspecting that it might have been the act of one of the house boys, or that some one might have known about the theft, Stevenson called a bed of justice. With his cousin Balfour on his right, Henry Simele on his left, Lloyd behind him and all the native servants sitting on the floor around the walls, Stevenson, looking like a solemn chief, opened the proceedings with a Samoan prayer: "Our God, look down upon us and shine into our hearts. Help us to be far from falsehood so that each one of us may stand before Thy Face in his integrity."

The prayer over, Henry Simele followed by the other eleven natives, came forward, laid their hands on the Bible and repeated clause by clause after Stevenson the following oath: "This is the Holy Bible here that I am touching. Behold me, O God! If I know who it was that took away the pig, or the place to which it was taken, or have heard anything relating to it, and shall not declare the same—be made an end of by God this life of mine!" All the servants took the oath with utmost seriousness, for, as Stevenson believed, it "struck direct at the most lively superstitions of the race." He was so impressed with the attitude of the servants that he went no further and the solemn scene ended. It may have closed with something like this: "We live only by the high-chief-will of God, nor must we be cruel to one another when the High-Chief Son of God is so good to us all. One word must still be said. Let the story of the wicked business be buried in your hearts, lest strangers talk of it . . . Think of your own sins and hold your peace. This trial is finished. Sosimo, Mitaele and Pulu will make *'ava* for us all, and it will be called on the front verandah."

At first it was customary to discharge the culprit, and through this survival of the fittest only the most loyal remained. Stevenson, however, adopted the policy of substituting large fines for discharges. The substitution was also made to develop the character of the clan. No native was fined unless he first admitted that the decision was just. Usually the verdict was accepted, often cheerfully, even when the fine amounted to half the culprit's wages. When he refused to accept the decision he was paid in full and discharged. Funds derived from fines were usually donated to the missions, depending upon the denomination of the miscreant. The fact that most of the servants willingly, and often with a smile, accepted a fine of half their wages, was an indication, in Stevenson's opinion, that the natives had accepted him as their chief, for ordinarily they would quit rather than accept a cut of even a few shillings.

It may be of interest to point out that many of the native servants seldom took the wages that were due them, but left the money standing to their credit. The reasons were these: in the first place, the natives had no pockets in which to put their money; secondly, if they went down to Apia with their money, their friends and relatives would expect them to spend it or divide it all among them.

There is no question that Stevenson greatly enjoyed his part as laird of the Vailima clan. To him the native workers were like the Highlanders, their plaintive songs reminiscent of Highland Farewells. When one of his men wore a bonnet with a little tartan, Stevenson reminded him that the hat belonged to his native country, "Secotia." "Yes," replied the big Samoan, "that was the place that he belonged to right enough!" The reply amused Stevenson greatly. He often bragged that, with the exception of Fanny, everybody on the Vailima premises had some Scotch blood in his veins. He beamed when he watched his retainers march proudly in their Royal Stuart tartans and saluted them as *tama ona,* which he translated into his own Scotch as "Mac Richies," children of the rich man! He enjoyed the pageantry when his Catholic servants kneeled and kissed the ring of a visiting French bishop. "You should have seen our twenty-five

Popes," he wrote Colvin, "squatting and peering in the rays of forty-eight eyes through the back and the front door of the dining room."

Among the most important of the native servants at Vailima was Henry Simele. This Savaiian chiefling joined the Stevenson household when a mere boy, to learn "long explessions," and the manners of an English chief. He succeeded in learning English so well that his master often used him as an interpreter. As for English manners, the most effective expression of disapproval was to remind him "that is not *alii* England," (not in the manner of an English chief). He enjoyed Stevenson's account of life in London: blocks of tall buildings, the underground, theaters, universities, and night life. The latter especially appealed to him.

Henry was usually dressed in a red and white waistcoat and *lava lava,* a necklace of red berries around his neck, hanging low upon his chest. His hair was cut close, but over his forehead he left a tuft in which he stuck a big scarlet flower. He was a curious sight as he stood on a stump and gave orders to the native laborers, especially the black boys, in the strong tones of a superior. He was a great help to Fanny in supervising the laborers.

The Stevensons thought very highly of their Henry; he was exceedingly useful, their stand-by. "He is civilized beyond oiling down," remarked Fanny. Once Stevenson suggested that Faale, a native servant girl, would be a suitable wife for him. "I do not know yet," replied Henry, "I will tell you next week." "But," said Stevenson, "will not your family be angry if you marry without asking them?" "My village?" cried Henry, "what does my village want? Mats!"

One day, in September, 1891, Henry informed his boss that he must quit in order to be with his "poor old family in Savaii." Suspecting that he was planning to return to Savaii to be tattooed and get married, Stevenson advised him to do what he thought was his duty, though he frankly hated the idea of losing him. In fact everyone in Vailima was sorry to say goodbye to Henry.

Before Henry's departure Stevenson invited him to lunch at the Chinaman's restaurant in Apia. Henry appeared in his kilt of gray, blue jacket, white shirt and black necktie, looking "like a dark genteel guest in a Highland shooting box." The climax of the farewell party was a visit to the circus with its ponies and dogs.

After a short absence, Henry returned to Vailima with a spear wound in his neck. Stevenson suspected that Henry's love affair had been unsuccessful. One wonders how young Samoans who loved gaiety and being in a crowd telling stories, passing jests and amusing themselves with the girls, could be happy with the quiet environment of Vailima and with its diet of decimals, grammar, and the mariner's compass. Vailima, however, was not altogether a lonesome place. The natives often stayed up till eleven talking, singing and dancing. They amused themselves also with cricket and other games.

The chief cook of the household was Talolo, a tall, handsome native with a drooping mustache. Stevenson called him "the Colonel," for he resembled an officer in the Life Guards. One day Lloyd had noticed him sitting outside. The Stevensons were badly in need of a cook. "Chief," said Lloyd, "you are he that I have been looking for so long. You are going to stay in Vailima and be our cook!"

"But I don't know how to cook!" he replied.

"That is no matter, two months ago I was as you are today . . . I will teach you my skill," Lloyd assured him.

"But I don't want to learn," protested Talolo.

"There is no good making excuses. This is a psychological moment in the history of Vailima. You are the man of destiny," said Lloyd.

"But I haven't my box," pleaded the young native.

"I will send for it!" asserted Lloyd, who also added that the chief of the Vailima clan rewarded his workers with money every Saturday evening and entertained his faithful servants as well as visitors with tinned beef and other delicacies.

Thus was Talolo initiated into the secrets of cookery for which he showed not only great aptitude but also a willingness to learn. He visited the kitchen of the French priests to perfect his art and to learn how to make salads, omelettes and *pot-au-feu*. Since cooking was considered a man's art in Samoa, Talolo was proud of his accomplishments and of his position as the chief of the Vailima kitchen for four years. He was especially proud of his biscuits. To Isobel Strong he said: "You make him black fellas. Loia make him white fellas. My fellas good Samoan brown." He took a great interest in the kitchen utensils which he kept well polished and gleaming. The egg-beater and the waffle-iron especially fascinated him.

Talolo, however, had contempt for the white man's bleached complexion and his strange manners. "White people lack wisdom," he blurted out, "I cannot endure them. All their cups and little plates, foolish. Those implements they eat with one for this kind of food, another for another one. For what then God gave them fingers!" When he accompanied Stevenson to Honolulu he was greatly impressed with the wonders of civilization: pavements, streetcars, electric lights and ice cream.

Talolo was of a good Samoan family and when gorgeously arrayed in his *lava lava,* white shirt and wreaths of flowers, he looked imposing. He brought into the Stevenson household a number of his Catholic relatives who proved very trustworthy. When he got married he brought his wife, Sigua, to work in the household. The family was fond of the gentle, modest, pretty young Samoan woman and treated her well. When she first arrived, her room was decorated with flowers and everyone in the house had gifts for her.

Stevenson's valet, Sosimo, was very devoted to his master. Once when Stevenson was too tired to help himself to tobacco, Sosimo sensed it and immediately appeared with what his master had been longing for. *Qel e le potu!* (how great is the wisdom) exclaimed Stevenson gratefully. Sosimo's quick reply was "How great is the love!"

Then there was the "Archangel" Lafaele (English Raphael), a veritable Hercules, a sturdy oarsman and good with the ax, but hopelessly dull. One day when Fanny was writing in her room Lafaele, wearing a colorful *lava lava,* his thick curly hair dyed red, entered and sat down on his heels before her, a posture expressing respect. Then he began to relate his troubles: "Everybody say me old man. Please you tell me what you think. Maybe you think me old fella?" Fanny sympathetically assured him that his face and vigorous body did not seem to show signs of age. "No," she added, "you are not old, Lafaele. When the great heavy pole we were putting up for the native house fell, you caught it on your shoulder. You held it, but it took three men to lift it off. Only a young man could do that. Then the big root in the lawn—no one could pull it out but you. Anybody call you old man you laugh, Lafaele. You young fellow." The "Archangel" left relieved and beaming with delight.

Lafaele was not fortunate with his wives. His first one was killed in a fall from a cliff. It was rumored that she had been shoved off by a group of workers whom she served as harlot. His second wife, Faauma, a dainty creature as "beautiful as a bronze candlestick," came to Vailima when she was a mere slip of a girl. Stevenson, whom she reverently called "papa," regarded her dainty limbs, arms and little hips as "veritable masterpieces." He admired "the minx" when she entered his room to wash his windows, dressed in a *lava lava* and a red handkerchief hanging around her neck between her breasts.

When Faauma left Lafaele's bed and bosom, the Archangel, feeling disconsolate, threw himself at Fanny's feet saying: "I belong to you now." "No you don't belong to me, you can't unless I say so," replied Fanny. "That's all right," retorted Lafaele, "you all the same my mother now. You savee I no belong this island. I Fituna man. Long time ago, I leetle young boy, one American whaler man he stealeee me. Long time I go catch whale. By and by Captain he go home, no want me any more; he put me ashore in Apia. I no got father, I no got mother, I no got brother, I no got sister. I no got friend neither. My wife, she Samoan girl, she no good; she no like me any more; she like Samoan man. I no got nobody; I allee same one fellow." Lafaele did not, however, seem to take his loss too much to heart. When Talolo was asked by Fanny why the natives do not seem to feel bad very long after such a piece of hard luck he replied: "Yes we do. When a man's wife runs away a native will feel bad for two or three days!"

Lafaele began to look for another wife. He soon brought one to Vailima for approval, but when he realized that she "had no conversation," he decided to take back his repentant Faauma who was decorative and good-natured. Henry, as go-between, listened to the confessions of both Lafaele and Faauma, and a happy reconciliation took place.

Despite his herculean physique, Lafaele was desperately afraid of ghosts and dared not walk alone in a dark forest. When Fanny sent him to work in the garden at some distance from the house, he refused to stay there alone for fear of devils. The natives believed that ghosts haunted Vailima. Like all Samoans the Vailima boys believed that the woods were filled with spirits or *aitus* who took the form of pigs, or flying creatures. The most dangerous spirits came in the shape of beautiful women and handsome young men who dressed in fine kilts and necklaces and scarlet seed flowers. Woe to one who spoke to these *aitus*, for the victim would be "hexed" out of his wits and die.

It was told that a handsome young man passing through the mountains was met by a female *aitu*. She tempted him and shortly afterward he died. One of the brothers of a village *taupo* was assailed by a female spirit; he returned half-crazed and never recovered. It was also reported that two beautifully dressed young women asked a native for some of the fish he was cooking in his house. In accordance with the Samoan custom the man complied with their request. When he asked one of the women for her red necklace, she replied: "I will give it to you by and by," and immediately vanished. During the night the man heard the voice of the woman crying to him to come out and get the necklace. When the man looked out he beheld the woman standing on the sea, as one might stand on a table. Frightened, the man fell upon his knees and prayed. When he looked out again the woman had disappeared. This was a "devil of the woods."

The natives believed that these spirits fished on the reefs alongside the living fishermen. They would step silently from canoe to canoe; their presence could be felt as a draught of warm or chilly air. Some believed that the spirits had their own canoes, just out of reach of human hands; others maintained that the spirits walked on water. They made for the shore and disappeared in the woods the moment their presence was suspected. They might be recognized by their lanterns, in the trackless mountains, and later by their tracks. Hence the natives were afraid to walk in the dark, especially in the wooded sections.

Lafaele's superstitions found other expressions. One day he announced that he had a devil in his toe and asked for a Samoan medicine-man. When the medicine-man arrived he did not resort to incantations, but put on a dressing of leaves soaked in coconut oil. The following morning Lafaele announced happily that his foot was "more better, and he sleep all right."

When any of the native servants were sick, Fanny acted as nurse and often as doctor. Frequently there was rivalry between her and the native medicine-man. When Sigua had a sore foot, Talolo's mother arrived to exorcize the supposed devil. When Paatalise of Wallis Island became delirious and kept shouting that he must go to his people who were waiting for him in the bush it took the combined efforts of all the men on the premises to keep him from escaping. Lafaele repeated some incantations "to drive away the devils." Then he chewed some leaves and put the juice into the patient's eyes, ears and nostrils, half choking him, to force him to draw it in. A quarter of an hour later the patient fell into a comatose state and lay quietly till morning when he got up and seemed as well as usual.

In addition to the regular Samoan servants there were at Vailima some natives from the Solomon and Hebrides Islands who had been "recruited" and brought to work on the German plantations. Most of these young blacks were gentle and sweet-smiling, though often melancholy and homesick. Their garb consisted of scarlet *lava lavas.* Having no pockets, they tied a string about their upper arms or around their necks on which they hung their pipes. Some wore ivory rings in their noses. The Samoans feared them, believing them capable of savage cruelty.

Stevenson thought them shabby and sorrowful, like sick monkeys. Their outcries when pushing a heavy cart sounded like those of a large strange bird. When he met them on the way to Apia he would shout: "Good morning!" Very few would answer him and those who did would do so with a piglike grunt. He often thought of discontinuing his practice of greeting them, but when he saw their melancholy look he continued the usual salute. As time went on more answered him. One called out in English: "You good man—always say 'Good morning!' " "It was sad to think that these poor creatures should think so much of so small a piece of civility," reflected Stevenson.

To make these blacks work harder, the German overseers often mistreated them. Some of the poor creatures would run into the forest, where they would build little sheds of leaves and feed on nuts, roots and fruits. When the scanty food supply failed them, they would often come into the village to steal. Their existence was miserable. Tracked and hunted by their German masters and denounced by the Samoans who feared and suspected them, they often reverted to ancient, ferocious habits. The Samoans accused them of practicing cannibalism, especially of catching and eating women.

One stormy day, when Stevenson was reading aloud Kinglake's *Charge of the Light Brigade,* a figure appeared on the verandah. Upon opening the door, Stevenson saw a slim, black lad with limed hair, who pleaded nervously: "I come here stop." He was given food and lodging.

Another time the servants dragged into the house a thin, terrified black boy whom they had found behind the trees of Vailima. This black boy, called Arrick, fell upon his knees and begged Stevenson to give him his protection. On the following day Stevenson visited the German firm for which Arrick had worked, and made the necessary arrangements to keep the runaway boy.

In a short time Arrick began to fill out and became plump and strong. The Samoans, who considered the black boys savages and cannibals, were, however, fond of Arrick. The girls, especially, treated him as if he were a pet monkey. Talolo reprimanded the mischievous girls, saying: "You must not despise him because his skin is black. His soul is as brown as yours and mine." When the girls discovered that Arrick did not bathe, they dragged him into the pool where they gave him a good scrubbing, limed his kinky hair and polished his body with oil until it glistened like ebony. Pleased with this beauty treatment, Arrick grinned and giggled. He now developed a veritable passion for bathing and went every morning and evening to the pool under the waterfall.

One day Arrick begged Stevenson for a gun. "What do you want with a gun, Arrick?" asked Stevenson. Smiling good-naturedly he replied that if he had a gun he would go into the bush and shoot black boys. Asked why he wanted to shoot runaway blacks, he replied, "What for he run away, then?"

At another time Arrick was sent on an errand to the German firm. He returned late with a bandage around his head, but all smiles and excited. When asked what had happened, he explained with pride how some of the blacks, who were his enemies back home, had attacked him; one of them had cut his head and back with a knife. However, in spite of the odds against him, he boasted that he had fought them all, and would have killed the boy with the knife had he not been rescued by his companions, three of whom had ended up in the hospital. "I knocked them down, three-four!" he boasted. He himself, however, had to be taken to the doctor to be bandaged. The following day Arrick was still too excited to work. The glory of his great victory was still undimmed. He was so elated that he came to Fanny's room to sing and dance a war dance. Accompanying himself on his one-stringed harp he enacted a head-hunting scene.

Occasionally Stevenson had complaints about "his boys." One day a missionary reported that Iopu was not married to his "wife," mother of his child, thus setting a bad example for the other young people in Vailima. Stevenson assured the missionary that he would investigate the case. When Iopu and his "wife" were questioned, the gentle and considerate couple assured their master that their intentions were strictly honorable, but whenever they had three dollars, the cost of the marriage ceremony, the native pastor was either away fishing or off elsewhere, and that whenever the clergyman was at home the couple did not have the money. Stevenson then gave Iopu three dollars and instructed him to go to the village and get married at once. Several weeks passed. When Stevenson asked Iopu whether he had gotten married, "No," he replied, "but it's all right; we had the baby photographed!"

There were whisperings about Helen, the washerwoman, wife of the tall, handsome Tomas of Fiji who moved like a marionette. Helen was a healthy, chaste, industrious and attractive young woman, full of energy and seriousness, a splendid worker. During prayer meetings she acted as the preceptress, leading the singing of hymns, for it was customary for a woman to start the singing, with the men following. Helen was fully familiar with the whole repertory of hymns and was delighted to train the chorus. She had a good taste in hymns, which she read aloud with a "great sentiment of rhythm." But while the others of Stevenson's native retainers were of "chief people," Helen was of no family at all, just a common woman. The natives in Vailima plotted against her and deputations came to Stevenson with sobs and outcries about her low social estate. The maligned woman finally agreed to leave, and happiness was restored to the Vailima household.

In general Stevenson found the Samoan women more ornamental than useful. The men spoiled their women by not permitting them to do hard work. When one of the women was assigned a difficult task, such as polishing glass or cleaning silver, she always managed to coax one of the men to do the work for her.

Stevenson's fame as a great chief of many retainers spread throughout the Samoan islands. One day there arrived at Vailima a native Methodist pastor accompanied by his son and daughter. The pastor, dressed in white clothes and wearing shoes and stockings, made a long speech saying that he had heard that Tusitala loved *faifeaus* (ministers) and always had *lotu* (worship) in his house. Now that he was at Vailima he felt like the Queen of Sheba who, when she visited King Solomon, of whose wisdom and greatness she had heard, exclaimed: "Behold the half was not told me!" He had also heard much about the beauty of the land and the splendor of Tusitala's house, and now that he had seen all he was fain to use the same words as the Queen of Sheba: "Behold the half was not told." The beauty and eloquence of the speech could be attributed to the fact that the visitor, Tale Papapanga, was a "talking-man." He begged Stevenson to take one of his sons as a Vailima "boy" and was tremendously delighted when the answer was favorable. Asuelo, his son, who had inherited his father's "gift of gab," later became the poet laureate of Vailima. He planned sivas, composed songs, including a plaintive chant for Graham Balfour which reminded Stevenson of the Highland Farewells.

Alii Vailima took a deep interest, a personal interest, in the selection of his retainers. The fact that among the household servants were always a number of the most attractive Samoan women, gave rise to some ribald jesting among the white residents. They referred to the female Vailima servants as "Stevenson's harem," and chuckled at the author's gallant attentions to the Samoan beauties at balls and festivals. However Reverend S. J. Whitmee, the novelist's friend, asserted that "the honor of a native girl was as dear to Stevenson as the honor of a white woman." It seems rather that Stevenson had an eye for the beauty of the human body whether male or female.

He was devoted to his people and took great pains to educate them. He spent especially much time teaching Henry Simele. In a letter to Conan Doyle Stevenson told about the difficulties he encountered in his attempt to re-narrate *The Engineer's Thumb* to Henry. It was necessary for the narrator to go farther afield than Conan Doyle had done; to explain what a railway was, "what a steam hammer, what a coach and horse, what coining, what a criminal, and what the police." Judging by the boy's "drawn, anxious features, and the bright, feverish eyes," he believed that he had succeeded with his pupil. Such camaraderie existed between Tusitala and all his native retainers.

A somewhat similar spirit prevailed between the rest of the Stevenson family and the Vailima household servants. Since the English names were difficult for the natives to pronounce, each member of the Stevenson family happily assumed a Samoan name. Stevenson was Tusitala or "Le Ona" (the rich one); Fanny was "Aolele" (the flying cloud); Isobel, "Teuila" (beautifying the ugly); Aunt Maggie, "Tamaitai Metua" (the old lady); and Lloyd, "Loia."

CHAPTER XIII

ALII VAILIMA

AT VAILIMA STEVENSON spent the last five happiest years of his life. Vailima was his home, his workshop, his show place, the center of entertainment and gaiety. Here he lived a patriarchal and semi-feudal life, presiding over his immediate family and a retinue of natives who loved and adored him.

In general the current of life at Vailima ran serenely but with sufficient variety to add zest to Stevenson's existence. One day he would spend writing, weeding and playing, in an atmosphere of absolute tranquility, only now and then interrupted by the laughter of his brown boys or by the conch shell of the distant German plantation. On the following day Vailima might be resounding with the arrival of important visitors: tourists, chiefs, naval officers, missionaries, or just plain people. All were his friends: from the simple native to the king; from the bluejacket to the naval captain; from the brown pastor to the Catholic bishop. They came to pay their respects; they came to consult him on important matters. Then there were gay parties, balls, native feasts, birthday and Christmas celebrations. Trumpets proclaimed the march of native warriors; booming cannon announced the arrival of a warship in Apia Harbor. During the tense war days there were exciting secret rides to the armed camps to confer with the rival kings and high chiefs. There were urgent visits to the hospital to nurse the wounded; to the gaol, to feed prisoner chiefs.

Stevenson's flair for the grandiose qualified him for such an exciting and adventurous role. He enjoyed knight-errantry. "It is a life that suits me but it absorbs me like an ocean," he confessed. He was flattered to hear that the fame of Vailima had spread even to Europe and America.

His friends wrote him that not since Byron's adventures and tragic death in Greece had a British author succeeded in so greatly arousing the romantic enthusiasm of his readers. His life on a tropic isle in the South Seas, his "castle," his household of Polynesian savages, all contributed to make Stevenson an even more glamorous figure than the hero of Missolonghi.

Stevenson was an industrious, methodical craftsman and an early riser. Long before the conch shell awakened the rest of the household he was already at work. His mind was most keen at dawn when man and nature were awakening. From his verandah he could see the skies brightening into gold; he could listen to the distant steady pounding and roar along the reef or to the call of the *manu-iao,* "the bird of dawn." After a breakfast of eggs, bread and tea—brought in by his devoted servant—he was busy at his desk, or, with a pad on his knee, making notes until about eight. After a short rest he resumed his work until his stepdaughter, Isobel, came in to take dictation. Barefooted, in white duck trousers and shirt open at the neck, Stevenson paced up and down the room, pushing chairs aside, kicking at the piles of books on the mats. He continued his dictation until about eleven.

At noon the entire household assembled in the large hall for a meal of two or three courses. The afternoon hours were devoted to recreation: reading aloud, chatting, playing piquet, or the flageolet, sitting on the verandah smoking, drinking coffee, or entertaining visitors. At two o'clock the clapping of hands announced *kava.* Each member of the household came for his cup; according to Samoan custom, the master received his first. Stevenson flattered himself that, in the ceremony of *kava*-drinking, with its correct libations and salutations, he was a past-master, and that perhaps not twenty whites in the entire world could claim as much.

After *kava* he would return to his writing-desk, or some sort of diversion: a game of croquet or tennis, a stroll into the woods of his estate, or weeding and clearing. Often he saddled his dark brown Jack, a Samoan-bred pony which he purchased from Moors in 1890, and rode to Apia on business or for recreation or to bring back town gossip. He was an excellent horseman and his light weight of some 110 pounds was undoubtedly greatly appreciated by Jack who was gentle but for his disagreeable "habit of shying and sitting down on his tail, if he sees a basket in the road, or even a bunch of bananas." Stevenson was very fond of his pony, and when the "master" died, Jack was never mounted again; he was allowed to spend his remaining years in a paddock at Apia.

At dinners, served between five and six, Stevenson always presided. His mother sat on his left, Fanny on his right, Isobel and Lloyd opposite him. Talolo did the cooking; Fulu, his assistant, brought in the food and handed it to Faauma, who was the head waitress. The table attendants, in their colorful *lava lavas*, with fresh flowers beautifully arranged in their hair, stood in attendance like statues, ready to respond to the slightest signal. On important occasions the table glittered with massive silver and glowing red china. The servants were colorful in their Royal Stuart tartans. Fuming braziers under the table kept the mosquitos away. As the laird and the son of a Scotch Covenanter, Stevenson was recognized by all to be the absolute head and center of interest: everything revolved around him; he dominated the conversation; he was truly the autocrat of the dinner table. It was his wish that no controversial topics be brought up during the meal; dining was to be the occasion for pleasant conversation and laughter.

After dinner there were relaxing hours on the verandah, lounging in easy chairs or squatting on mats, smoking, chatting, or card playing. When any of the visitors present could sing or play the piano, he would be invited to perform. On an ordinary evening all the members of the Vailima household scattered to their rooms at eight o'clock,

After a snack Stevenson, the early riser, was ready to turn in for the night. His bed consisted of a chest, mat and blankets, "No mattress, sheets or filth." Quite frequently he would read himself to sleep; in fact he did most of his reading between eight and ten in the evening.

Vailima was the only white man's home in Apia other than the mission, where daily prayers were said. This was done to please Aunt Maggie and the native servants. After the day's work was finished the war conch was sounded summoning the members of the household to prayer. *Lotu! Lotu!* was the cry. Soon the Stevenson family formed one group at the end of the great hall, while the natives trooped in quietly, often with their lanterns, and with great decorum seated themselves in a semicircle on the floor under the big lamp suspended from the ceiling. This patriarchal scene delighted the would-be Highland laird and would have greatly pleased old Thomas Stevenson.

Alii Vailima felt deep satisfaction as he watched these reverential gatherings, with the natives kneeling under the gaze of his Scottish ancestors. Aunt Maggie sat in her arm-chair with her back toward Rodin's *Spring*, listening intently to her devoted son as he read a chapter from the Bible and then the prayers, some of which he had composed for the occasion: "Lord, behold our family here assembled. We thank Thee for this place in which we dwell; for the love that unites us; for the peace accorded us this day; for the hope with which we expect the morrow; for the health, the work, the food, and the bright skies, that make our lives delightful; for our friends in all parts of the earth, and our friendly helpers in this foreign isle. Let peace abound in our small company. . . . Give us courage and gaiety and the quiet mind. Spare to us our friends, soften to us our enemies. . . ." These utterances expressed in beautiful English prose the sentiments of a restless, wandering spirit which had found contentment in its new home. The services concluded with the singing of one or more hymns in Samoan and the recitation of the Lord's Prayer in Samoan by the entire group.

Although the natives failed to comprehend and observe the moral and ethical ideals of Christianity, they were very punctilious about the rites and ceremonies of religion.

They enjoyed especially hymn-singing, and it was impressive to hear the "long rambling Samoan hymn rolling up," wrote Stevenson. "Many of these hymns were set to ancient tunes very wild and warlike." Even in pagan days, when the evening fires had been lighted and the proper libations had been offered to the gods, the Samoans would pray: "Sail by O Gods! and let us be; ye unknown Gods, who haunt the sea." With the coming of Christianity hymn-singing became even more popular. At twilight, when the fires were lighted, and preceding the evening meal, the head of each native household would read the prayers and sing hymns. The omission of this ceremony would have indicated not only a lack of religious training in the house chief, but a shameless disregard for all that was most highly regarded in Samoan social life.

In Vailima, as in most isolated places, news was always eagerly received. Everyone coming even from nearby Apia was plied for the latest reports and latest gossip, the "merrier the better." And in Samoa, as an Irishman once remarked: "You can be in a new conspiracy every day."

The entire household relished discussing the news, the scandals and the gossip. When Sosimo brought the mail from Apia he took it up immediately to Stevenson's room. There the head of the house would empty the waterproof sack and distribute the mail to the members of the family who would be sitting on the floor in great expectancy. No one dared snatch up a piece of mail without the master's approval.

Life in Vailima was quiet and idyllic. No trains, no carriages disturbed the silence; everybody walked barefooted. This life was made to order for Stevenson, although its daily routine and placidity were interrupted on numerous occasions. When work was pressing, when the author felt the spur of inspiration and a story was in process of gestation, or new episodes were being introduced into one that was already under way, he would continue at his desk the entire day, and even into the night. On the other hand, when he was ill or not in the proper mood for writing, he would spend the greater part of the day loafing or busying himself around the estate with all sorts of odd jobs—helping to feed the calf, drive out a bull, or nurse sick servants. His cousin, Graham Balfour, relates an incident he witnessed during his visit to Vailima. A hogshead of claret had arrived from Bordeaux in such condition that it had to be bottled immediately. Stevenson was in his utmost glory that day when he supervised the washing of the bottles, the tapping of the cask, the pouring of the red wine into bottles which were then dipped into green sealing wax. The whole operation and the part he played in it delighted him greatly.

Much of Stevenson's time at Vailima was taken up by frequent visitors, native and white. Though he honestly enjoyed them and felt proud that people cared to come from near and far, he found the interruptions interfering with his work and considered setting aside one day a week for an "at home." This would leave him the balance of the week for writing.

The spaciousness and lavishness of decoration of the "flash house" called Vailima, dazzled the Samoans, from the common man up to the highest chief, including the king and queen, for such luxury was not to be seen anywhere else in Samoa, not even in the king's "palace." Little wonder that Tusitala was known among the natives as *le ona,* the man who owned great possessions. When one of the native ministers saw in Aunt Maggie's room an old oak cupboard dated 1634, he exclaimed, "surely it must be as old as Noah!" A chief who gazed intently at two gilded Buddhas whispered, "Are they alive?" A more sophisticated Samoan looked puzzled at the nude figures of a young man and a young woman embracing, then remarked: "It is very beautiful. But I don't understand it. Do these figures tell a story? Is there some legend connected with them? What is the meaning?"

The natives saw in Tusitala not only a man of great riches, but one also very wise and genuinely friendly; one who always had their welfare at heart, ready to battle for their cause. His stepson, Lloyd Osbourne, tells of the frequent visits of the natives: "Government chiefs and rebels consulted him with regard to policy. Old gentlemen would arrive in stately procession with squealing pigs for the chief-house of wisdom, and would beg advice on the capitation tax or some such subject of the hour; an armed party would come from across the islands with gifts, and a request that Tusitala take charge of the funds of the village and buy the roof-iron for a proposed church . . . and poor war-worn chieftains, whose only anxiety was to join the winning side, and who wished to consult with Tusitala as to which that might be. Mr. Stevenson would sometimes sigh as he saw these stately folk crossing the lawn in single file, their attendants following them with presents and baskets, but he never failed to receive them or hear their story."

Among the most favored native visitors at Vailima was Laulii. Though not very young or blessed with regular features, her wit, sparkling eyes, gaiety, vitality, charm and tact made her the most popular native woman in the social circles of Apia. She was invited, without her oldish American husband, to all social affairs: balls, races, luncheons, dinners and tennis parties. On all of these occasions she was the center of attraction, with many admirers around her.

When Stevenson was engrossed in work in his library no one was permitted to interrupt him except Laulii. He gave orders that he was to be notified when she arrived, and he would either come down to meet her or she would be conducted to his study. There her admirer would sit on his couch, watching intently the dramatization by Laulii of the latest gossip of the beach, or her description of an important scene. Her English, too, was picturesque: the bride's dress was "silk sadine dreamed in flowers." Of the Samoan chief who was rewarded by the United States Government with a watch and chain for his heroic services during the hurricane of 1889, she said: "You see that chief, you laugh. He wear no coat, he got no pocket. Round his bare belly he wear a belt to hold that watch and chain."

Another native belle of whom Stevenson was fond was Fanua, the former *Taupo* of Apia.

Alii Vailima took a great interest in the social life of the natives and half-castes. When the latter complained that the foreigners in Apia held themselves aloof, not caring to mingle with or teach them the ways of the white man, Stevenson agreed to organize a club for natives and half-castes only; he and Fanny were to be the only whites admitted. On the evening of March 10, 1892, some twenty-five native men and women came to Vailima for the organizing party. Some of the native women, married to whites, brought their husbands, but the latter were not permitted to join.

The Stevensons received their guests on the front verandah, which was beautifully decorated with flowers and Chinese lanterns. Tusitala opened the meeting with an address on the objectives of the organization: namely, amusement and improvement. He spoke deliberately and restated each idea in a number of ways, so that every one in the audience could understand. It was agreed that the name of the club was to be "Royal Vine-ula," *vine-ula* being the name of a native flower, emblematic of Apia. It was necessary to get the king's permission to use the word royal. Fanny was chosen president with the power to expel any recalcitrant member. When the organization was completed the Stevensons entertained the group with refreshments of cake and lemonade. The members were given their first lesson in dressing neatly, and in the ways of meeting as ladies and gentlemen. Before departing one half-caste stated that this was the first time that any white man tried to do anything for them socially; he and his friends felt deeply grateful to Tusitala and his wife.

During the regular meetings that followed the members of the club were taught the mysteries of the waltz, the lancers and the schottische. Belle taught the natives how to bow, how to ask their partners for a dance, and how to lead them back to their seats. Nor were the activities confined to dancing. At the third meeting Fanny read a much appreciated paper on good manners. Alii Vailima enjoyed the meetings and danced with the members of the group. Unfortunately friction developed; some members took umbrage at the fact that the native cook was taken into the club, and the organization was discontinued.

Vailima was the center of attraction not only for the natives but also for whites. There one could meet consuls, land commissioners, naval officers, bluejackets, traders and missionaries. Many tourists who stopped at Samoa made it a practice to visit Vailima, the "show place" of the islands and the home of the popular novelist. One afternoon, forgetting that it was steamer-day, Fanny found herself busy at work in a blue *holaku* and a big native straw hat. One of the tourists inquired, "Is this Vailima? Are Mr. and Mrs. Stevenson at home?"; whereupon she shouted from the roof of a carriage house, "No spik English!" The visitors were received at the house and served tea, and as they departed, expressed regret at not having seen Mrs. Stevenson.

When visitors arrived at Vailima, the native retainers would announce them. The Stevensons would then assemble on the verandah to welcome their guests with kind words and refreshments. The host liked to see visitors come, but they were not to be encouraged to linger after they had begun their leave-taking. Members of the household were to refrain from starting a new topic of conversation if the visitors were ready to depart. In honor of guests who stayed for dinner the laird had the attendants wear their uniform; he loved the contrast between western evening clothes and the colorful *lava lavas* and the garlands of the half-naked attendants. Here in the great baronial hall decorated with sculptured works of Rodin and August St. Gaudens, paintings by Hogarth, Sargent, Lemon and Will H. Low, were also rifle-racks, revolvers and trophies of native warfare. Surrounded by this unique juxtaposition of things Stevenson sat at the head of the dinner table and dominated the conversation which ranged from literature to trade, from European politics to native head-cutting.

Stevenson enjoyed good company so much that he encouraged visitors who afforded him diversion and entertainment to come often and to stay long. Again and again we hear him urging his friends in Europe, Charles Baxter, Sidney Colvin, Conan Doyle, Rudyard Kipling and others, to visit Vailima. He assured them that they would fall in love with the place. When he heard that the Doyles were planning to visit Vailima, he wrote: "Delighted to hear . . . Are you Great Eaters?" He assured them that a fortnight "of Vailima diet could kill nobody." Kipling, too, planned to come but gave up the idea, to Stevenson's sorrow. Charles Baxter was actually on his way when he was notified of the death of his friend.

Many interesting personalities showed up at Vailima. There was the American author, Henry Adams, the painter, John La Farge, the actor, Nat Goodwin and the Countess of Jersey. There were soldiers of fortune, such as Count Wurmbrandt, a very polished Austrian ex-cavalry officer, and Jack Buckland from the Gilbert Islands, commonly called "Tin" Jack and as handsome as Apollo. He became the Tommy Haddon of *The Wrecker*. And there was Signor Nerli, an Italian artist who painted the Stevenson portrait now in the National Portrait Gallery in Edinburgh. After dinner, Fanny would sit at the table and turn the hurdy-gurdy while the rest danced. Stevenson would waltz in triple time and dance the Highland schottische with much earnestness.

Then again there were visitors of an entirely different sort, the notorious Shirely Baker of Tonga, a former missionary who resembled the John Bull of cartoonists. Baker was considered one of the most colorful characters of the South Seas. He was accused of dictatorship, theft, rape, judicial murder, poisoning and misappropriations. Realizing, however, how readily suspicions and accusations were circulated in the South Seas, Stevenson refused to believe all the charges against him. Besides, both being extensive travelers and highly interesting talkers, they found many common interests to discuss.

When the Stevensons were informed that their cousin, Graham Balfour, would stop over in Vailima on his way around the world, they began to prepare for their illustrious guest. Out came the best china, the table cloths with "lighthouses interwoven in the damask —a gift to Thomas Stevenson from Queen Victoria, the silver tea service with its famous sugar bowl from which Robby Burns had sweetened his toddy and Sir Walter Scott his tea, the linen sheets and pillow cases embroidered with a hand holding a laurel wreath —the Stevenson crest."

To receive their cousin the Stevensons trekked to Apia with seven horses, for the party and baggage, and for several nights they slept in the hotel awaiting the arrival of the steamer. When the ship finally cast anchor, they sat in the hotel boat trying to spot their guest, whom none of them had seen for many years. The passengers seemed an unprepossessing lot, but then there appeared on deck "the Simon Pure," a tall, handsome young man. "There he is!" exclaimed Stevenson. "You can't mistake a Balfour," added Aunt Maggie. It was not very long before the future Oxford Don and knight became a regular member of the household. He took to the ways of Vailima "like a duck to water," appearing with bare feet. "He is a damn fool like the rest of us!" chuckled Stevenson.

Of the many white visitors most graciously welcomed at Vailima were the missionaries, both Protestant and Catholic. Brought up as a child by a devout mother, a severely religious governess, and an intolerantly ardent Covenanter father, young Louis was passionately religious. He loved his Biblical stories, prayers and hymns. As a student, however, he lived in the agnostic atmosphere of Tyndall, Huxley, and Spencer. He rebelled against the faith of his ancestors and flaunted his unorthodox views. "I pray to God, if there is such a gentleman," he once wrote. Now at Vailima, after years of sickness and much reflection on human destiny, after contact with a number of missionaries, many of whom he admired and loved, after playing the part of "father" to his large number of pious servants, Stevenson's religious views mellowed.

It is doubtful, however, whether he ever did become a religious man in the strict sense of that term. He loved to read the Bible as a great piece of literature, but he refused to accept many of the theological interpretations. He confessed that he did not believe in hell nor "in a lake of fire, anyway, nor in a remorseless, unappeasable God." At Vailima there was no "odor of sanctity," testified Moors. Cant and religious pretensions were abhorrent to the Stevensons.

Though Robert Louis found much in the theology of the Catholic Church with which he could not sympathize, he admired the French missionaries for the way they encouraged the natives in those of their customs and traditions that were not incompatible with Christianity. He also liked their policy of favoring increased influence of the chiefs; he agreed with them that it was wiser to concentrate on people of rank than to follow the policy of the Protestant missionaries, of attempting to impose democracy upon the masses. As a confirmed royalist he was convinced that the hope of Samoa lay in the men of rank, the chiefs. Furthermore, to a romantic like Stevenson, the pageantry and warmth of the Catholic Church ritual had a strong appeal.

Although the majority of the Samoans were Protestants, Mataafa, Stevenson's hero, was an ardent Catholic, and the best boys of the household were Catholics, too—which may have accounted for the especially cordial welcome awaiting the French priests and nuns at Vailima. Stevenson enjoyed their conversation carried on in lively French over a stimulating glass or two of sherry. To Tusitala the French bishop with his white beard and violet girdle over his white cloak was a "splendidly episcopal" figure. And when at a luncheon at Vailima "three lads came one after another and kneeled before him in the big hall, and kissed his ring, it did me good for a piece of pageantry." The Sisters of the Sacred Heart Convent were also always welcome at Vailima; frequently horses would be sent to the convent to bring them over. Sister Cecelia, who was the most liked, was very much impressed with Stevenson's large library, and borrowed Victor Hugo's *Hunchback of Notre Dame,* possibly thinking it a religious work. She soon returned it without comment.

For a number of obvious reasons Stevenson was on most congenial terms with the members of the London Missionary Society, the greater number of whom he considered to be excellent men. Among his favorites were Reverend J. E. Newell, with whom he made several excursions and who was the first to introduce him as "Tusitala," and Reverend S. J. Whitmee, who taught him the Samoan language. He adored the fiery little James Chalmers who was renowned as an explorer as well as a missionary in New Guinea, where he was later murdered by the cannibal natives. He admired Chalmers' freedom from narrowness and his daring to smoke a pipe—one of the seven deadly sins—and his dancing a Highland fling on the mission verandah before a large crowd. Louis was so impressed with the missionary's humor and charm, that when Chalmers departed for New Guinea, the former agnostic wrote: "O Tamate (Chalmers' Samoan name), if I had met you when I was a boy and a bachelor how different my life would have been."

Another one of the missionaries much admired by Stevenson was Reverend Clarke, whom he had met the first day of his arrival in Samoa. He greatly appreciated Clarke's open-mindedness. He considered him not only a good churchman—one of the best in the world —but also a man whom he could "esteem and like to the soles of his boots."

He was pleased with the way Reverend Clarke handled the question of the *siva.* When the new Chief Justice, Henry C. Ide, arrived from the United States, a great official reception was prepared for him. Among the invited guests were King Malietoa and his court, the foreign consuls, the officers of the warships, the leading white residents, including the missionaries, and Robert Louis Stevenson. The honor of arranging the reception was entrusted to Seumanu, high-chief of Apia and *persona grata* to the Americans for his outstanding services in saving American lives during the fatal hurricane of 1889.

Now the embarrassing part of the reception was the request of the white officials that a *siva* be made part of the entertainment. Seumanu was in a real predicament: as a deacon of the church he could not possibly witness a *siva,* for any church member present at a *siva,* with its elements of what was alleged to be obscenity, was to be formally excluded from church fellowship. True, the white missionaries had made several unsuccessful attempts to amend this prohibition, but they were overruled by the ill-educated and strait-laced native pastors. Greatly distressed because of the embarrassing predicament he was in, Seumanu confessed to Reverend Clarke that he, Seumanu, would have "to bow the knee in the house of Rimmon." He assured the missionary that when his offense had been duly expiated he should again be "a seeker of church fellowship."

Reverend Clarke realized that here was a poser not only for poor Seumanu and other members of the church, but also for him. To have refused the request of the white officials for a function which appeared to them an innocent ceremonial, was to place himself in an invidious position. He assumed the responsibility, and advised Seumanu to arrange a good *siva,* but to see to it that there was no impropriety. He assured the high-chief that not only would he not forfeit his church membership, but that he, Clarke, himself intended to attend the reception with his *Misi tamaitai* (my wife). The *siva* was duly performed before a large audience to the great enjoyment of all present, including Stevenson.

On the following day Reverend Clarke received a letter from Stevenson expressing his conviction that the permission to present the *siva* was wise and should produce good results; that the "only honest thing is to discriminate boldly between the use and the abuse in this as in all things. Cowardice lies in the extremes, whether of severity or of indulgence." He offered the good and courageous Reverend his pen and influence should that become necessary. Fortunately no occasion for his intervention arose; for not only did Reverend Clarke not have to face censure, but, on the contrary, the native pastors actually agreed to modify the prohibitory edict so as to permit dances if performed with due propriety.

Indicative of the interest that Stevenson manifested in the missions and the religious life of the community, were his frequent monetary contributions and the several addresses he delivered before the students of the pastors' training school at Malua. When Aunt Maggie was at Vailima her devoted son frequently accompanied her to the little English chapel at Apia where services were held every Sunday evening. Here the author found himself in a motley crowd of consuls, naval officers, beachcombers and half-castes.

We do not know whether it was to please his mother or the American Land Commissioner, H. C. Ide that Stevenson decided to teach a Sunday school class. At any rate the announcement of his intention to do so surprised and amused the Apia community no end. "The Sunday school racket," he wrote Colvin, "is only an experiment which I took up at the request of the late American land commissioner; I am trying it for a month, and if I do as ill as I believe, and the boys find it half as tedious as I do, I think it will end in a month." Even Tusitala found the squatting, wriggling urchins staring at him with their dark goggle eyes, impenetrable and uninspiring. He was certain that no one understood him. When he invited the youngsters to ask questions by offering sixpence to the first boy who would ask a question on the lesson, there was stolid silence. He then raised the offer to a shilling and later to half a crown. Finally a youngster raised his hand and in trembling tones said: "We learned in the Sunday school that the illustrious God created the world, but who made the High-Chief God?" Tusitala considered that question well worth the half crown. His career as Sunday school teacher was short-lived.

According to Reverend Clarke, Stevenson was deeply interested in a little monthly magazine, *O le Sulu O Samoa* (the Torch), published by the London Missionary Society. To enliven the dull religious periodical Tusitala offered a story which he entitled *The Bottle Imp.* The offer was eagerly accepted by the missionaries, for the tale taught a good moral: namely, one must not risk eternal damnation in the next world for the sake of wealth and a good life in this one. The story was translated into Samoan and appeared as a serial in the *Sulu.*

This was the first bit of fiction ever to be read by the Samoans, and it had a great success; it was read with wonder and delight in many a native house. The old European legend, decked out in Polynesian clothes, told the tale of a Hawaiian, Keawe, who lived in a house on a mountainside. The house was three stories high, with large rooms and verandahs, and was lavishly furnished. His wealth and his beautiful house Keawe acquired through his possession of a little devil in the shape of an imp kept in a bottle. The imp enabled one to acquire wealth but not to prolong life or to enjoy happiness. The way to happiness was to get rid of the bottle and the imp by selling it to someone else for less than the sum paid for it by its owner. The moral—to be happy one must not enter into a pact with the devil. When the natives who had taken the story literally visited Vailima they would stare at the big safe in the corner and very politely ask whether the High-Chief Tusitala would kindly show them the *Bottle Imp.*

Though Stevenson stood very high in the esteem of the Protestant and Catholic missionaries, and though, on the whole, he was very sympathetic with their work among the natives, he was, nonetheless, a candid critic when he felt criticism was justified.

"I do not think all missionaries are equally wise, and of some missionary methods I do not approve," he wrote Reverend Whitmee. He frequently complained about the missionaries' meddling in politics and against their trying to enforce a strait-laced code of morals upon the natives, particularly in connection with the *siva,* the favorite national dance.

Apia's society provided various opportunities for entertainment. There were invitations to weddings. A memorable occasion was the marriage of Mr. Gurr, a banker and one of the prominent members of the community, to Fanua, the former *Taupo* of the town and the adopted daughter of Chief Seumanu and his wife Faatulia. All the women were native; all the men, with the exception of Seumanu were white. "The bride and bridesmaids were all in the old high dress." Stevenson enjoyed the ceremony and the party that followed, especially the dance with the beautiful Fanua.

There were dinners at the homes of the leading residents of Apia or on the German plantations, and the standing invitation to the officers' messrooms of the visiting warships. Then there were nights at the circus which came often to Apia. At the entertainment hall the

Stevensons, the naval officers, and other prominent whites, whom an "embittered" correspondent of the Samoa *Times* called "the shoddy aristocracy of Apia," occupied the reserved seats in the front row. Even though the circus was second-rate, it was greatly appreciated. Stevenson clapped, Captain Foss "hollered 'wunderschön!' and threw himself forward in his seat, and how we all in fact enjoyed ourselves, like school-children."

In addition to entertaining frequent visitors, Stevenson welcomed every excuse for larger and gayer festivals, and Vailima became the liveliest place in the Samoan islands. The annual Christmas party was usually celebrated with great ceremony. In the large hall a gigantic tree would be set up and covered with carefully selected gifts for everyone in the household, from the head of the clan to the humblest native servant. Months before the holiday season Stevenson would order many of the gifts from London: jewelry, umbrellas, tobacco pouches and various trinkets. Often he would go down to Apia where he bought anything that caught his fancy.

Tusitala enjoyed the preparations and the decorations. This was to be a surprise party for the servants, or rather, his retainers. When the tree was lit and the doors of the large paneled hall were thrown open, the gong was sounded and all trooped in. For a moment all the members of the household stood in hushed reverence, then tiptoeing into the room, seated themselves cross-legged on the floor around the tree. Though good taste demanded that the natives manifest only mild enthusiasm, they nevertheless were captivated by the magnificent sight, their sparkling eyes rivaling the brilliance of the candles on the tree. The Laird of Vailima would then step up and with dignity and graciousness distribute the gifts. When anyone's name was called he would step forward to receive his package. With intense eagerness the natives would examine each other's gifts, almost to the neglect of their own. After the Christmas dinner there were usually recitations or dances by the Samoan girls, all of which Stevenson enjoyed hugely.

Another occasion for celebration was Stevenson's birthday, on November 13th. Since a large number of natives and whites were usually invited to these parties, there was, naturally, a great deal of preparation, decorating, polishing the silver and blending the "preliminary cocktails." Everybody in the household was assigned a definite task. Tusitala's favorite job was cleaning the "crystal." The table supplies were ample and they came from various sources: the pigs and chickens from the stable; the pigeons from the woods; the prawns from the stream; sea fish from the coast; bananas, pineapples, breadfruit, coconuts, mangoes, avocado pears and oranges from the Vailima gardens. The storeroom was well supplied with wines and other delicacies from London and Sydney. To supplement these the shops of the butcher, baker, and grocer in Apia were resorted to. Talolo, the cook, would be up at dawn to supervise the ovens where numerous pigs, chickens, and pigeons were roasted. The village girls, smelling a feast, would offer their services to help decorate the banquet house. As early as six in the morning the native guests would start arriving, bringing gifts of pigs, breadfruit, fowl, taro, tapa, necklaces, shell wreaths and other articles. They would come to spend the day and possibly assist the cook with the preparation of the food as well as to partake of it later.

For his birthday party of 1892 Tusitala invited the relatives of his house servants, natives from the neighboring villages, and about twenty of his white friends. This was the first time that the houseboys appeared in their "Vailima livery," Royal Stuart tartan, *lava lavas* and white shirts. The native women of the household wore *lava lavas* with chemises, and flowers in their hair. The feast began with *kava* and its customary ceremonies and speeches. In addition to the usual food, spread on leaves in *faa Samoa* (Samoan style), was a highly-prized delicacy, fried *palolo*. This consisted of long, thin, green salt-worms which appear early in the morning three days in the year. Fishing for *palolo* was great sport. The natives caught them with their bare hands or in nets. When cooked with coconut mea they look like a green mass of spinach and taste like *foie-gras*.

After the feast Tusitala told his guests how happy he was to see them present on his birthday and thanked them for their good work The father of one of the servants expressed gratitude for the host's interest in the natives and in their customs, of "which the white men on the beach know nothing."

After the feast the audience was invited to a *siva* staged by the servants. The raised part of the great hall was used as a stage, with candles in tin boxes for footlights. The orchestra consisted of a log of wood on a mat on which the boys kept time with drumsticks. The performers sat on the floor cross-legged and sang their songs, many of them composed for the occasion. They sang about Tusitala, how he fed them with beef, salmon and biscuits; about Tamaitai who cured them when sick; about Teuila who gave them fine rings; about Loia who scolded them when they were lazy. They also sang about a white man who objected to all he had seen in Samoa. At first the performers sat for their dance; all the principal movements were done with the arms, though the whole body swayed in graceful motion. When the sitting dance ended two performers stood up and engaged in a mock fight and pantomimed a game of cricket. Then the women rose and danced, swaying their arms and their bodies, displaying their supple figures to perfection.

These birthday celebrations recurred annually despite the fact that Stevenson had transferred all his rights in his natal day to a young Vermont girl. Ide, the Samoan land commissioner and later chief justice, told Tusitala that his daughter, Annie, often complained that to all intents and purposes she was always being cheated out of birthday parties and birthday presents because she had the bad luck to be born on Christmas day. Tusitala sympathized with her in her misfortune, and, since he, himself, no longer had any use for his birthday, which served only to remind him and everyone else that he was getting old, decided to give it to someone who could use it. Accordingly he drew up a legal document in which he solemnly declared: "I, Robert Louis Stevenson, Advocate of the Scots Bar . . . civil engineer, sole owner and patentee of the Palace and Plantation known as Vailima . . . a British subject, being in sound mind, and pretty well, I thank you, in body. In consideration that Miss Annie H. Ide . . . was born, out of all reason upon Christmas Day, and is therefore out of all justice denied the consolation and profit of a proper birthday; And considering that I . . . have attained an age when O, we never mention it, and that I have now no further use for a birthday of any description . . . *Have transferred* . . . to the said Annie H. Ide, *all and whole* my rights and privileges in the thirteenth day of November, formerly my birthday; now, hereby, and henceforth, the birthday of the said Annie H. Ide, to have, hold, exercise, and enjoy the same in the customary manner, by the sporting of fine raiment, eating of rich meats, and receipt of gifts, compliments, and copies of verse . . . *And I direct* the said Annie H. Ide to add to the said name of Annie H. Ide the name of Louisa."

The "Will" was dispatched to the Ide family at Vermont, with all due formality, where it was published in many newspapers. Shortly thereafter the gallant Tusitala received a letter from Annie "Louisa" thanking him for the gift and relating happily that for the first time in her life she had a birthday party—November 13, 1891! The chivalrous cavalier replied that he was very happy to bestow his birthday on such a clever, pretty young girl. Mother Stevenson reminded her son that, since he had given away his birthday, he had no right to expect presents. However for the sake of *Auld Lang Syne* she was willing to give him a bathroom. Tusitala warned his mother that Annie Louisa might have a legal claim to the gift.

The annual Christmas and birthday festivals did not exhaust the opportunities for gay celebrations at Vailima or Apia, or perhaps on board the warships stationed in the harbor. There were balls in honor of Queen Victoria, the Fourth of July, the Fourteenth of July and the *Blumen Corso* or flower fête given by the Germans. These balls were usually cosmopolitan affairs, attended by over one hundred members of Apia's society: diplomats, naval officers, traders, barkeepers, clerks, mechanics, whites, half-castes and full-blooded natives. Tusitala always favored festivities in which natives could take part. These affairs were generally colorful, too. At the fancy dress ball, November, 1891, in honor of the Prince of Wales' birthday, Mrs. Gurr, the former *Taupo,* wore a Greek dress with a gold belt; another native lady wore a pale green dress and was supposed to represent a water-witch. Isobel was dressed as a Spanish lady with a black lace skirt trimmed with gold, a black bodice opening over and under one of white, a high comb and a crimson flower in her hair. Stevenson appeared in black trousers and white mess-jacket. Some of the other whites came in evening dress: most of the native girls wore bright colors and wreaths of sweet-scented flowers which covered what their clothes did not; the *Taupo's* outfit was even more scanty. The weekly Samoan *Times* commented on the good comradeship that existed among the members of the gathering and the "lack of starch and stiffness." One might see naval officers whirling with arms around the bare bodies of dusky native girls, including the village *Taupo.* Few enjoyed these affairs more than Tusitala. He took special dancing lessons from his stepdaughter, and at Vailima they used to say that he would be ready to get out of bed to dance a polka or a Highland schottische.

Often at these public balls Alii Vailima would come face to face with his political foes. In September, 1892 the "spinsters" of the town invited a group of Apia's élite to one of their balls. And whom should Stevenson meet there but Chief Justice Cederkrantz, his political enemy. When the two shook hands all present remarked that they were the only ones who wore real red sashes, "all the hue of blood, sir, blood." The audience was greatly amused to see the two rivals in the same set of a quadrille. When they found themselves in the dancing, prancing gambado, crossing hands, kicking up and being embraced, in turn, by the same large and respectable females, they tried to preserve some form of dignity. They exchanged glances, then grins, and pranced in competitive agility. "Hard to imagine my position more ridiculous," wrote Stevenson, "a week before he had been trying to rake up evidence against me by browbeating and threatening a half-white interpreter; that very morning I had been writing most villainous attacks upon him for the *Times;* and we meet and smile, and damn it—! like each other. I do my best to damn the man and drive him from the islands; but the weakness endures—I love him. . . . But if I don't make hay of him, it shall not be for want of trying." Politics took a holiday at these gay parties, but only for their duration.

CHAPTER XIV

THE CRAFTSMAN

POLITICS AND THE gay life in Samoa, however, did not absorb al of Stevenson's time and energy. He had always been a diligent worker Now life in the Pacific had not only restored his health; it had als stimulated his creative energy. "I do not think my health can be s hugely improved," he wrote Colvin, "without some subsequent im provement in my brains. Though of course, there is a possibility tha literature is a morbid secretion, and above health." He laughed at th doctors who spoke of the debilitating South Sea climate. "Why th work I have been doing here with all the interruptions would be in credible in Norway." He wondered "if anyone had ever more energy upon so little strength." Indeed, in spite of numerous interruptions he wrote prolifically, and some of his best work was produced during the years 1888–1894, which he spent in the Pacific.

Why did frail Robert Louis Stevenson work so feverishly when he was aware that his physical resources were limited? Was it th need of money? His annual income between 1888 and 1894 range from 3,000 to 4,000 pounds, and it was constantly increasing. True

ıe demands of his expensive Vailima establishment with all its re-
ainers, and his generous contributions to various causes and friends
onsumed much of his income. Quite often he complained of the
ıcreasing need of money. He also often expressed a fear that his
reative powers were declining and that the sources of his inspira-
on might dry up entirely. "If only the public will support me," was
is plea. In one of his letters he says that if some one would pay him
wenty dollars a day, he would rather become a farmer and work
o more on the "damned literature." One need not, however, take
tevenson's letters too literally; they might be the expression of a
ıomentary mood or just a pose.

Stevenson was neither mercenary nor money mad. He once com-
lained that American publishers paid him too liberally for his literary
vork. Moreover, why should he have had to worry about financial
ecurity? His estate of Vailima, his royalties, and his inheritance
vould be more than ample to care for his wife and himself. His adult
tepchildren were perfectly capable of looking out for themselves.

In 1888 he wrote to Burlingame of Scribner's: "I tell you I do
lislike this battle of the dollars. I feel sure you all pay too much here
n America; and I beg you not to spoil me any more. For I am get-
ing spoiled: I do not want wealth, and I feel these big sums de-
noralise me." On another occasion he jokingly remarked, "I am now
. salaried party; I am a bourgeois now . . . I am to write a weekly
monthly) paper for Scribner's, at a scale of payment which makes
ny teeth ache for shame and diffidence . . . I am like to be a mil-
ionaire if this goes on, and be publicly hanged at the social revolu-
ion: well, I would prefer that to dying in my bed."

No, Stevenson was an indefatigably industrious writer because he
oved to write; he was impelled by the urge to create. As a child he
ısed to say, "Gee me the Bible, Gee me the Bible!" As an adult his
ry was, "Gee me the novel, gee me the novel!" Although he often
romised himself a deserved rest after the completion of one work,
ıis active mind could not resist the temptation to sketch out a new
ne almost on the heels of the one just finished. "No rest but the grave
or Sir Walter! O the words ring in a man's head," he wrote in 1893.
That money was not, by any means, the sole driving force behind
Stevenson's ardent devotion to his craft is indicated by the toil he

willingly lavished on his *Letters* to the London *Times* and on hi
Footnote to History. He realized fully that they would not bring i
any considerable financial rewards. Also S. S. McClure recalled tha
when in 1888 he offered the author $8,000 for the two novels to b
written: a sequel to *Kidnapped* and *St. Ives,* Stevenson blushed
looked confused and stated that his price was $4,000, that he did no
think any novel of his was worth as much as he was being offered
He apologized for accepting that much money for his work; only th
expense of chartering a yacht for a long cruise made it necessary.

Stevenson was a methodical, and meticulous craftsman. In hi
letters to his friends, he described the bizarre scenes and the nu
merous projects with which his fertile imagination teemed. Many o
these he never used. In his opinion there were three ways, "and thre
ways only, of writing a story or a novel. . . . You may take a plot an
fit character to it, or you may take a character and choose incident
and situations to develop it, or lastly . . . you may take a certai
atmosphere and get action and persons to express and realize it."

He worked as precisely as an architect. When ready to write a
novel he would commence with its foundation by making as it were a
blue-print of his plan, sketching the plot, the incidents and characters. He would then build the superstructure. He did not, however, always stick dogmatically to his original plan, often departing
from it when new developments and incidents suggested themselves
After outlining the plot and studying local color minutely to enable
him to tell the story accurately and picturesquely, he wrote the first
rough draft. This he considered as preliminary spade work. Then
followed writing and rewriting, often more than ten times. Each re-
vision aimed at greater conciseness. "There is but one art, that art to
omit," he said. To him a writer was only an amateur, "who says in
two sentences what can be said in one."

After a light breakfast at six, he would settle down, propped up in
his bed or at his desk and begin his work. Belle arrived a few hours
later to take dictation until lunch-time. A few hours of rest after lunch
and he would resume work, that is, whenever there were no interruptions. At times when he felt the inspiration of a new novel or story, as
when he was writing *Weir of Hermiston,* he would work long hours
without a break.

Isobel Strong, his step-daughter, who served as his amanuensis, tells that when Stevenson dictated he would pace up and down the room barefooted, pushing aside chairs, kicking at the piles of books on the mats. He dictated deliberately, occasionally starting a sentence then pausing. He dictated every comma, every semi-colon, every period, and even the spelling of difficult words. He seldom repeated a word or sentence. Frequently, when dictating, he unconsciously, or perhaps consciously, acted the part of the character he was describing. Unless he lived the part, he felt the writing would be merely ink on paper. When he described a Scot, he pronounced even the "coma" in broad Highland accent. He would mimic the part of an old lady, slouch as a drover. He swaggered, bowed gallantly and twirled his oversized mustache when he dictated *St. Ives.* He forgot himself so completely in *The Master of Ballantrae,* that, when he looked into the mirror, he was startled to see, not "the powdered hair and aristocratic features of the Master, 'but my own ugly mug!' "

According to *Scribner's Magazine,* which published some of his works serially, Stevenson was a difficult problem for the proofreader. His copy was often obscure and difficult to decipher. He violated many of the rules of punctuation observed in well regulated printing offices, and he was in the habit of searching out unusual words. Yet not a single punctuation mark, not the spelling of a single word could be changed without his permission. When once a proofreader dared make a correction, the author sent him the following scorching letter: "To the reader: If I receive another proof of this sort, I shall return it at once with the general direction 'see me.' I must suppose my system of punctuation to be very bad; but it is mine; and it shall be adhered to with punctual exactness by every created printer who shall print for me." That put the fear of the Lord in the printing office. On the other hand S. S. McClure, in his *Autobiography* and in *McClure's Magazine* of March 1914, states that when Stevenson began to send him the *Letters from the South Seas,* he told him to use his "own judgment about editing them and to cut wherever I thought it would be advantageous."

In 1890 Stevenson complained of the great load he was carrying. In addition to his numerous personal letters and the monthly contribution to McClure's Syndicate, he completed *The Wrecker,* wrote a *Footnote to History* and a number of other works. He wrote 66,00 words in thirty days, about 2200 words a day; "the labour of an ele phant!" he exclaimed. Yet it made him envious to think of Scott turn ing out *Guy Mannering* in three weeks. "Heavens!" he cried, "Wha thews and sinews!"

First on the agenda in Samoa was the completion of *The Wrecke* which was to appear in serial form in *Scribner's Magazine*. Stevenso and Lloyd found the writing of the last part of *The Wrecker* har going. Some chapters had to be rewritten eleven times. Stevenso complained about the disadvantages of collaboration: "You can't ex plain what you mean. I know what kind of effect I mean a characte to give, what kind of a *tache* he is to make; but how am I to tell my col laborator in words? Hence it is necessary to say, 'Make him So-and so'; and this was all right for Nares and Pinkerton and Loudon Dodd whom we both knew . . . I, as a personal artist, can begin a charac ter with only a haze in my head . . . These are the impossibilitie of collaboration. Its immediate advantage is to focus two minds to gether on the stuff, and to produce in consequence an extraordinaril greater richness of purview, consideration, and invention." Stevenso felt weary when he finished the novel and celebrated it with a "whoo of joy."

It is not difficult to determine which parts of *The Wrecker* ar Stevenson's and which are Lloyd's. "Superficially," Stevenson wrot "the work is all mine"—that is, the last copy was in his hand. Som of the incidents in France and in San Francisco were his own experi ence. They are thus somewhat autobiographical. His were also th character sketches of Loudon Dodd and Jim Pinkerton. But the whol skeleton of the adventure novel, the bloody, lurid events at sea and th character sketches of Captain Nares, who was a portrayal of Captai Otis of the *Casco*, were Lloyd's contributions. Lloyd was an impres sionist and a writer of picaresque novels.

Stevenson was generally a reliable critic of his own works. Whe he sent a copy of *The Wrecker* to Henry James, he apologized. H warned him not to expect too much. "It's a machine, you know—don expect aught else—a machine, and a police machine; but I believ the end is one of the most genuine butcheries in literature; and w point to our machine with a modest pride, as the only police machin

ithout a villain. Our criminals are a most pleasing crew, and leave
ie dock with scarce a stain upon their character."

He maintained, however, that there was more in *The Wrecker*
ian some might think; that the best part of it was Captain Nares, a
enuine character. In fact he believed it to be a good, long, tough
arn with some horrible pictures of the manners of the greater world,
ot "the shoddy, sham world of cities, clubs and colleges, but the
vorld where men still live a man's life." He was pleased with most of
ie reviews, which were favorable. Though a little piqued that *The*
Vrecker outsold *The Master of Ballantrae,* he was nevertheless grati-
ed that it earned over ten thousand dollars.

It ran in *Scribner's Magazine* from August, 1891 to July, 1892.
'here was always some anxiety in Scribner's office lest the next in-
tallment should be lost in the mails, or not be finished in time because
f a breakdown in Stevenson's health. It was always a red-letter day
vhen the precious contribution did arrive.

For a number of years *The Wrecker* was in great demand, out-
anking *Kidnapped, The Master of Ballantrae,* and *David Balfour.*
t continued to earn about $1000 a year. However, though financially
uccessful, *The Wrecker* is definitely not among Stevenson's best
vorks. It is poorly integrated and loosely constructed. It is an exciting
arn of ships, of ruthless men committing horrible deeds at sea. It is
hell let loose!"

The sea story was followed by the *Footnote to History,* which is
n account and an interpretation of Samoan affairs from 1883 to 1891.
ince Stevenson deals largely with the period before his arrival in
amoa, he was actually a direct observer of only one year of those
urbulent times. He was, therefore, forced to depend on information
upplied him by whites and natives. Collecting, sifting and evalu-
ting material and writing the *History* consumed much of his time.
'requently he complained of the strain. He often wondered, "how
o journalists fetch up their drivel!" when it had taken him two
nonths to write 45,000 words, "aiming only at clearness and the most
bvious finish."

He wondered whether many people would actually read his *His-*
ory. "I fancy not," he wrote in a discouraged mood, "people don't
ead history for reading but for education and display—and who

desires education in the history of Samoa, with no population, no past no future, or the exploits of Mataafa, Malietoa, and Consul Knappe? Then he concluded: "Well, it can't be helped, and it must be done and better or worse, it's capital fun."

While Stevenson may have hoped for some financial succes of his *History*, he wrote Burlingame of Scribner's: "To me it is no business at all. I have to publish anyway, you understand; I have a purpose beyond; I am concerned for some of the parties to this quar rel." He considered it his duty to his conscience to expose the evils o imperialism and to champion the cause of the exploited natives. Orig inally he planned to donate all profits from the book—should there be any—for the welfare of the Samoans, but on further thought he felt that for the time and energy expended he was entitled to half o the proceeds. When Baron Tauchnitz's German edition of the *History* was confiscated and the publisher fined, he offered to pay half of the fine.

Stevenson did not think lightly of the *History*. He wrote Burlin game: "Here is, for the first time, a tale of Greeks—Homeric Greeks —mingled with moderns, and all true; Odysseus alongside of Rajah Brooke, *proportion gardée;* and all true. Here is for the first time since the Greeks (that I remember) the history of a handful of men, where all know each other in the eyes, and live close in a few acres, narrated at length, and with the seriousness of history. Talk of the modern novel; here is a modern history. And if I had the misfortune to found a school, the legitimate historian might lie down and die, for he could never overtake his material."

The *Footnote to History* may not be among Stevenson's mos popular literary productions. In fact, he often considered it "a kind of journalism." Neither can it be considered as entirely objective scientific history. Stevenson was not by temperament objective; he was prejudiced against the Germans and very sympathetic toward the natives, especially the Mataafa faction. Nonetheless it is a valuable contribution and the best account we have of what he calls "the Sa moan racket," the play of imperialism in the South Seas. It is fairly good history, too, and brilliantly, often eloquently written.

On his initial cruise in the Pacific which brought him to the Mar quesas, Paumotus, Tahiti, Hawaii and the Gilberts, Stevenson succumbed to the lure of the exotic material in which this region was so rich. What a storehouse to draw from! Here were inexhaustible sources for a remarkable book of travel, strange, almost unbelievable stories of unforgettable characters, heroes of ancient legends in Polynesian poetry. He saw the Pacific as a "strange place; the nineteenth century only exists here and there in spots; all around, it is a no man's land of the ages, a stir-about of epochs and races, barbarism and civilization, virtues and crimes."

Fanny with her innately shrewd, practical mind, bitterly complained: "I am very much exercised by one thing. Louis has the most enchanting material that any one ever had in the whole world for his book, and I am afraid he is going to spoil it all. He has taken into his Scotch Stevenson head, that a stern duty lies before him, and that his book must be a sort of scientific and historical impersonal thing, comparing the different languages (of which he knows nothing, really) and the different peoples, the object being to settle the question as to whether they are of common Malay origin or not. Also to compare the Protestant and Catholic missions, etc., and the whole thing to be impersonal, leaving out all he knows of the people themselves. I believe there is no one living who has got so near to them, or who understands them as he does. Think of a small treatise on the Polynesian races being offered to people who are dying to hear about Ori a Ori, the making of brothers with cannibals, the strange stories they told, and the extraordinary adventures that befell us:—suppose Herman Melville had given us his theories as to the Polynesian language and the probable good or evil results of the missionary influence instead of *Omoo* and *Typee*, or Kinglake instead of *Eothen*. Louis says it is a stern sense of duty that is at the bottom of it, which is more alarming than anything else. I am so sure that you will agree with me that I am going to ask you to throw the weight of your influence as heavily as possible in the scales with me."

Stevenson, however, was tremendously excited about his South Sea book. From the *Equator* he wrote Colvin that the work was practically modeled, and if he would be able to execute what he had planned there would be no novel like it; in fact few better books in existence, bar the epics, big tragedies, histories, and a novel or so. "At least, nobody has had such stuff; such wild stories, such beautiful scenes. . . ."

The plan provided for a book of some sixty chapters, totaling about 500 pages. He labored on the *Letters,* the monthly contribution to McClure's Syndicate which were ultimately to form the South Sea book. The deeper he got into it, the more he found the job immense. "Gracious, what a strain is a long book!" he complained. "The time it took me to design this volume, before I could dream of putting pen to paper, was excessive; and think of writing a book of travels on the spot, when I am continually extending my information, revising my opinions, and seeing the most finely finished portions of my work come part-by-part to pieces. Very soon I shall have no opinions left. And without an opinion how to string artistically vast accumulations of fact?"

The load began to weigh upon him and at times he found the work distasteful. "As for the Damned literature," (the *Letters*) he cried "God knows what a business grinding along without a scrap of inspiration or a note of style." The information taken from the notes and journals of his South Sea cruises was disjointed and uninspired. In England and in the United States readers of the newspapers which carried the *Letters* felt greatly disappointed. Instead of sprightly picturesque descriptions of scenes and personalities, and interesting personal experiences, they found dull, impersonal, disconnected accounts of native beliefs. Many of the readers complained: "What on earth has come over Robert Louis Stevenson that he gives us stuff like this?" "So this is your great stylist, your great writer, the genius who sits on the Olympian heights just a little above Shakespeare." Many of the newspapers discontinued the publication of the *Letters*.

When Stevenson was informed of the "damnatory" criticism, he gladly discontinued the undertaking in June, 1891, though he felt that there was a "hell of a want of money this year." The most interesting parts of Stevenson's South Sea book, the parts dealing with Tahiti and King Apemama, never did get into the *Letters.* After reading over some of his material he was convinced that there was sufficient merit in it for making a good book. The student of the South Seas is grateful to Stevenson for this volume, for his having collected and recorded in such interesting fashion the facts and observations of a civilization that is rapidly disappearing. Even students of literature will find in it beautiful descriptions and good character analyses. No less a mariner-writer than Joseph Conrad considered the South Sea volume among Stevenson's best.

Although Stevenson felt exhausted, and deserved a rest, he plunged immediately into a new story which he first called *The High Woods of Ulufanu* and later *The Beach of Falesá*. It was in 1890, when he was exploring the woods, that the story "shot through me like a bullet in one of my moments of awe in that tragic jungle." It is not a typical romantic story of the South Seas, but rather a realistic yarn of the natives, their dread of spirit devils, of the intrigue and debased actions of the white adventurers on the beach, all "nourished with facts," vividly and skillfully contrived and convincingly told by a simple, uneducated white trader, Wiltshire.

This short novel, of fewer than one hundred pages, is one of Stevenson's most successfully plotted and integrated stories. Background, atmosphere, character and action are masterfully collocated. In addition to some fascinating descriptions of the islands and their environment—mostly the Gilberts—there are realistic, brilliant character delineations. The three important characters are the two white traders, Wiltshire and Case, and the simple native woman, Uma, who married Wiltshire. Throughout the story the reader is gripped by the elements of dread, mystery and impending danger. The tragedy culminates in the death of Case.

Stevenson considered *The Beach of Falesá* one of his best. Of it he wrote: "It is the first realistic South Sea story; I mean with real South Sea character and details of life. Everybody else who has tried, that I have seen, got carried away by the romance, and ended in a kind of sugar candy sham epic, and the whole effect was lost—there was no etching, no human grin, consequently no conviction. Now I have got the smell and look of the thing a good deal. You will know more about the South Seas after you have read my little tale than if you had read a library. As to whether any one else will read it, I have no guess. I am in an off time, but there is just the possibility it might make a hit; for the yarn is good and melodramatic, and there is quite a love affair—for me; and Mr. Wiltshire (the narrator) is a huge lark, though I say it. But there is always the exotic question, and everything, the life, the place, the dialects—trader's talk, which is a strange conglomerate of literary expressions and English and American slang, and Beach de Mar, or native English—the very trades and hopes and fears of the characters, are all novel, and may be found unwelcome to that great, hulking, bullering whale, the public."

Stevenson feared that financially *The Beach of Falesá* would prove a great disappointment on account of some "immoral" incidents. "It seems," he wrote, "it's immoral and there's a to-do to make the young folks married properly before 'that night.' I refused; you will see what would be left of the yarn had I consented." He maintained that the fraudulent marriage contract was the heart of the whole story. He bitterly resented the narrow-minded prudish attitude of public opinion toward his work. "This is a poison bad world for the romancer, this Anglo-Saxon world; I usually get out of it by not having any woman in it at all; but when I remember I had *The Treasure of Franchard* refused as unfit for a family magazine, I feel despair weigh upon my wrists." Stevenson had a legitimate complaint. His point of view has prevailed; we have traveled a long way in this direction since his day. Today we consider *The Beach of Falesá* as one of the best South Sea stories.

Sophia Scarlet promised to be another appealing story of the South Seas. It was to have been a typical novel with its hero, heroine, false accusations, love, a dying poet-planter, and finally marriage. In addition to Sophia Scarlet who comes to the plantation from an English school, there were to be two other women and seven men. The plot was to take place on a large South Sea plantation, managed by ex-English officers. The labor trade in the story was to give it an "Uncle Tom flavour." Unfortunately Stevenson never got to writing this story, though he was very much in love with the theme.

Again Stevenson turned to his native land, Scotland, for his next novel, *David Balfour*, or *Catriona* as it is called in England. When he published *Kidnapped* in 1886 he had a great deal of extra material which he felt could be used for a sequel novel, "should the long-eared public" show any desire to have one. The favorable reviews of *Kidnapped* encouraged him greatly and he was confident he could do it with "ease and pleasure."

It is amazing that Stevenson should have postponed for years the writing of this novel. But that was typical of him. "David," he said, "has been kept for five years within the British Linen Company's Bank of Edinburgh," but "he still has a kick in his shanks." Then one night when he tossed with colic, thinking how to end the troublesome *Footnote to History*, the *David Balfour* novel got hold of him. Within a short time he drafted a good part of the story. It drove him at such a pace that he complained the "tale interferes with my eating and sleeping." He worked at full speed and finished it within four months, in 1892.

The novel is not organically well constructed; it is rather a series of episodes that fall into two parts. An irrelevant but interesting episode is the "Tale of Todd Lapraik," the religious hypocrite, "a muckle, fat white hash of a man, like creesh, wi' a kind of a holy smile that gar'd me scunner."

Nevertheless, the novel is more than an ordinary adventure story; it contains good characterization and psychological penetration into the emotional state of its heroes. It is a cross between adventure and drama. It is quite possible that the hero, David, is somewhat autobiographical, even to the point of appropriating Stevenson's mother's name of Balfour.

Stevenson admitted that the novel suffered from several weaknesses, but he was well satisfied with it nevertheless. He was confident that "there has been no such drawing of Scots characters since Scot; and even he never drew a full length like Dave," with his shrewdness and simplicity and charm. He liked Lowlander David, yet he felt that the public would want more of the Highlander, Alan Breck, a man possessing splendid qualities, but a vain, proud, quarrelsome swashbuckler. Stevenson was in love with both feminine characters. Catriona he considered a simple, and "respectable young woman, as virginal as billy, oh!" "But o dear me," he confessed, "I came near losing my heart to Barbara Grant." Barbara is indeed a more live, vivacious character than the vaguely-drawn heroine, Catriona. Stevenson thought well of his story. But, he wondered, "will it do for the young person? I don't know, since the *Beach*. I know nothing except that men are fools and hypocrites, and I know less of them than I was fond enough to fancy." When the novel was published in 1893 the reviewers and the reading public received it favorably. Henry James thought it was splendid; Bret Harte applauded it as "simply delightful."

From Scotland Stevenson turned again to the South Seas; the result was *The Ebb Tide.* The plot was drawn by Lloyd who was fond of adventure stories replete with action and lurid scenes. Stevenson, who did the rewriting and the character portrayal, found the task difficult. He complained: "I break down with every paragraph." Nor was he pleased with the "sensational" style and the characters. To Henry James he wrote: "The grimness of the story is not to be depicted in words. There are only four characters, to be sure, but they are such a troop of swine! And their behaviour is really so deeply beneath any possible standard, that on a retrospect I wonder I have been able to endure them myself until the yarn was finished."

He thought that if Zola's work could be admired for its ugliness and pessimism, then *The Ebb Tide* should be admired also. However, those readers who like Zola, not for his art but for his "rancidness," would likely be disappointed with *The Ebb Tide*'s healthy brutality. The reception of the novel by the reading public was disappointing. The public could not see why the writer of wholesome, entertaining adventure stories should now offer them novels of ugly criminals. However, people who were familiar with the South Seas felt that Stevenson described real experiences of people with *Beach.*

As a relief from *The Ebb Tide,* Stevenson turned to the *History of a Family of Engineers,* the story of his grandfather, and to a short novel, *St. Ives.* The latter was in the strain of an adventurous romantic comedy. It will be noticed that both of these themes took him back to his native Scotland and to his own early experiences. The escape of *St. Ives,* the English-speaking French officer of the Napoleonic army, from his prison in Edinburgh Castle and his travels through familiar places in Scotland might be somewhat autobiographic and parallel the author's own "exile."

Stevenson was not pleased with the style or content of *St. Ives.* To Colvin he wrote: "I must not let you be disappointed in St. I. It is a mere tissue of adventures; the central figure not very well or very sharply drawn; no philosophy, no destiny, to it; some of the happenings very good in themselves, I believe, but none of them bildende, none of them constructive, except in so far perhaps as they make up a kind of sham picture of the time, all in italics and all out of drawing. Here and there, I think, it is well written; and here and there it's not . . . 'tis my most prosaic book." Even the petticoats in the story, he thought were "Damned bad ones, too." He even called it a mere "pot boiler," a "mere story to tickle gudgeons and make money for a harmless family." Though he found the writing of *St. Ives* difficult and, in fact, never finished it, *St. Ives* has more depth and perception than the usual cloak-and-dagger adventure story of Dumas.

Then came the last and the best, the *Weir of Hermiston,* a semi-historical novel of late eighteenth and early nineteenth century Scotland. The central character of the novel was the notorious Lord Braxfield. For years the cruel personality of Robert Macqueen, Lord Braxfield, fascinated Stevenson as it had many others. A number of stories and anecdotes had been centered around this coarse, inhuman "Hanging Judge."

Once, pointing to a house in George Square, Edinburgh, Stevenson exclaimed: "Braxfield lived there; hot stuff in his day!" In his essay "Some Portraits by Raeburn," Stevenson described the "Hanging Judge" thus: "The tart, rosy, humorous look of the man, his nose like a cudgel, his face resting squarely on the jowl, has been caught and perpetuated with something that looks like brotherly love. A peculiarly subtle expression haunts the lower part, sensual and incredulous, like that of a man tasting good Bordeaux with half a fancy it has been somewhat too long uncorked . . . Out of the bar, or off the bench, he was a convivial man, a lover of wine, and one who 'shone peculiarly' at tavern meetings. He has left behind him an unrivaled reputation for rough and cruel speech; and to this day his name smacks of the gallows." As a young man Stevenson took long walks to Swanton, Glencorse, and Cauldstone Slap, associated with the moorland and the "Four Black Brothers," of the *Weir of Hermiston.*

For several years Stevenson toyed with the idea of writing the *Weir* novel. The idea simmered until September, 1892, when he finally began writing. From the outset he expected the *Weir* to be his masterpiece. For three full days he was in a seventh heaven. He worked day and night, writing, debating points about his characters and reading aloud to the family, as was his custom, the first draft of a few chapters. He was convinced that "it ought to be a plum."

At first he was overpowered by enthusiasm and a burst of energy. A hemorrhage, the old enemy, forced him to relax. To lose no time, he began to dictate to Belle with his fingers in the deaf and dumb alphabet. At that he managed to dictate about six pages a day. To recuperate he went for a six weeks' journey to Sydney, hoping for a speedy return of his health and deeper insight into the story.

The question has often been asked, why did Stevenson make so comparatively little use of the wealth of interesting material surrounding him in the South Seas and with which he was so fully familiar? The strange customs of the natives, and such striking unforgettable personalities as Ori, Tembinoka, Mataafa, Shirley Baker and Theodore Weber, and a host of others, should have appealed to his adventurous and romantic nature. Yet during these six years he wrote only a few stories with their settings in the South Seas. He planned to write a number of South Sea stories but somehow never got around to them. Instead, he turned inevitably to his native Scotland for locale and material.

Stevenson himself was conscious of this paradox. To Barrie he wrote in 1892: "It is a singular thing that I should live here in the South Seas under conditions so new and so striking, and yet my imagination so continually inhabits that cold huddle of grey hills from which we come." It was to the hills of his home that Stevenson returned for material and characters for his *David Balfour*, *St. Ives*, and *Weir of Hermiston*. However, it is not unusual for writers to draw upon their early experiences and native environment. Early impressions become heightened in retrospect. The autobiographical element figures prominently in *David Balfour* and *Weir of Hermiston*.

Stevenson had an additional reason for setting many of his novels in his native land. It was a sort of compensation for his feeling of enforced exile. He loved the South Seas, the beautiful islands, the climate, which met him more than half way, and the handsome, hospitable, poetic Polynesians. He knew he could not have been happier anywhere else, even in his native Scotland. Yet throughout all the years in the South Seas he felt the deep, aching sorrow of the life-long exile. He was haunted by the "memories of the wet moorland," and the smell of heather. "It is singular that I should fulfill the Scot's destiny throughout, and live a voluntary exile, and have my head filled with the blessed, beastly place all the time!" He longed for civilization, society, friends, his native Edinburgh, the Lothian Road. When hearing the bells at Pago Pago he was carried back to the cold, windy, misty Metropolis of the North. "Touch me! and you will find a thistle!" he cried. "No stars like the Edinburgh street lamps" he reminisced. He begged his friends to write him gossip from Edinburgh. Distance in time and space from Scotland with its beloved moorland and heather enhanced the nostalgia he felt for his native land. When he had a premonition of the end, he cried out that his final resting place was destined to be Mount Vaea, in the far away South Seas, and not upon the "purple hillsides," amidst the heather,

> Where about the graves of the martyrs the
> whaups are crying
> My heart remembers how!

One final question. What part did women play in Stevenson's works? In his early stories and novels women are definitely excluded, or when admitted at all, are so only by courtesy, as it were, or in deference to tradition. Some critics have been inclined to believe that Stevenson was unable to draw a real, strong feminine character. His women are not creatures of impulse and passion. Even in his later novels, with the exception of *Weir of Hermiston,* there is little sentimentality and even less of tender passion. "The wooing is done to an accompaniment of sword-play and the angry bark of horse pistols."

Henry James adds: "It all comes back to his sympathy with the juvenile and the feeling about life which leads him to regard women as so many superfluous girls in a boys' game. They are almost absent from his pages . . . for they don't like ships and pistols and fights, they encumber the decks and require separate apartments, and almost worst of all, have not the highest literary standard. Why should a person marry when he might be swinging a cutlass or looking for a buried treasure?"

One thing seems certain: the omission or under-emphasis of feminine characters in his novels was not due to such misogyny as distorted Strindberg's work. On the contrary, Stevenson was always a ladies' man. At the age of twenty while on a summer trip aboard a steamer to the Orkneys, he saw a pretty lass in conversation with an old gentleman. "*Eh, bien,*" he said to himself, "that seems to be the best investment on board." Immediately he sidled up to the pair, shoved the old gentleman aside, and spent a delightful journey with his new companion. In a lyric he wrote:

> Who talks to me of reason now?
> It would be more delight
> To have died in Cleopatra's arms
> Than be alive tonight.

There is some evidence that as a hot-blooded youth he fell in love with a street waif in Edinburgh. Claire, as Stevenson called her, was very young, "slim, dark, very trim, neat, with jet black hair." This Highland girl was eager to be redeemed from the tragic estate to which she had sunk. She recited stories and sang songs from her native Highland country which captivated young Stevenson's imagination. Her grace, charm, and devotion touched a responsive chord in the sensitive, sensual and chivalrous lover. He proposed marriage but his Covenanter father, who supported him, was unalterably opposed to such a shocking misalliance.

With a pathetic cry: "My God! if I marry you, I would drag you down," Claire passed out of Stevenson's life, but not out of his memory. He mourned: "The relic taken, what avails the shrine?" "I have left all upon the shameful field, Honour and Hope, My God and all but life." He never forgot this blighted romance. In his dreams he saw his beloved coming to meet him "in the dawning and the dew."

Soon Stevenson with his great capacity for falling in love met Mrs. Sitwell, who, having been unhappily married, was divorced from her clergyman husband. Fanny Sitwell, a woman of great understanding and intelligence recognized in her youthful admirer, "a young Heine with the Scotch accent." How intense were Stevenson's sentiments toward this stately, beautiful woman, eight years his senior, may be judged from the numerous letters he wrote her expressing adoration and love for his "Madonna." "You don't know how I yearned today to see you all"; "I do not fail to think of you nor shall ever"; "I kiss your hand with affection; I cannot think of what life would be to me if you were gone; a great hole, without form and void."

There was also his flirtation with Madame Gerschine, an accomplished aristocratic Russian woman whom he met on the French Riviera. Madame Gerschine, though his senior by some fifteen years, did not hesitate to display her romantic sentiments quite openly. Stevenson was ready to reciprocate and carry on the flirtation, though he feared that the lady might make a fool of herself and him. He addressed a poem to Madame Gerschine and was very sad when the time came for her departure. He promised to visit her at her home in Poland.

Stevenson's keen interest in the "eternal feminine" is reflected in many of his poems and letters. His thoughts on viewing the three deep-breasted women among the Elgin Marbles, in the British Museum, reveal this aspect of his nature. "And think, if one could love a woman like that once, see her once grow pale with passion, and once wring your lips out upon hers, would it not be a small thing to die? Not that there is not a passion of quite other sort, much less epic, far more dramatic and intimate, that comes out of the very frailty of perishable women; out of the lines of suffering that we see written about their eyes, and that we may wipe out if it were but for a moment; out of the thin hands, wrought and tempered in agony to a fineness of perception."

Lamenting his lack of feminine society, Stevenson wrote Mrs. Sitwell: "Oh, I do hate this damned life that I lead. Work-work-work; that's all right, it's amusing, but I want women about me and I want pleasure." Again: "John Knox had a better time of it than I, with his godly females all leaving their husbands to follow him; I would I were John Knox; I hate living like a hermit." He envied John Knox, the staunch, gloomy moralist, author of the *Monstrous Regiment of Women,* who, as a widower at the age of fifty-eight, married a seventeen-year-old girl who bore him three daughters.

Stevenson was always extremely susceptible to feminine charms, white or native. Dark women especially attracted him: witness his love for Fanny, Princess Kaiulani and Laulii. We have seen how he took an interest in the selection of feminine servants.

His views on sex relations were entirely too liberal for his day. "There is no harm in voluptuaries," he insisted, "and none, with my hand on my heart and in the sight of God, none—no harm whatsoever in what prurient fools call immorality. The harm was in Jekyll, because he was a hypocrite—not because he was fond of women." He felt greatly offended and hurt by the objections of his narrow-minded publishers to *The Beach of Falesá*.

The critic must, therefore, look for other reasons why Stevenson excluded women from his early novels. One explanation he himself gave when, in a sanitarium at Saranac in the Adirondacks, an American lady asked him why women did not play a greater role in his books. Stevenson replied frankly, that the human quality which appealed to him most strongly and which he loved to write about was physical courage of the adventurous kind, even when found in a pirate, and that women were lacking in it. All the efforts of the lady to prove with numerous instances that women were not devoid of the quality were in vain.

In his essay *Some Portraits by Raeburn*, Stevenson confesses that "Raeburn and the rest of us labour under an obstinate blindness in one direction, and know very little more about women after all these centuries than Adam when he first saw Eve." Once when King, an employee, complained that the women at Vailima "were too much for any man," Stevenson put his pen down, clasped his hands behind his head and remarked: "Well, King, you know what women are! You understand their ways!" Then, after a slight pause, he exclaimed. "By jove, no! How can you? Show me the man who does!"

According to his friend Moors, Stevenson was often critical of marriage. "Marriage," he said, "is a field of battle and not a bed of roses." Once married, "there are no more by-path meadows where you may innocently linger, but the road lies long and straight and dusty to the grave." "It is better to face the fact and know, when you marry, that you take into your life a creature of equal if unlike frailties; whose weak, human heart beats no more tunefully than yours."

There is some evidence that, at the persistent goading of his wife, Stevenson burned a novel revealing his love affair with "Claire." If true, this might have been prompted not only by personal jealousy and fear that it would cause pain to his parents, but also by the desire to perpetuate among his readers, mostly belonging to the younger generation, the legend of Stevenson "the seraph in chocolate." Fanny was a practical woman, not averse to substantial royalties.

At any rate, if Fanny or public opinion would not let him create women characters as he wished, then he would ignore them. To quote him again: "This is a poison bad world for the romancer, this Anglo-Saxon world; I usually get out of it by not having any women in it at all." But toward the end of his life, at the height of his fame, Stevenson yearned to write for art's sake, not merely for royalties. He wanted to be free to write novels with real, live women characters, though some people might think them "dreadfully improper."

To his friend Colvin he made the following confession: "I am afraid my touch is a little broad in a love story. I can't mean one thing and write another. I am a realist and a prosaist, and a most fanatical lover of plain physical sensations plainly and expressively rendered; hence my perils." "There was a time," he continued, "when I did not dare draw a woman; but I have no fear now." His attitude to sex became bolder and more radical: "As for women, I am no more in fear of them; I can do a sort all right; age makes me less afraid of a petticoat, but I am a little in fear of grossness." Writing to his cousin in 1894, shortly before his death, he deplored the sex complex of Christian society. "If I had to begin again . . . I believe I should try to honor sex more religiously. The worst of our education is that Christianity does not recognize and hallow sex. It looks askance at it, over its shoulder, oppressed as it is by reminiscences of hermits and Asiatic self-torturers. It is a terrible hiatus in our modern religions that they cannot see and make venerable that which they ought to see first and hallow most."

Now with his reputation in literature firmly established, with annual royalties mounting to fifteen or twenty thousand dollars, Stevenson gained greater courage to rebel against compromising with the ideals of his craft. He now succeeded in carrying out his dream of writing vigorous novels including alive feminine characters. Whatever the cause, Stevenson undertook to deal with life in a more profound manner than in the purely masculine adventure story. His Barbara Grant and Catriona may not be great feminine characters; but who can question the power, the passion, the aliveness of the two Kirsties in *Weir of Hermiston.* Though the central theme of the novel lies in the relations between the son and his father, the love scenes between Archie and the Kirsties are among the finest in literature.

CHAPTER XV

THE KNIGHT-ERRANT

FRIENDS AND ADMIRERS of Robert Louis Stevenson regretted his meddling in the political squabbles of Samoa, a mere tempest in a teapot. They believed that his valuable time and energy could have been devoted far more profitably to literature. But considering the conditions in the islands and the temperament of Stevenson, one can readily understand and expect his involvement.

For here, on a few remote islands in the romantic and picturesque South Seas, was enacted a drama packed with farce, comedy and tragedy. The drama was enacted by dusky chiefs and warriors, led by one of the most heroic personalities of the time, battling for justice against a weakling puppet king moved by strings held in the hands of haughty, bombastic Swedish and German officials, rival consuls, naval commanders and foreign offices. This melodrama was a story of *fonos,* proclamations, marching warriors, with blackened faces, imprisonment, secret trips to rival camps, war, shelling of villages, and exile.

For Stevenson, the impulsive knight-errant in quest of adventure and eternally battling for fair play and justice, the Samoan fiasco "filled the bill." It was to him a Waverley novel and Arabian Nights tale combined. He deeply regretted that, instead of blessings, the white man brought his beloved Polynesians discord, conflict and despair. When a principle of justice was involved, it did not matter to him whether it affected a large group or a small, "civilized" people or "savage." Fanny realized that Stevenson liked politics; the constant excitement stimulated him. He wrote, "Why, you madman, I wouldn't change my present installation for any post, dignity, honor, or advantage conceivable to me. It fills the bill; I have the loveliest time. And as for wars and rumors of wars, you surely know enough of me to be aware that I like that also a thousand times better than decrepit peace in Middlesex. I do not quite like politics. I am too aristocratic, I fear, for that. God knows I don't care who I chum with; perhaps like sailors best; but to go round and sue and sneak to keep a crowd together—never." His opinion of politics is expressed as follows: "Politics is a vile and bungling business. I used to think meanly of the plumber, but how he shines beside the politician!"

The Act of Berlin, adopted at the Berlin Conference, June 14, 1889, by the three interested powers did not settle the Samoan problem. It embodied contradictory provisions and established a government that was too complex and too extravagant. It recognized, in theory, the independence of the Samoan Government and the right of the natives to choose their own king and to be ruled according to their own laws and customs. Malietoa Laupepa was returned from his exile on a German island and recognized as king. To "advise" the puppet ruler, a foreign chief justice, who was to enjoy extensive judicial and political authority, was to be appointed by agreement of the three treaty powers. A second foreign official, to be appointed by the three powers, was to be the president of the municipal government for Apia and to act also as "advisor" to the king. To investigate all land claims by foreigners in Samoa, each of the three powers was to choose a land commissioner. The three consuls retained the prestige they had enjoyed before the conference. Incidentally, with the Act of Berlin, the United States reversed its historic policy of "no entangling alliances."

It is doubtful whether this complex and contradictory form of government could have worked even under the most satisfactory conditions. As things turned out, conditions were far from satisfactory. At first, however, the political affairs in Samoa seemed to have been settled. The return of the exiled king was acclaimed by the natives. Even Tamasese's followers expressed their allegiance. The natives looked forward to the arrival of the foreign officials with a "childishness of trust." Even among the rival foreigners in Samoa there was a vastly improved feeling. Unfortunately the appointment of the foreign officials was delayed too long. When the three powers could not agree on the choice of a chief justice the King of Sweden and Norway was asked to designate a suitable person for the office. His choice was Conrad Cederkrantz, a Swedish assistant-judge, who did not arrive in Samoa until December 30, 1890. The President, Baron Senfft von Pilsach, a German official chosen by his government, arrived even later.

The unaccountable delay in the appointment and the delayed arrival of the two officials aroused suspicion among the natives who were beginning to distrust the sincerity of the three powers. They began to smell trickery. Various superstitious stories, expressions of discontent and fear were circulating among the native: "rivers had come down red; unknown fishes had been taken on the reef and found to be marked with menacing runes; a headless lizard crawled among chiefs in council; the gods of Upolu and Savaii made war by night."

Finally, on the afternoon of December 30, 1890, the cry went up that the *Faamasimi Sili* (Chief Justice) had arrived. The illustrious personage was welcomed by three consuls, crowds of civilians, troops and chiefs in their uniforms and finery. Stevenson, who sat on his horse watching the ceremony, looked as if he "were commanding the manoeuvres." On the following day, when the consuls presented the chief justice to the king, there was a full dress reception with natives in war array. From many districts natives arrived bringing the customary presents of food for the chief justice. All promised that they would abandon plans for the war that would have broken out had this foreign official not arrived. Chief Fau addressed the chief justice: "Good are the words which you our chief justice has spoken. The people of Samoa are ignorant and in the darkness but now the sun will shine and all is light. The light we refer is you. All will be united for the welfare of Samoa." In proof of their sincerity the natives began once more to spend their money, which for months they had been accumulating, for the surreptitious purchase of guns and ammunition.

Unfortunately the foreign officials who were received by the natives with a great deal of consideration, lacked the initiative and tact necessary to carry out the delicate powers which had been granted them. The natives wished action, but the chief justice had an aversion for haste and announced that he would delay action rather than do amiss.

The two officials quarreled with the land commissioners, the whites and the natives. As a commentary on the grasping policy of the foreigners in Samoa, it is worth noting that out of the entire 832,000 acres in the islands, the Germans claimed 134,419 acres of which 75,000 acres were confirmed by the land commission; the British claimed 1,250,270 acres; were allowed 36,000; the Americans, who claimed 302,746 acres, were granted only 21,000 acres, mostly to one San Francisco corporation.

The natives belived that they were being cheated out of their land. They resented also any centralized authority, and felt humiliated that their king was being treated shabbily by the foreign officials. As Stevenson pointed out, the chief justice, who received an annual salary of $6,000 and the president, who received $5,000, had been in Samoa for months and had accomplished nothing. They lived in beautiful new houses, while just across the street the native king lived in a wretched shanty or what his opponents called *Fa le-moa* (a henhouse), on a salary of $30 a month, and that not paid regularly. It was even rumored, falsely, that the poor king couldn't get credit at the *papalangi* stores and had to send out his queen to do washing in order to help replenish his empty purse. And this was the titular king of 30,000 natives! The situation made Stevenson's heart burn.

The natives also resented the fact that none of them were given positions in the government; that the foreign officials evidently forgot that the Samoan people existed. They complained against acts of injustice and oppression. In the outer districts many refused to pay taxes. They cried: "Who asked the great powers to make laws for us; to bring strangers here to rule us? We want no white officials to bind us in the bondage of taxation!" They asked their foreign friends to explain to them the peculiarities of white government and white man's justice.

To make matters worse, the government was soon beginning to have trouble with Mataafa and his followers. In the eyes of almost all natives and foreigners Mataafa was by far the outstanding personality of the Samoan race. To Stevenson he was the nearest thing to a hero in Samoan history, who by his patriotism, statesmanship and military skill was able to defend his country against German aggression. Even Henry Adams considered Mataafa one of the most heroic figures of the nineteenth century, as well as a genuine aristocrat and gentleman.

Mataafa was blessed with the physical and spiritual attributes of greatness. He was of commanding stature: tall, powerful, erect as a shaft, white-haired and moustached. His deep-set eyes were bright, his face a study in sensitivity and dignity, his jaw underhung, which gave him "something of the expression of a benevolent mastiff." Clad in linen of spotless purity, without any ornaments save a rosary or a holy symbol, he looked grave, often sad, the essence of dignity, serenity, superiority and gentility. He gave the impression of being a great warrior or a distinguished prelate. An ardent Catholic, he attended mass daily, and from his house could be heard the singing of *Ave Maria.* He had never married, but a natural daughter attended him. He had in later life taken a vow of chastity and, what was more remarkable, had kept it.

Mataafa was the idol of his people, holding an unrivaled position in their eyes. During the war against the Germans he was acclaimed by the American Admiral Kimberley as the George Washington of Samoa. While Malietoa Laupepa was in exile Mataafa was crowned king of Samoa; the district of Malie conferred upon him the title of Malietoa; in fact he held all the titles necessary for the kingship. During the war he had lain with his warriors in the bush and had shared all their privations. He was, therefore, convinced that he was entitled to enjoy the fruits of victory. When the Germans returned Malietoa Laupepa from exile, he was graciously received by his cousin Mataafa. They embraced; they related their experiences—one in captivity, the other in war. Laupepa, worn in body and mind, urged Mataafa to retain power and the kingship; Laupepa longed to lay down the burden of his office and retire to private life so that he could indulge his love of study. The very word Laupepa, meaning "the sheet of paper," derived from his studious habits.

A secret protocol in the Berlin Act, however, provided that Mataafa was not to be allowed to assume the position of kingship, even though he might be the popular choice. This was Germany's vengeance for the defeat of Fangalii; a punishment for daring to defeat the *Herrenvolk!* Stevenson blamed not only Germany but also England and America which treacherously agreed to the infamous protocol. Perhaps the three powers did not want a ruler with a will of his own, but a mere puppet whose strings they might pull when they wished to make him dance.

This situation was destined to create trouble. On several occasions native chiefs informed the foreign officials that their choice was Mataafa and not Malietoa Laupepa. In addition to the overt and covert rivalries between the two leading high chiefs, there were the old, though somewhat smothered, tribal animosities and the claims of the Tamasese faction which had for many years caused conflict in this little cockpit of the South Seas.

Tamasese, the former protégé of the Germans, died shortly after his defeat. It was rumored that he died of a broken heart. Others reported that he was killed by the "deadly barb of the sting-ray's tail" placed among his sleeping mats by an assassin. It entered his back, reached his vitals, and caused his death in a few days. His son, Tamasese the younger, an attractive young man, continued the intrigue to weaken the alliance between Laupepa and Mataafa.

There were also other sources of trouble. Two chiefs in Savaii and Atua were conniving to win the regency. And lastly, the irrepressible Maunga was having his own little civil war in Tutuila, which soon affected Upolu. All this combustible material was building up into a stockpile bound to explode into a general Samoan war.

Though refusing to recognize the justice and the legality of the Berlin protocol, Mataafa was willing to bide his time. He continued to live side by side with King Malietoa at Mulinuu, the native "capital." The beautiful relationship, however, was too good to last. Malietoa Laupepa was not popular with the natives: he was suspected of being a tool of the treaty powers. The natives challenged the right of the foreigners to interfere in their affairs and to dictate to them the choice of their own king. They resented the edict against playing their favorite cricket matches. Was this done to make them work longer hours for little pay in order to enrich the business community, especially the beer-drinking *papalangi* with "glass-eyes" who were interested only in dollars and cents! Thus ran popular sentiment against the *matagalasi* (bespectacled Germans).

As Mataafa's popularity grew, the weak, well-meaning titular king became uneasy, and began to suspect his kinsman. Mataafa on his side felt offended by his "poor brother's" lack of faith, and was disgusted with the spectacle of mismanagement. The bomb finally exploded on May 31, 1891, when Mataafa and his chiefs suddenly moved from the house at Mulinuu and took up their residence at Malie, down the coast seven miles west of Apia, a place much revered by ancient tradition. Here Mataafa made his headquarters; here he was visited by many well-wishers, both native and white.

The expressions of popular sympathy, particularly by the French Catholic priests, who were desirous of seeing their most prominent convert in power, undoubtedly bolstered his self-confidence and raised his hopes. He may have suspected that the Germans would not seriously oppose his return to power. He even hoped that he might be supported by the American and British consuls who frequently clashed with their German colleague. In fact the Germans did accuse the British and Americans of encouraging Mataafa to rebellion. It appeared, however, that Mataafa overestimated his strength among the natives, many of whom in the end chose to align themselves with the government in power. Others remained neutral for fear of punishment by the foreign powers, especially by the German warships stationed in Apia Harbor.

Mataafa's removal to Malie was regarded with great apprehension by the government at Mulinuu; it was feared that it might be the precursor of rebellion and war. The significance of the move is better understood in the light of Samoan customs; for Malie, the central division of Samoa, had the right to grant the name Malietoa, an honor which it soon conferred on Mataafa. The foreign officials went to Malie to point out to Mataafa the significance of his move and to persuade him to return to Mulinuu.

Mataafa disclaimed any intention of making war or causing any trouble; the move to Malie was simply in obedience to the wish of a number of districts. He renewed his profession of loyalty to Malietoa Laupepa, but complained of the latter's jealousy of him. He insisted that he was acting within the provisions of the Berlin Act, providing for the free right of the Samoans to elect their own king according to the customs of their country; he favored submitting the question of the choice of the king to the people of Samoa. "For myself I ask nothing," he insisted. In a voice choked with emotion, he confessed to Henry Adams, that his "only hope was in Christ and in America."

At Malie, meanwhile, many native houses were going up daily. Speakers were sent out all over the islands to exert their influence in behalf of Mataafa. Some chiefs, who visited the camp at Malie, held off, deciding on armed neutrality and reserving the right to join the stronger faction when the critical moment arrived. But a number of recruits with blackened faces, a sign of war, continued to pour into Malie. In fact Mataafa had some difficulty in keeping the growing number in check. The young braves from Savaii and Manono were itching for glory. He was justly proud of the discipline and order that prevailed in his camp; of the obedience to the code of laws which he had drafted with his own hand, which threatened offenders not with corporal punishment only, but also with loss of caste. Moreover, he pointed with satisfaction to the number of huts, plantations and gardens, and to the canoes drawn up on the beach. Mataafa impressed all visitors equally with his courtesy and goodwill and his great capacity for leadership and sense of law and order. His habitual expression was sad. The source of his sadness was to be found in his thwarted ambition. He felt his high lineage, heroic services and great devotion to his people entitled him to aspire to the kingship.

In spite of his assurances that he harbored only peaceful designs, well informed people, including Stevenson, were afraid that Mataafa might not be able to restrain his overzealous braves; that his confidence might prevail over his better judgment, and that hostilities would break out. This would mean famine for the natives and attacks upon the whites.

Stevenson inspected his own premises with a view of defense. His supply of weapons consisted of eight revolvers, a shotgun, and "swords galore." He found the whole business of preparedness a lark, for it "filled the bill." To Colvin he wrote: "As for wars and rumours of wars, you surely know enough of me to be aware that I like that also a thousand times better than decrepit peace in Middlesex?" Nevertheless he decided to take a more active part in an attempt to prevent hostilities. "I had stood aside, and been a loyal, and above all, a silent subject, up to then; but now I snap my fingers at their malo (government). It is damned, and I'm damned glad of it . . . The sense of my helplessness here has been rather bitter; I feel it wretched to see this dance of folly and injustice and unconscious rapacity go forward from day to day, and to be impotent!" He looked upon the situation as a real tragedy. He did not glorify the natives whom he considered like other folk, "false enough, lazy enough, not heroes, not saints—ordinary men, damnably misused."

Stevenson denounced an edict issued by the Mulinuu government against anyone's visiting the rebel camp at Malie. He advised Lloyd and Moors to defy the law and to visit Mataafa, though the German and British consuls besought them not to make the journey. He also defied the decree that no one was to interview King Malietoa Laupepa, "the sacred puppet," without permission from the consuls, and then only in the presence of an approved interpreter—a spy, in his opinion. As was to be expected, Stevenson's defiant attitude caused a row in Apia; he was considered a trouble-maker by the Germans and the "idiotic President." He even suspected that, in the hope of securing conviction for some subversive act, his letters were opened by order of the chief justice.

Trouble soon broke out; some of the Mataafa men at Manono burned houses and destroyed crops belonging to the followers of Malietoa Laupepa. The German President visited Manono and persuaded some of the accused chiefs to come to Apia for trial. When the latter of their own accord or on the advice of Mataafa surrendered, they were summarily sentenced to six months imprisonment under "gentlemanly conditions," and were immediately clapped into jail. As the chiefs marched along the street a number of their friends cried, "Shall we rescue you?" Being surrounded by some thirty soldiers with loaded rifles, the condemned men shouted, "No!"

Soon rumors spread throughout Apia that the Swedish commandant distrusted the loyalty of the armed guard around the jail and conceived a plan to put dynamite under the building to be set off in case of an attempted rescue. It was rumored that the German President agreed to this pernicious scheme, and that, when an American warship refused to supply the dynamite, the material was secured from a wrecking vessel.

All Apia was a hotbed of rumors. The unpopularity of the foreigners mounted. Henry Simele declared that he was "weary of whites upon the beach. All too proud!" One of them, he insisted, had threatened to cut off his head with a bush-knife. Stevenson, true to form, protested vehemently against the dynamiting designs. "I loathe politics," he wrote to Colvin, "but at the same time, I cannot stand by and have the natives blown in the air treacherously with dynamite." He was determined to take action, even though the other whites in Apia might hesitate to join with him for fear of retaliation by the Mulinuu government. Supported by a few of the whites in Apia, Stevenson sent a letter to the President asking for an assurance that the rumors of dynamiting the gaol were unfounded. He warned the officials that "the rumors in their present form tend to damage the white race in the native mind, and to influence for the worse the manners of the Samoans," for rumors uncorrected or unexplained acquire almost the force of admitted truth.

Though the letter was couched in true diplomatic and friendly language and signed by a number of the leading white residents in Apia, haughty Baron Senfft snubbed the petitioners and questioned their right to speak in the name of the whites. He advised them, if afraid of the natives, to seek the protection of their consuls. Needless to say, the President's answer did not allay the suspicions of Stevenson or his supporters. They wrote again protesting the baron's imputation on their honesty and the accusation that they were promoting scandal. They further pointed out that the signatories were not seeking protection but information, "that it was not a sense of fear that moved them, but a sense of shame . . . not fear of suffering by the hands of the Samoans, but in their good opinion." The President replied in a scornful and incoherent letter that he was not to be trifled with and that he would not stoop to explanations. Stevenson characterized the letter as a "roulade of gabble," and urged the recall of the two foreign officials.

He sent copies of the exchange of correspondence to the London *Times*. The great "Thunderer" published the letters and in a vigorous editorial characterized the Samoan situation as a comedy which could well turn into a tragedy. "Baron Senfft Pilsach," said the editorial, "whether he is a designing despot or only a reed shaken by every wind of panic, or both, may play what risks he likes without much risk to himself. There is pretty sure to be in the offing a ship of war to which he can put off if things get too hot on shore!" It pointed out that the natives if convinced of the truth of the rumors about the dynamiting of the gaol might put into practice what Stevenson calls "an object lesson in the arts of peace and the administration of the law," and renew, with fresh atrocities, the trouble which once disturbed the islands. Under such conditions the "carpet-bag president will have an unfair advantage over the white residents who must stay, whatever fires their ruler's folly kindles, to protect and save from the flames their goods and chattels. He stakes nothing but his salary; they their property and lives."

The *Times*, agreeing with Stevenson, demanded that "this Offenbach fanatic tyrant" be removed or taught to stop his dangerous gambadoes. The old native government was weak but cheap; the present government was equally weak but expensive. "We do not like to meddle in Samoan politics," asserted the editor, "the country is volcanic and the temper of the people, white and native, are in harmony with the country. But Samoa is not a place for 'cocksparrow revolutionaries' to have their fling. The natives there are in Stevenson's words: 'famous in battle, feast, marvellous eaters and smiters.' We cannot expect a busy novelist to devote his precious time to tame the wild functionaries. The Foreign Office should look into the matter; and if guilty, the exalted baron should be retired into fiction, for he is too exaggerated for real life."

The publisher of the only local newspaper, the Samoa *Times*, declared that he was "literally astounded by the romantic conclusions arrived at by their author (Stevenson)," "our only literary shining light." It denied that the Samoa *Times* was controlled by the foreign officials as charged by Stevenson. "The gentlemen charged with these grave offences," continued the editor, "are responsible only to those who appointed them, and it would be undignified for them to defend themselves from the criticisms of Mr. Stevenson, or any person of similar importance." The editor concluded his long tirade against the author by saying: "It seems to us, that, had Mr. Stevenson employed his time and exercised his undoubted talents in his legitimate business, instead of dabbling in Samoan politics and discovering mare's nests in the administration . . . he would have gained more legitimate *kudos* . . . Mr. Stevenson is, we confidently assert, no friend to Samoa, although he poses as the champion of the oppressed and long-suffering inhabitants."

According to Stevenson the haughty President, realizing that he "had been an idiot," sent emissaries to him to "kiss and be friends." A personal interview was to be arranged. Stevenson, however, thought it was useless: the Baron had had his chance but had failed to exploit it. The German colony in Samoa suspected Stevenson's motives in attacking an official countryman. When the German naval captain, a former constant visitor, was about to leave Samoa, he wrote that "as a German officer he could not come even to say farewell."

Meanwhile the plot was thickening. The President issued a proclamation declaring Mataafa a rebel. The British and German consuls, with the concurrence of the Mulinuu government, suggested to their respective Foreign Offices the desirability of capturing Mataafa and disarming his troops. The American Consul-General Sewall and the State Department, however, opposed such extreme measures; there had been so far no outbreak of violence. They believed that Mataafa could be restrained from overt action if the three treaty powers would each send a battleship to the Samoan islands.

Stevenson deplored the decision to proclaim Mataafa a rebel, the only man who could hold the warriors in check. "We sit upon a volcano which is being stoked by bland incompetent amateurs," he wrote. It was no "thanks to our idiot governors," that Mataafa had not yet moved. It was said that Mataafa's forces did not have ammunition, but "where there are traders, there will be ammunition." In fact boat loads of ammunition had already arrived at Malie. He was, however, of the opinion that none of the natives really wanted war and that every day that passed was solid gain, for the Samoans thus had opportunity to dissipate their energy in oratory.

Reverend S. J. Whitmee, an experienced missionary who had recently returned to the islands, wrote to Stevenson suggesting a one-man rule as a solution for Samoa's ills. He proposed Chief Justice Cederkrantz as the person to hold that position. Stevenson opposed this idea as dangerous. If it were possible to have a Gordon or a Lawrence, he held, it would be well; but in a place as isolated as Samoa, an experiment as extreme as this would prove most unwise. He was definitely opposed to Cederkrantz for the position. He was convinced that neither Laupepa nor Mataafa singly could govern successfully; the separation of the two chiefs was bound to mean war or a stalemate. He was determined to bring about a reconciliation between Laupepa and Mataafa as the only door of hope; they were once friends and they must be friends again. "Only fools and meddlers set them at odds."

Stevenson expressed the same idea a few months later in a letter to Reverend R. Wardlaw Thompson. Peace in Samoa, he insisted, could come only with a reconciliation between Laupepa and Mataafa; neither could be king without the cooperation of the other. He regarded all those who helped to prolong the estrangement of the two high chiefs as the real enemies of Samoa. He denied the right of the Congress of Berlin to exclude Mataafa from the kingship which he held *de facto*. He criticized the Protestant missionaries, whose task was to promote religion, culture and social improvement, for being involved in politics and aligning themselves with either side.

There were reports that in order to bring about a reconciliation Malietoa was willing to give Mataafa a place in the government. Since he could not receive him as a son, because then he could take the king's name and claim the right to the succession, he was willing to receive him as a daughter. "Imagine," wrote Mother Stevenson, "the grey-headed elderly man to be accepted as a pure virgin and cannot marry without the consent of his new family!"

Early in the spring of 1892 Stevenson decided to visit Mataafa at Malie. "To live within a few miles of the rebel camp," he wrote, "to be a novelist, to have all my family forcing me to go, and to refrain all these months, counts for virtue." He was encouraged when he heard that several people had visited Mataafa without the government's taking action against them.

According to La Farge, Stevenson had wanted to meet Mataafa, but the question was who was to call first. "It is always difficult," commented La Farge, "for those of us who have the cosmopolitan instinct to realize how fundamental are the views of the Britisher . . . I know how that would be settled in England. No one would expect the Queen or the Prince of Wales to call first, even though they cannot have for themselves the sense of 'dignity and sacredness which must envelop Mataafa.' " The two finally met when both happened to be visiting their mutual friends, Adams and La Farge, who were living then in Apia. Stevenson was at once won over by the "delicate courtesy of the great chief." Mataafa expressed a keen interest in Tusitala, the man of great distinction.

Stevenson sent a message about his plan to visit Malie. Immediately a messenger arrived with an invitation. But before the journey could be undertaken Tusitala had a visit from King Malietoa with a guard of three soldiers dressed in white coats and trousers, and armed with rifles and bayonets. The visitors were invited to stay for lunch and during the meal the King was loud in his praise of everything at Vailima. When he asked Stevenson why he had not visited him at Mulinuu, he was reminded of the law passed by the white officials that no one was to visit the King without permission. He did not care to ask leave of the consuls and perhaps be refused. The King advised him to pay no attention to the law and to come when he pleased. Malietoa's pleasant manners and mild nature impressed the Stevensons. Evidently the favorable impression was mutual, for some time later the Queen visited Vailima, accompanied by two unarmed men dressed in *lava lavas* and shirts. The Queen herself, a woman of about thirty or forty years of age, was quite pretty and dressed in a *kolau* of cream-colored muslin trimmed with dainty lace. She had never ridden on horseback and the undertaking was really difficult for her, but since the King spoke so favorably of Vailima, she felt that she would not be satisfied until she too had been introduced to the beauties of the "flash-house." She admired everything about the house: the pantries, the bedrooms, and above all the statues. She stared in amazement at the big stuffed heads of the lions.

To demonstrate his impartiality Stevenson decided to return the visit of King Malietoa Laupepa. At Mulinuu he was met by a guard of native soldiers in white uniforms, and taken to the King's house. It made Stevenson bristle with indignation when he saw the beautiful houses of the foreign officials which were in marked contrast to the low shanty where the King resided. The "royal palace" was a typical, squatty, oval-shaped hut supported on wooden posts. The eaves were so low that Stevenson had to stoop to enter. The venetian blinds were kept down at both ends of the house, but in other places they were entirely drawn up to let in air and light. The floor was covered with handsome, thick, soft mats; the furniture consisted of an iron bed, a washstand, several wooden chests and a lamp, but no chairs. The Queen came out to meet the visitors, while the King awaited them within. There he stood dressed in black trousers, white flannel shirt, black tie, and white shoes and stockings. He received his visitors with his usual dignity and courtesy.

Soon the *kava* bowl was brought out by three pretty girls dressed in skirts of tapa with bright-colored low bodices and wreaths on their heads and round their necks. They shook hands with everyone, then seated themselves behind the bowl at the far end of the room to prepare the drink. When it was ready to serve, a "talking-man" in dark blue entered and took his place beside the bowl. He called out the King's name and title, filled a cup by squeezing the liquid from the fibre, and handed it to His Majesty, who bowed to the visitors and drank. Then *kava* was served to the honored visitors. There was some discussion as to which *Tamaitai* (high born lady) should be served first. The King favored old age, so it was decided to serve Aunt Maggie first, then Tusitala, next followed the Queen, then Fanny, and finally Belle. The King was friendly and conciliatory. He complimented Mother Stevenson on her beautiful white cap which was like that of Queen Victoria. He thought she looked younger than her son and must be very strong to be "the mother of such an old son."

After *kava* was served the guests were led to the dinner table, banana leaves spread on the floor, on which were a number of roasted ducks and chickens. The King seated Aunt Maggie on his right and Fanny on his left. After the meal the guests were presented with baskets filled with food to take home. The Stevensons found Malietoa gentle, amiable, and most courteous, as was to be expected of the king of a courteous people, but unlike most of the natives, who were light-hearted and gay, he looked sad. His exile and the uncertainty of his future had, no doubt, crushed his naturally buoyant spirit.

Stevenson was eager to have a confidential talk with the King and try to bring about a reconciliation with Mataafa. It was arranged that the two were to meet the following day, but at the appointed hour the King failed to appear. After a considerable time the Queen arrived with a message that a government function had been scheduled which the King was obliged to attend. Stevenson suspected that the foreign officials counseled the King against the meeting.

Tusitala decided to visit Mataafa in the effort to reconcile the rival claimants to the throne, and thus bring "a little chance of peace." Early on a May morning in 1892, the family started out for Malie: Fanny on Musu, Belle on Jack, and the Laird himself on Donald, the huge gray cart-horse which made him look like a "sweet little cherub that sits up aloft." At Apia the group was transferred to a boat belonging to the Roman Catholic Mission. Malie with its well built houses reminded the Stevensons of Tautira in Tahiti.

The party was welcomed by Mataafa with most friendly consideration. As a special honor Tusitala was served his *kava* together with the King himself. Before the bowl was presented to Mataafa a libation was poured from it. Fanny, in her dark red silk *haloku,* trimmed with Persian embroidery, and Belle, in her green silk dress, were also served together in order not to offend either one, for they were taken to be Stevenson's wives. Alii Vailima's interpreter, Talolo, was a great disappointment. He was unable to translate the orations by Mataafa and his talking-man, for he could not speak high chief language. Instead of saying "they were very much obliged," he used the word "surprised." Since the Stevensons were in the habit of referring to Mataafa as "Charley over the water," and toasted him by waving their glasses over the water bottle, Talolo, not completely understanding the meaning of this, thought it was a good time to emulate his master and waved his hands in the air, exclaiming "Charley in the water!" Stevenson understood enough Samoan to catch the error. Dinner was served in "civilized" manner with plates, tumblers, spoons, knives, and forks. Mataafa, a devout Catholic, crossed himself and said grace. When Tusitala offered a present of a hundred-pound keg of beef, the talking-man stepped outside to announce in a stentorian voice the nature of the precious gift which it would have been considered a breach of custom to refuse.

After a serious talk with Mataafa, the Stevensons departed from Malie by boat. To keep up their spirits they sang hymns to the accompaniment of the water gurgling against the ship's prow.

A few days later Stevenson returned to Malie for further talks with Mataafa. He arrived early in the evening when he could hear the clanging of the bell in Mataafa's chapel. When the High Chief Mataafa returned he greeted Stevenson most heartily. He felt deeply grateful for the latter's desire to help his people to a lasting peace and introduced him to his chiefs as "a man who had risked deportation to serve their master." They were advised to study his face and remember on all occasions to help and serve him no matter what the cost to themselves. Stevenson was compared with Jesus Christ. After dinner and talks on politics, Stevenson retired about midnight upon a pile of mats prepared by Mataafa's daughter, Kalala. Throughout the night Stevenson was disturbed by the patrol of armed guards and a drummer who "stood to arms from sun-down to sun-up." About four in the morning he heard the sound of a whistle pipe playing a pleasing, simple air in the dark which sounded very sweet and soothing. He was later informed that this music was a part of the routine in Mataafa's camp to provide pleasant dreams.

Stevenson maintained that his visits to the rival camps were made, not because of a desire to interfere in the affairs, but from a sense of duty; because of his great affection for that sweet and beautiful soul, Mataafa. Incidentally, he was proud of his physical ability to undergo the sea journeys in all kinds of weather.

Late in May the entire Stevenson family visited Malie. The party arrived when the war dances were over, but the elaborate ceremony of food presentation was still in full swing. The village lawn was completely surrounded by oblong sheds of flapping canvas cut from old boat sails or of green palm boughs stuck into the ground and roofed with green palm branches. These were crowded with some thousands of gaily dressed natives wearing their colored tapas. Their heads were gilded with powdered sandalwood or ornamented with purple flower petals. In the middle of the large field were spread out piles of food gifts brought in by chanting deputations, brandishing their contributions aloft. The delegates from each village marched in procession, every man carrying a gift. As the delegation passed, an orator from each one of the villages rose and delivered a conventional speech. In spite of the distance, beyond ear-shot for the average person, Stevenson could hear the description of his gifts, and of himself, as the *Alii Tusitala O le alii O malo tetele* [the chief White information, the chief of the great Governments].

The gifts were accepted, according to law and custom, by the official king's receiver, dressed in a spotless *lava lava* and wearing scarlet flowers. When he picked up each article and turned it round to show it off to the crowds, he accompanied the gesture with a rapid fire commentary which amused the audience no end. Meanwhile the king's officers were making lists of all the gifts brought in. Mataafa sat watching the proceedings, his lips moving and the "beads of his rosary slip stealthily through his hand." The only other ones in the house with Mataafa and the Stevensons were the great talking-man, Popo, and his son and granddaughter. Eighty-year-old Dantesque Popo, who had worshipped idols before the coming of the missionaries from Tahiti, was of a high chief family. When the *kava* was served, Popo and his son rose and proclaimed loudly the praises of King Mataafa. To the experts it meant, said Stevenson, "Long live *Tuiatua!* to the inexpert, it is a mere voice of barbarous wolves." Mataafa was highly gratified, for it was of great significance to him that Popo and his son had now for the first time openly joined his forces and accorded him Mataafa, as was their hereditary right, the due cry of *Tuiatua,* one of the eight royal names in Samoa.

After the dinner Mataafa and his guests returned to their posts to watch the ceremony of the public announcement of the gifts. The audience was convulsed by the humorous orator who in sing-song called out: "6,000 roots of taro, 319 cooked pigs, 200 live chickens, and pieces of tapa, one of them one hundred years old and has been worn by a great number of natives."

Stevenson then witnessed a most strange and weird performance: Popo and his son rose, rushed out of the house and with long staves, which "talking-men" carry, commenced to perform a bizarre dance. Along the piles of food the old man capered with outstretched arms, while his son crouched and leaped beside him. Whatever they leaped over and called for became theirs by right. They later returned to the King all they had claimed, except some tapa and a box of biscuits which Stevenson had brought.

The ceremony aroused considerable amusement and laughter. Mataafa himself took care of the gifts for "his excellency Tusitala": five live hens, four gourds of oil, four beautiful tapas, a hundred head of *taro,* two cooked pigs, a cooked shark, *kava,* and a turtle which soon died from sunstroke. The entire family returned delighted with their visit. Aunt Maggie agreed that Mataafa was the most gracious gentleman in the world.

Stevenson's last journey to Malie was made in August, 1892. He was accompanied by the charming Lady Jersey and her brother Captain Leigh, "a very nice kind of glass-in-his-eye kind of fellow," who were visiting Samoa. In order not to compromise the wife of the governor at Sydney, who might be accused of siding with the rebel, Mataafa, it was agreed to call her "Cousin Amelia Balfour," so that no one of the Mulinuu government would be aware of the visit. Stevenson was afraid that, since there were no secrets in Apia, it would be difficult to conceal the identity of Lady Jersey, or "Queen of Sydney" as she was often called. He was fearful lest her journey to Malie might even prove the signal for war. The plot, however, appealed to him enormously, a veritable lark, an adventure that admirably suited his book.

On the appointed day the party set out from Vailima: Stevenson in a white cap, velvet coat, cords and yellow half boots; Isobel in a white suit and cap; Lloyd in white clothes, straw hat and long yellow boots; Graham in khaki. Henry Simele, in a blue coat and black kilt was to officiate as Stevenson's "talking-man." After reaching Apia the party turned westward to a trysting place where they were to meet "Cousin Amelia" who was to travel thither by a more circuitous route.

When the arrival of the lady was delayed, Stevenson became nervous; he began to suspect that the secret had leaked out and that the lady and her brother had been arrested. But even the possibility of the discovery of the conspiracy added zest to the adventure. Soon he was overtaken by the riders who almost bore him down, shouting "Ride, Ride!" like characters in a ballad.

Heading the march, Stevenson and his "Cousin Amelia" thoroughly enjoyed this spice of adventure: the journey of some seven miles crossed through banana plantations, past native villages with their inevitable coconut palms, through plots of *taro,* and forests with their pink flowers. The pig fences were the only disagreeable obstacle. When the party approached one of the Mataafa villages, the beating of a wooden drum sounded their welcome; then the whole population came out to meet them with their customary salutation, *talofa!* Some asked, "Which is the great lady?" The inquiry made Stevenson wonder whether the disguise was really a success.

At Malie the party passed a guard of powerful men in native costume, for Mataafa had not adopted Malietoa's practice of having his army wear regular uniforms. Escorted by the guards blowing their bugles and a large crowd, mostly children, the Stevenson party finally reached headquarters. There they were welcomed with great dignity and genuine satisfaction by Mataafa, dressed in a white shirt and a *lava lava.* During the conversation Mataafa exhibited proudly a gold watch which the United States Government had presented to him in acknowledgement of the services which his men had rendered in helping to rescue American sailors during the great hurricane. He then begged to be excused while he attended evening prayers, for he was always devoutly Catholic.

At dinner Mataafa invited Stevenson to say grace; for a moment the latter felt embarrassed. Fortunately Cousin Graham came to his rescue by reminding him of *Benedictus Benedicat.* The meal, consisting of pigeons, chickens, *taro,* yams and coconut milk, proved very enjoyable. While Mataafa himself used his fingers, the Stevensons were provided with plates, knives, and forks. When dinner was over Popo rose and howled across "Cousin Amelia's" shoulder; this naturally startled her. "There," shouted Stevenson, "we have been giving you a chapter of Scott, but this goes beyond the Waverley Novels!" At the private *kava* service the first cup was offered to the great lady with blue eyes from across the waters. When the King drank his cup, Popo shouted in his stentorian voice the royal names of Mataafa. Mataafa and Stevenson then retired for an interview. Henry Simele was dumfounded to hear the great king addressing the Alii Vailima as *alioga* (his excellency), give him his own staff and bid him to pass on ahead of him.

Though the custom among the Samoans was for all the members of the household to sleep in a common room, in consideration of his guests' peculiar prejudices Mataafa ordered that large tapa hangings partition off a portion of the house for the women. The natives were, however, surprised that the men and women slept separately. The guard also watched curiously when the women came out to brush their teeth. Before dawn Stevenson heard good singing from Mataafa's chapel; when he went out to listen he was saluted by the guards. It really pleased Stevenson to know that there was a place where sentinels saluted him.

After a protracted breakfast the party moved to the guest house, the largest native house in Samoa, which was elaborately constructed on cross beams and decorated inside with wooden birds, in memory of Mataafa's father who was called the "king of birds." Here they witnessed an interesting ceremony. A number of speeches were made and it was an unusual experience for Henry Simele to translate the orations made in honor of Tusitala and then to translate Tusitala's own speech. He had to speak loudly to be heard; he blushed and trembled but covered himself with glory.

When the *kava* was served first to the king, he poured one drop in libation, drank some and poured the remainder outside the house. This was followed by serving the *kava* to two orators. One of them took his drink down straightway; the other, who feigned illness, was packed under tapa, and his neck, resting on a bamboo head-rest, was massaged by his friends. At last, groaning, he lifted his head, then lifted himself on his elbow to drink. The beverage immediately restored the sick man to health. Now came the turn of a great hereditary war leader. Five times the cup bearer filled the cup, marched up and down the hall announcing the name and titles of the important personage. Each time the mighty warrior looked into the cup and refused it as too scanty a portion. Finally the sixth cup was offered and found satisfactory. This custom might have stemmed from the time when Malietoa as head of his army suffered from the lack of supplies—food as well as drink. The warrior finally asserting the dignity of his office drained the six cups of *kava,* each denoting a great name. He played his part very well and in harmony with the occasion. The drink was then offered to a few more high chiefs, to Tusitala, to his "cousin," and to the other members of the Stevenson party, to all, in fact, except Henry. He was served after the family and guests. Stevenson observed: "I thought it had like to have made Henry Simele angry: he is really a considerable chief." Henry was, nonetheless, regarded as one of the household—a retainer.

When the festivities were over the Stevenson party bade Mataafa and his courteous daughter, who acted as his hostess, farewell, and rode back to Vailima. They were much pleased with their escapade. The secret, however, leaked out, and rumors were circulated in Apia respecting the visit and the subsidies furnished the "rebels" by the Stevensons and their guests. Lady Jersey was of the opinion that, while Malietoa's claim to the kingship was somewhat stronger than that of Mataafa, the latter was, nevertheless, much admired by the people; that without the interference of the consuls he could have easily defeated his rival at Mulinuu. But even then there were several districts that would continue to oppose Mataafa, and the confusion could become worse. In her opinion, both Malietoa and Mataafa were honorable and well intentioned, deserving of respect and sympathy. It was regrettable that they were ever permitted to drift asunder; a reconciliation could have been effected.

Stevenson's open sympathy for Mataafa's cause, and his several visits to the "rebel" camp, aroused considerable suspicion at Mulinuu. He was accused of meddling in Samoan politics, of fomenting sedition among the Mataafa people, and even of illicit importation of arms. Stevenson suspected that the Mulinuu government posted spies to watch him, to open his mails, and to cross-question the Vailima servants and seduce them into betraying his secrets. The Samoa *Times,* accused by Stevenson of being a tool of the Mulinuu government, criticized the novelist for writing numerous letters to the London *Times* attacking the local newspaper and the government.

Moors and Stevenson informed Chief Justice Cederkrantz that they were friendly with both Mataafa and Malietoa and that they had a right to speak in public or in private in disapproval of all the government measures which they deemed unwise. Government officials, they maintained, were public servants and all their acts were open to criticism. "It is not our opposition that is bringing your government to its end; it is the want of our support, which we cannot give you," they concluded.

A rumor spread in Apia that the Chief Justice and the President were planning to kidnap and deport Stevenson. The local newspaper quoted an article in the German *Vossische Zeitung* suggesting the "complete disarming of the whites who meddle in the internal affairs, including Mr. R. L. Stevenson, the novelist." This did not seem to alarm Stevenson, for he wrote to Colvin: "There is great talk in town of my deportation; it is thought they have written home to Downing Street, requesting my removal, which leaves me not much alarmed; what I do rather expect is that H. J. Moors and I may be hailed up before the C. J. to stand trial for lese-majesty. Well we'll try and live it through."

Early in November Apia was startled by the firing of guns on the British warship *Ringarooma* which had just arrived. As soon as Stevenson rode into town, people surrounded him and told him excitedly that he was going to be arrested and deported. He was shown the German newspaper calling loudly for his removal from the Samoan islands. When Stevenson boarded the *Ringarooma* to find the reason for her unexpected visit, he was informed by the captain that he did not know why he had been sent to Samoa; he was waiting for further instructions. To Colvin, Stevenson wrote: "It is hoped the same ship that takes this off Europewards may bring his orders and our news. But which is it to be? Heads or tails? If it is to be German, I hope they will deport me; I should prefer it so; I do not think that I could bear a German officialdom, and should probably have to leave *sponte mea,* which is only less picturesque, and more expensive."

In fact Stevenson seemed to be amused by the deportation rumors. "It is a strange life I live, always on the brink of deportation," he wrote. "And well have you known my character: If I were to pretend to you that I was not amused, you would justly scorn me. For, say what you please, it has been a deeply interesting time. You don't know what news is, nor what politics, nor what the life of man, till you see it on so small a scale and with your own liberty on the board for stake. I would not have missed it for much. And anxious friends beg me to stay at home and study human nature in Brompton drawing rooms!"

Sir John Thurston, British High Commissioner of the Western Pacific, issued a regulation which rendered any British subject guilty of sedition against the government of Samoa liable, on conviction, to imprisonment. Stevenson was convinced that the order was aimed at him, but he refused to be intimidated. "If those are the laws of Great Britain," he said, "the Lord deliver us; and I have reasons more than one for believing that this regulation was mainly directed against me . . . Is it seditious to say a word likely to tend to bring about discontent or dissatisfaction with the existing state of affairs . . . What Samoa really wants is to get rid of the leading white officials; that is, the Chief Justice and the President of the Council." When asked whether he intended to leave Samoa, he replied: "Certainly not—that is, unless I am deported. The regulation smells of martial law; but there is no sign of war in the islands."

Stevenson's reactions to the regulation were cabled to London. In Sydney Sir John Thurston was shown the Australian newspaper that printed the London cable, and, when interviewed by a newspaper reporter, the commissioner stated that the order "may have some connection with the impression conceived by Mr. Stevenson that the Regulation had a reference to him. . . . It is just conceivable that the sensitiveness of Mr. Stevenson on this point may be due to the prickings of conscience . . . It is natural if (which, however, is not suggested) Mr. Stevenson has been directly inciting the Chief Mataafa to resist the authority of the recognized King of Samoa."

No action, however, was taken against Stevenson. Sharp comments in the British press and challenging questions in the House of Commons, influenced the reasonable colonial secretary, Lord Rippon, to intervene and instruct his underlings to modify their orders, and cease their "opposition to Mr. R. L. Stevenson." There was a rumor that England proposed laying cables to Samoa at the expense of the signatory powers, for under the existing mode of communication it took four to five weeks for dispatches from Samoa to reach Europe. The Cologne *Gazette,* however, advocated the annexation of the islands by Germany.

Meanwhile a very official-looking letter arrived at the Apia post office; it was sealed in a heavy envelope on which were printed in large sharp letters, "British Foreign Office," and addressed to "Robert

Louis Stevenson, Esquire." When Isobel called for the mail, everyone who stood around her stared at the impressive, official-looking package. Immediately the rumor spread throughout Apia that the Foreign Office in London was taking action against the stormy petrel, Stevenson. Actually it was a friendly letter from Foreign Minister Lord Rosebery, requesting the author to send him his autograph. An additional triumph for Stevenson was the dismissal of Chief Justice Cederkrantz and President Baron Senfft von Pilsach by the three treaty powers. Though he knew that they were his enemies, and he had often accused them of incompetence and injustice, he did not gloat over their fall. "There was no man born with so little animosity as I," he declared, and with some justice.

Conditions in Samoa, however, were growing worse, not better. The two armed camps grew increasingly restless. Stevenson decided to try to encourage a reconciliation between Mataafa and Malietoa and thus bring peace to "this distracted archipelago of children sat upon by a clique of fools." He offered to invite the two rival leaders to Vailima during the negotiations. He realized that his interest might arouse suspicions, but he was willing to take the risk. Unfortunately, Malietoa Laupepa refused Stevenson's intercession. The powerful Chief Lautai, deeply concerned about the situation, tried by great personal exertions and charms of oratory to bring about a compromise by which Malietoa Laupepa was to continue to be king while Mataafa was to be the prime minister, but this, too, was rejected by Malietoa Laupepa. "What else is to be done for these silly folks?" Stevenson implored. "O," he cried, "if I could only talk to the home men! But what would it matter? none of them know, none of them care. If we could only have Macgregor here with his schooner, you would hear of no more troubles in Samoa. That is what we want; a man that knows and likes the natives, *qui paye de sa personne,* and is not afraid of hanging when necessary. We don't want bland Swedish humbugs, and fussy footering German barons. That way the maelstrom lies, and we shall soon be in it." He was even more disgusted with King Malietoa: "that triple-headed ass in his plenitude of ignorance prefers to collect taxes and scatter Mataafa's force of arms."

There were, however, many in Samoa and elsewhere, who criticized Stevenson's meddling in politics and espousing the cause of the "arch rebel," Mataafa, declaring that he had mistaken his vocation and besides had been "backing the wrong horse." Said the Leeds *Mercury* of April 8, 1893: "Mr. Robert Louis Stevenson, who has now climbed to the very topmost rung of the ladders, so far as fame and popularity as a novelist are concerned, has been before the British public this week; and surely never before has a British storyteller figured in a more curious fashion. Here is a gentleman who ought to be spending his day at the Athenaeum of the Savile Club, drinking tea of an afternoon in the goodly company of bishops or art critics; a gentleman who, if he were alive to the privileges which successful authorship brings in its train, would not now be figuring largely in the natives' troubles."

As an escape from work and politics Stevenson, accompanied by Fanny and Belle, made a brief visit to Sydney. Here he found that his reputation as a writer and South Sea personage had grown greatly since his last visit. He was lionized by Sydney intellectual and artistic society. He enjoyed the publicity he received in the press as well as the receptions, dinners, and even the numerous invitations to address clubs and societies. He lectured on literature, on reading, and on the art of writing, and, of course, on Samoan politics. When he marched into the dining room of the Victoria, the leading Sydney hotel, looking distinguished in his specially tailored evening clothes, with Fanny by his side in a handsome black velvet evening gown, all the patrons turned to look, and the waiters murmured, "Stevenson!"

During his stay in Sydney Stevenson ran about town purchasing anything that attracted him, irrespective of price. Among the articles he bought were three topaz rings. On his own were engraved the initials, "F" and "B." On those of the women were the initials, "R. L. S." One day Stevenson stopped at the hotel to send a message to Fanny. When he found the bellboy or "buttons" so absorbed in reading a book that he did not even reply when spoken to, Stevenson snatched the volume out of the boy's hands, glanced at it but immediately returned it saying: "Go right on reading, my little man. Don't let anybody disturb you." It was *Treasure Island!*

The highlight of his trip was a lengthy visit with the "Great pro-Consul" of Australasia, Sir George Grey, whom Stevenson so much admired. The old gentleman received him in the quietest, coolest manner, listened patiently to his account of the Samoan situation, urged him to go on with his story, then said: "Let me give you a piece of advice from my own experience—pay no attention to attacks, go on doing what you are doing for the good of Samoa; the time will come when it will be appreciated, and I am one of the few men who have lived long enough to learn this." While examining him with his impressive blue eyes and a ripple of a smile on his lips Grey went on: "The worst of my anxiety is over, I thought you were an invalid. When I see the fire in your eye and your life and energy, I feel no more anxiety about Samoa." When Stevenson assured him that nothing but deportation would induce him to abandon Samoa, and that he was determined to put his hand to the plow, Grey, nodding his head for a considerable time, said:

"You may have thought me old-fashioned, but I believe it was Providence. There is something over us; and when I heard that a man with the romantic imagination of a novelist had settled down in one of these islands, I said to myself, these races will be saved!"

Stevenson was flattered and deeply gratified by this interview, and as he and George Grey walked out arm in arm to the hotel door, his mind was made up. "I'll not give up the fight!" he told himself.

CHAPTER XVI

THE TENDER HEART

IN SPITE OF Stevenson's efforts the two armed camps drifted toward civil war. The older natives regarded war as an unpleasant but inevitable experience; the young braves looked upon it as an escape from ennui and an opportunity for excitement and glory. Battle gave the hero his opportunity to show his prowess in taking the heads of his slain enemies.

During the spring of 1893 there was considerable excitement in the Mulinuu and Malie camps. Messengers came and went; *fonos* were held to which the village chiefs were invited to send delegates; the important question of war and peace was discussed. Each side dispatched its most eloquent talking-men to the various village districts to induce the natives to come over into its camp. The orators met the chiefs of the villages at the *faletele* or guest-house and presented their arguments persuasively. The Samoans, like the ancient Athenians, were eager to meet and discuss politics.

At the appointed time the great *fono* opened at the Mataafa camp, while a similar one took place at the Malietoa headquarters. Before dawn all the villages were astir. The young men from each family gathered at the village green with the staffs of their orators. At the *malae* they drove the staffs into the turf at designated places and then seated themselves beside them awaiting the arrival of their talking-men. When the chiefs and their orators arrived they seated themselves beside their respective staffs under the shade of breadfruit trees. Since dignity did not permit the kings and high chiefs to speak for themselves, each had beside him his "mouth-piece." To each group was assigned its proper place, with the chiefs, understandably, occupying the most honored positions. Several thousand attended the great *fono.* The path running through the *malae* was closed during the sessions so that the delegates would not be disturbed by passers-by. The chiefs and the orators sat cross-legged around the open village green, which was about one thousand feet in circumference.

The *fono* was opened in the cool of the morning. The leading orator in his half-hour speech gave the "keynote address." He rose, placed his fly-flapper over his shoulder, leaned forward upon his six-foot pole, the insignia of his office, and gazed upward as if imploring heaven for inspiration. Then in a low voice he began his normal address which consisted largely of an elaborate series of greetings to the delegates from the various districts. No one was overlooked; everyone was greeted according to an elaborate system of priorities. The speaker had to remember the exact titles of the various districts by which the delegates were always known and saluted. An omission of any title could be interpreted as an insult.

The first orator was succeeded by others with their fly-flappers and tall staves. As each one in his turn rose to address the gathering, a number of the other orators of the village stood up and contested among themselves as to who should have the honor of making the speech. This was a mere formality, for the order of speakers was known beforehand. The purpose of the simulated dispute was to let everybody know that there were other competent speakers present. After a short argument the colleagues of the orator sat down again and turned their attention to baskets of plaited coconut leaves and fibre from which they made sinnet while listening. Each orator spoke with grace and eloquence for a quarter of an hour, making allusions to his history and traditions. His voice seldom fell, but rose gradually so that the final word of the sentence was spoken in full volume. As the orators spoke their people sitting around them were not only attentive but also participated as prompters, refreshing the speakers' memories or suggesting new ideas. When a speaker wandered from his topic, his listeners brought him back to the subject. The spokesmen patiently and good-naturedly accepted the interruptions and often withdrew a statement in deference to the people's objections.

At noon a number of young men, decked out in their best, distributed refreshments in accordance with directions from the heads of the families. The discussion, however, continued during the meal. It was not until sunset that the *fono* ended.

The point of view expressed at the Mataafa camp was that the foreign governments had no right to interfere in Samoan affairs and dictate who should be king; this was a matter for the Samoans themselves to decide. It was maintained that even the Berlin Act recognized the right of the Samoans to choose their own government. It was also agreed that some compromise should be brought about with the Malietoa camp in order to prevent hostilities.

At Stevenson's suggestion Mataafa addressed a letter, May 8, 1893, to "His Majesty Malietoa Laupepa," entreating him to "put away that word—war!" and not to see Samoa torn to pieces. He reminded Malietoa that he had given him (Mataafa) the title of king in the presence of a great council meeting. "Take you the command, and confer with the people, for I am not strong enough," Laupepa had said when he returned from exile. Furthermore, the title, "Malietoa," had been given to Mataafa by the rightful districts. He begged the king to have a friendly meeting at any place he might designate. "Let Samoa choose him that it is unanimous for and is satisfied with. Let our country then construct in peace a government; and we shall be able to carry out our agreement with the Three Powers. Your Majesty, may you live long!"

George Pritchard, an authority on Samoan affairs, commenting on Mataafa's letter, approved the suggestion that the two Samoan high chiefs meet on Laupepa's *malae* to consider a settlement of their conflict. While the Europeans looked upon Mataafa as a rebel, the Samoans considered him the idol of the country, one of the greatest chiefs, who, were it not for the Germans, would have remained king.

Unfortunately, Malietoa Laupepa, at the advice of the foreign officials, in whose hands he was mere putty, refused any suggestion for conciliation with his rival. Stevenson and others held that the failure of any attempt at reconciliation, and the outbreak of the bloody civil war, should be laid at the door of the Three Powers.

By June both camps were busily engaged in soliciting help and collecting forces. Each district, each village had to be won over through diplomacy, eloquence, promises, or threats. Some chiefs made stipulations, demanding special concessions. Atua was one day off, the next day on; Anna was on and off; Savaii refused to move; Taumasaga was divided; Tutuila was rebellious. At one time each of the contending parties would feel reassured by promises of support, but the next day found that it had been deceived. At another time it appeared as if there would be no war and Samoans would "sit still and plant *taro*."

Apia, however, was in a state of turmoil. It was feared that the old lion would one day abandon his den and leap into war. Various rumors were afloat among whites and natives. As Stevenson rode from Apia to Vailima late at night, he noticed in the huts of Tuamanasaga fires burning, around which, he surmised, buzzed eager discussions of the latest rumors. It was reported that war drums were beating, that the woods were full of scouting parties, and that natives were carrying their prized mats to the missions for safety. It was rumored at one moment that King Malietoa Laupepa was dying; and then that he was perfectly well and riding, at night, with his face covered, through the back parts of Apia and up the Vailima road on an unknown mission. A report went the rounds to the effect that Mataafa was consulting with chiefs; that he was certain of the support of almost all Samoans; that he was already marching his men; that Germany would supply him with arms and make him king of the islands. Dr. George Brown, a missionary with considerable understanding of the natives, toured the islands to find out the truth. He assured Stevenson that "when the first shot is fired, and not before, you will know who is who." Stevenson believed that even after shots had been exchanged and men had been killed, many an important province might still be wavering. He wrote: "We wait, with a kind of sighing impatience, for war to be declared, or to blow finally off, living in the meanwhile in a kind of children's hour of firelight and shadow and preposterous tales."

June 28 was a very rainy day, but so anxious was Stevenson to hear the latest war news, that, after lunch, he and Graham got into their saddles and rode to Apia. There they found no signs of hostilities, but the place was rife with rumors. They were told that during the night drums had been heard in the distance; that men had run to arms from as far as Vaiala. In fact it was even whispered that battles had actually been fought. The whites in Apia were feeling so uneasy that they hoisted their national flags over their houses and places of business and drowned their fears in pots of beer or shots of brandy, depending on their nationality. A brother Scot, the Secretary of State, assured Stevenson that there was no genuine news.

Stevenson and Graham then decided to ride to the Mataafa camp where, according to rumors, there were real preparations for war. At Vaimusu, in rebel territory, they found the houses filled with unarmed men. A little farther, at a ford, they met a picket of seven men with Winchesters and cartridge belts. *Talofa!* exclaimed Stevenson. The commanding officer returned the greeting with a hearty *Talofa!*, and asked where they were going. "To Faamuina," Stevenson replied, and rode off. Every house on the way bristled with armed men. Over the European house of a Chinaman flew a flag of truce. The verandah, however, was crowded with armed warriors and garlanded, admiring girls. Down the road the adventure-seeking riders met a number of warriors marching with shining Winchesters and cartridge-belts girded around their big, bronzed, oiled bodies. "The cheerful alacrity and brightness of their looks set my head turning with envy and sympathy," confessed Stevenson.

At Vaiusu the houses around the village green were crowded with armed men. Outside of the big council-house stood an orator who was pouring out his political wisdom and exhorting his hearers to arms. The war spirit was infectious; even children were playing with spears. At the big house on the knoll Alii Vailima and his cousin were cordially welcomed by the former's good friend, elderly High Chief Faamuina and his wife Pelepa. The guests stayed long enough to smoke a cigarette, but refused to have *kava* made for them. They were afraid that their escapade was already too incriminating and "perhaps even blameworthy." As they left the house they were entertained by a man with his face blackened and his tattooed hips naked. He leaped, cut a caper, flung his knife high in the air, and caught it.

With some inward misgivings Stevenson and Graham rode back home, splashing through the miry paths, hurdling stone fences with dogs barking and nipping at their horses' heels. All along the road they were greeted by the Mataafa people. At the ford the commander of the sentries asked if there were many warriors on the Malietoa side. "Very many," Stevenson assured him. "That is well!" he replied to the great amusement of the picket. After five hours in the saddle, riding hard in a squall of rain, the anxious adventurers returned to Vailima at six to a bowl of *kava* and a warm dinner.

The sight of the "ardent, happy faces" of the armed warriors had made Stevenson's head whirl. "War is a huge *entrainement;* there is no other temptation to be compared to it. The old aboriginal awoke in both of us and nickered like a stallion," he confessed. For a moment he was even overcome by a temptation to ride to Malie, become the general officer, seize Mulinuu and have the Chief Justice arrested. "And yet I stay here! It seems incredible, so huge is the empire of prudence and the second thought," he lamented. To his friend Colvin he complained: "It is dreadful to think that I must sit apart here and do nothing; I do not know if I can stand it out. But you see, I may be of use to these poor people, if I keep quiet, and if I threw myself in, I should have a bad job of it to save myself."

Three days later Stevenson, Fanny, and Belle rode out toward Malie. To their great surprise they found at Vaiusu, instead of armed pickets, a cricket match in full swing on the village green! This time they all stopped at Faamuina's for *kava.* That same night at a ball at Apia Stevenson heard that one of the chiefs had stated that Tusitala was the source of all the trouble and that he should be punished. He also found considerable panic among the whites in Apia and talk that in the event of hostilities they would seek refuge on the two German warships in port. One effect of the threats to Vailima and its occupants was that it cooled Stevenson's ardor and "childish temptation to go out and fight." He felt that he would need his energy to protect his home.

As the war clouds darkened the natives at Vailima became restless and succumbed to superstitious fears. Lafaele and Arrick reported that they had seen Tusitala on the road, yet when they reached Vailima they were assured that their master had not left the house. Some of the servants drew out their wages in readiness for an emergency. When Fanny asked one of them whether he would be cowardly enough to take the heads of slain and wounded men, if war should break out, he replied that he would take all he could. When she attempted to reason with him, he stubbornly insisted that each people had its own peculiar customs. One good old fellow who felt that he had had enough of war in the past campaigns, took refuge from conscription by joining Stevenson's household. The trick did not work, for although there was no standing army in Samoa, every man and boy who was old enough to be tattooed, was presumed to be able and ready to fight if war came. Each village looked out for any absentees. Refusal to fight meant the loss of lands, even banishment. Several messengers visited the "slacker" and under pressure of argument and threats, he was prevailed upon to join the others. Off he marched, laden with a basket of food, *kava,* and tobacco. Later, on another occasion, when Talolo and Sosimo were called out, Stevenson insisted that Sosimo's heart was too weak to stand up to the hardships of war. When the father of the boy came to urge his son to join the armed forces, Tusitala exclaimed: "Who is the true father of this boy, you who wish to send him where he may be killed by the sword or die of exposure in the woods, or I, who wish to save his life by keeping him safe at home?" Lowering his head, the father replied, "It is true."

Early in July a number of war boats from Atua began to arrive at Mulinuu. When the canoes were about to land, a champion jester stood up on the nose of one of them performing various stunts: he danced, he leaped and capered while the bugles and the drums kept time. To add to the wild scene and the discordant notes of the bugles, the crew uttered savage howls at intervals. The shops of Apia soon sold out their supply of red handkerchiefs, the rallying sign of the royal army. Apia and Mulinuu assumed a martial air. Troops of young braves with blackened faces and oiled bodies marched with their rifles on their shoulders to the sound of bugles, whistles and drums. Stevenson saw six men march out from a neighboring hamlet equipped with tobacco, matches, and the inevitable red handkerchief. They marched to the nearby hill, but when dusk came they returned to their more comfortable homes.

On July 5 news reached Mulinuu that Mataafa's warriors had left their Malie camp and swarmed in full force to the west of Apia where they took up a position in a semicircle. Swiftly the royal braves marched out to meet the enemy. A large body of riflemen from Atua was stationed at Mulinuu point, looking across the bay where the "rebels" were lying encamped behind the orange and coconut groves belonging to the German firm. Women, including the *Taupos*, accompanied the braves, carrying cartridges and water, ever ready with their bright eyes to "rain influence and reward valour." The war parties moved in a body; each chief took the lead among his own people. Some of the younger chiefs, wearing headdresses of false brown hair, enjoyed the privilege of taking the lead in the "glory of dying," though seldom did the casualties in a Samoan battle exceed fifty. The natives sensibly considered it folly to sacrifice too many good lives. Killing a few dozen, cutting off some heads, burning several villages were sufficient. In fact before the advent of the *papalangi* and the introduction of firearms, all fighting was carried on by hand-to-hand encounter with clubs and spears. The exchange of amenities would consume much time and call for the most polite language. After the exchange of *kava* the opposing forces would discuss the question of fighting. If they decided to fight at once, one would say: "Well! let us trample the grass, and may we both be equally successful." If they decided to postpone the fray because it was getting dark, one would ask the opposite party when hostilities should commence. The other would reply: "It is not for us to speak of such things in the presence of chiefs and warriors such as you." Such bantering would continue for some time, for neither side wished to appear to be dictating to the other side. Finally one would say: "Well, if that is your mind, then we will trample the ground tomorrow." The two parties would then retire to their positions without fear of treachery. However once hostilities commenced, all exchange of courtesies ended. Then each side would use scurrilous language: "Where is that Savaii pig, that I may kill him?"

About noon the opposing forces stood facing each other in an extended line. One of the King's men shouted jeeringly to his foes: "Wait a bit, wait a bit. You will very soon all be dead!" "Very well we are ready!" replied the Mataafa men. One fearless old royal warrior shouted: "Get you gone, rebels, return to Malie; there will be no fighting today. The men of Atua have not joined us yet, and we wait them!" An armistice was agreed upon and a number on either side began to fraternize, even going so far as to take *kava* together which the women of both camps had prepared. One old chief on the royal side, named Patu (hit-hard), ran into the fraternizing groups flourishing a stick and drove back some of the Mataafa men shouting: "Get back, rebels, into your fort, and back to your position, men of the king's party." One account states that Patu used the term *maile* (dogs) which was the common taunt the Protestant natives flung at the Catholics for wearing medallions around their necks. But no one paid any attention to old Patu. The natives believed that they were entitled to a little festivity even in war.

While the rival forces were intermingling, a shot was fired, accidentally or treacherously, and one of the King's Vaimungas men fell mortally wounded. His comrades, inflamed with the thrill of combat, rushed forward and captured the position of the "rebels." Though many had failed to join Mataafa's forces out of fear of the foreign warships, both sides were about evenly matched for numbers. The Mataafa forces were unwisely posted and poorly led. When the rebel army recoiled, the Vaimungas pounced on them, hacking off the heads of the killed and wounded. In the heat of the battle a woman on the royal side beat a drum and shouted: "Fight, fight valiantly, men of Vaimunga!" Then she rushed forward, attempting to snatch an ax and a rifle. Other women joined her, though with less ardor.

It was estimated that forty of the rebels lost their lives. All night the King's men fired on the rebel forces who hid behind a wall. When morning came and the charge was renewed, it was discovered that the rebels had fled their positions under cover of darkness. From the distance one could see smoke from Malie, where the fleeing rebels had put the torch to the houses which they had built so painstakingly during the past two years. The rebels fled to Savaii and then to Manono. The royal forces did not care to give pursuit. In fact there was a great stampede in the King's party when twenty barges with Mataafa men approached Mulinuu. They were, however, driven off and did not again return.

After dinner a messenger arrived in Vailima with the news that the wounded were arriving at the Mission House. Immediately the Stevensons saddled their horses and, guided by a lantern and a starlit night, rode to Apia. They found the town in a state of confusion and flustration. Stevenson felt by turns excited and gloomy; the others appeared sullen. In the long frame hospital a number of wounded natives were stretched out along the walls, surrounded by their relatives and sympathizers. One warrior, shot in the bowels, lay silent with contorted face. Another, a splendid-looking fellow, swarthy with a noble aquiline countenance, had been shot through the lungs and was lying on his side awaiting death. Seven natives stood around him speechless, fondling his hands and legs. A woman suddenly clasped his knee, burst into a wail for a moment, and then again relapsed into silence.

The only attendants present were Reverend Clarke and the little bespectacled angel of mercy, Miss Large, also of the London Missionary Society. Though a teetotaler, she ordered brandy for the wounded. There were also German orderlies in clean white uniforms. When Reverend Clarke suggested the advisability of using the public hall for a hospital, Stevenson, the chairman of the committee in charge of the place, immediately dashed away to secure the building. Though it was in the middle of the night, he awakened the members of the committee, and after using persuasive arguments, succeeded in procuring their consent. When he returned to the hospital he found the surgeons operating on the wounded. He was surprised that the hospital sights which once used to "murder" him, now struck him as a sort of "peep-show." He who had many times faced death, now watched calmly as others died. In fact he was more impressed with the efficiency with which things were managed than with the actual sight of the dying. A chill, however, went through him when he touched one of the victims. It was about two in the morning before the Stevensons returned to Vailima. They went to bed deeply regretting the defeat of their friend Mataafa, fearing that greater resistance might be offered later which could lead to a long and bloody war.

The following day Stevenson again went to Apia to gather the latest reports of the war and to help Miss Large in the hospital. There he found that the warrior who had been shot in the bowels had passed away, while Ulu who was shot in the lungs was still alive. Many of the wounded were asleep with their heads upon wooden pillows. In one corner he found a handsome youth who, though only slightly wounded, was attended by two girls, one of whom, with a most beautiful face, rested on his pillow. In another corner lay a far braver youth, but less handsome, wholly deserted. "Heavens, what a difference that makes; in our not very well proportioned bodies and our finely hideous faces," reflected Stevenson. In town he received the disturbing news that many bodies of the dead and the wounded had been brought to Mulinuu. The Mataafa forces had been scattered and his friends were facing disaster. It was painful to realize that his friend and hero, who only a few months ago might have controlled all the islands, was now a defeated man and a fugitive.

At Mulinuu, however, there was much rejoicing and celebrating. On July 15 the victorious king's party held a great *talolo* (feast) with military reviews and dances. Hundreds of warriors with faces blackened, backs streaked with white lines, wearing girdles of long leaves and armed with rifles, clubs and bushknives, marched and staged a mimic battle. They shouted, they leaped, and at intervals fired their guns into the air. While the drums and fifes made weird music, the braves swung their clubs and shouted in staccato cadence. Some of the warriors danced; others paraded by slowly with arms crossed. Ahead of the braves marched the leading *Taupo,* decorated in conventional style with flowers in her hair and a red necklace around her neck and a grenadier's cap on her head. She swung a club with both hands and danced slowly to the tune, crossing and uncrossing her legs. Slowly she advanced, escorted by two men clad in mats. Behind her came several other village maidens, repeating the same movements.

One of the most exciting scenes of these victory celebrations was the public presentation by the successful braves of their prized trophies, the heads of the enemy. No ancient Greek or Roman took greater pride in winning the chaplet than did Samoan warriors in the public display of the heads of their victims. As they marched through the village and reached the green where the chiefs were assembled, they would dance and caper, shouting out from time to time: "I am so-and-so; I have got the head of such a one." Each brave would place the head before the chiefs. It was the height of a warrior's ambition to receive the chief's thanks and congratulations. The heads were then piled up on the village green, the important ones placed on the top of the pile. After they were displayed a few hours the heads were either buried or returned to their relatives. Thereafter, when there was talk of certain battles, the accounts ran: "There were so many heads, surmounted by the head of so-and so."

King Malietoa and his chiefs who sat on the verandah of the President's house, greeted the brave warriors who carried the freshly severed heads of the rebel forces. Tauailao, the village jester led the procession, dancing and leaping and brandishing his knife. When the song and dance ended, and the heads were uncovered, a shudder ran through the crowd: three of the heads were those of women, and, what was more shameful, one was the head of a highly respected *Taupo* of Savaii! It must be remembered that one of the most faithfully observed customs in Samoa was the absolute immunity for women in war and in peace. They were permitted to go to the battlefields, to bring water and cartridges. Often they jeered at the faltering and nursed the sick and wounded. One woman, seeing her husband running away, dragged him back and compelled him to return to the battle. Another woman who saw her lover fall, seized his gun and kept the head-cutters away while she dragged the dead body from the battlefield. These brave women, however, had to risk death, for often stray bullets struck them. Moreover, in the fury of the battle an excited brave might mistake a woman for a man and decapitate her with his hatchet. Of course, as soon as the horrible error was discovered, the head was either buried or returned to her people. No brave would think of placing a woman's head at the feet of his chiefs. In fact the man who took a woman's head suffered the jeers of his fellow warriors.

There was humiliation in the King's camp; the women were afraid of reprisals. To soften the tragic blunder it was reported that the *Taupo* had cut off her hair to make a warlike headdress for her father, a high chief, and that during the battle she had carried her father's arms. It was even rumored that she carried a gun and fired on the enemy. Under such conditions it was easy in the fury of the battle to mistake her for a man. King Malietoa was deeply ashamed of the unpardonable act and ordered that the honored head be wrapped in costly mats and returned with apologies to her people.

Among the heads taken was that of Leaupepa, Mataafa's nephew, a splendid, brave young man and highly respected by his people. Tragic too, was the scene when a young brave with great pride, brought to Mulinuu the gory head he had taken. When the black paint and blood were washed away he recognized to his great horror the head of his own brother! He retired to his house to shed bitter tears while holding the gory trophy in his lap.

Stevenson was horrified. How often had he argued against this beastly practice with the natives. The latter admitted that head-cutting was indefensible, but insisted that it was necessary to continue the practice. How else could one demonstrate one's bravery? One young man admitted to being overcome with horror when he beheld his father taking a head in battle; nevertheless, he insisted that he would have to do likewise in some future war. Every one's country, the natives maintained, follows its own peculiar customs. Frequently Stevenson wondered how these kindly aborigines could become such savages in war time, and pouncing upon the wounded with whom they had only recently fraternized, decapitate them and then bring in the gory heads as trophies for public exhibition. "Barbarous war is an ugly business: but I believe the civilized is fully uglier; but Lord! what fun!" he reflected.

He blamed the king, the consuls, and the missionaries for failing to suppress the beastly practice of head cutting. He was greatly pained by the sad collapse of Mataafa's cause. "The sky looks horribly black for Mataafa and so many of our friends along with him," he wrote. The great chief overestimated his strength among the Samoans, many of whom chose to align themselves with the government in power or to remain neutral for fear of punishment by the German warships lying in Apia Harbor.

Apparently there was considerable indecision among the King's supporters. Some districts, such as Aana, instead of carrying out the plan agreed upon and blocking the fleeing Mataafa forces on their

way to Manono, chose to entertain an embassy from the rebels an
allowed their boats to escape from the narrow waters of the lagoon
Though the Savaii refused to support Mataafa, it was reported tha
they hesitated at joining the King's forces, and urged, instead, tha
both sides be invited to a *fono,* to promote conciliation. Even th
people of Tumuas, who were greatly responsible for the King's vic
tory, were, on principle, hostile to Malietoa. They were adherent
of the old Tamasese party and their great desire was to take reveng
on Mataafa for the losses which he had inflicted on them in the war o
1888–1889. There were "too many strings in a Samoan intrigue for th
merely European mind to follow," confessed Stevenson.

The Mataafa forces made one more attempt to strike back. Som
fifteen canoes carrying about fifty warriors in each, suddenly ap
peared before the King's capital. There was a short exchange of fir
between the men in the boats and the Atua rifle-men on land; th
former retreated and never returned.

The King's forces then marched to Malie, Mataafa's former strong
hold, and razed what was left of the deserted capital. On their wa
they burned houses, chopped down fruit trees, and pillaged planta
tions belonging to their enemy. Houses designated by flags as belong
ing to whites remained unmolested. In a special letter King Malieto
warned his defeated cousin of the futility of attempting to resist th
large forces assembled against him and urged the wisdom of surren
dering. The crushed rebel chief replied in a dignified but patheti
letter that he was ready to do what was right and fair and for the be
interests of his country. "But," he wrote, "you must give us a litt
time to take counsel, for many of the young men are grieved and an
gry at heart for their comrades slain in battle. Hot and eager the
are for revenge, and they are hard to keep in hand." The Frenc
priests, the *faifeau* popes also attempted to effect a reconciliatio
They visited Mulinuu in an effort to organize a meeting without sub
jecting Mataafa to the indignity of surrender. The King's party, how
ever, politely informed the priests that their efforts were fruitless.

While the three consuls were conferring on a common polic
toward the rebels, there arrived in Apia from Auckland the Britis
warship *Katoomba* with instructions from the three treaty powe
to support King Malietoa. On the following day, July 17, the thre

consuls and the naval commanders held a conference at which it was agreed, halfheartedly by the latter, to send three warships to Manono to bring the rebels to unconditional surrender. The warships were to be accompanied by a number of armed natives, in their boats, to carry out the land attack, should it be necessary.

Pursuant to this agreement the three warships, two German and one British, with the three consuls on board and accompanied by some 1,500 to 2,000 native warriors in their canoes, reached Manono on the following morning. The three consuls sent an ultimatum to Mataafa and his men, giving them three hours to surrender unconditionally or suffer bombardment. Realizing that any attempt to continue resistance would be suicidal, Mataafa and his chiefs accepted the terms. Shortly after eleven o'clock two French priests boarded the *Katoomba* with the announcement that the surrender would soon take place. A few hours later a canoe approached the *Katoomba,* and Mataafa and a number of his high chiefs capitulated to Captain Bickford.

Unfortunately, before the warships sailed away, government forces were permitted to land to disarm the rebels and establish order, with the understanding that there should be no reprisals. Toward evening flames and clouds of smoke could be seen rising from the island of Manono. When Mataafa saw what was happening to his unfortunate people, he flung himself upon his knees before Captain Bickford, appealing for protection of the women and children left on the unhappy island. Captain Bickford immediately dispatched the British consul to Manono to warn the government troops that the three powers were now responsible for whatever might happen and that any atrocities committed would be punished. On his return the consul reported that the chiefs of the two factions were fraternizing and making *kava.* Stevenson challenged the veracity of the report. When he presented the consul with evidence that the King's forces had burned houses, cut down fruit trees, stripped the women and left the former "garden island" in ruins, the official cried: "O! huts, huts, huts! There isn't a house, a frame house, on the island."

Captain Bickford treated Mataafa as if he were a guest on the *Katoomba* and not a prisoner. Pointing to the British ensign he said: "Tell them they are safe under that!" Mataafa's meals were brought to his cabin. Since there was no *kava,* his favorite beverage, on hand, he was supplied, before retiring to rest, with a tall glass of whiskey and water and three good cigars. Mataafa was not pleased with *Vaisma* or yellow water, but he considered the "fingers of rolled tobacco-leaf," equal to anything grown on Manono. He took his misfortunes philosophically; he had played for high stakes and lost. His parting words to one of his white friends and admirers were: "I love my Samoan people. I have fought and lost the day because God willed it. I am now in the hands of these men of Britain (*Peletane*), who will see right done, and Samoa shall yet rejoice one day."

The question now was what should be done with the leaders of the rebellion. The three consuls deliberated. Execution was too horrible, unthinkable. But, on the other hand, they considered it would be unsafe to set them free, because they might embark on another and more serious rebellion against the existing government which the treaty powers had decided to support. It was agreed, therefore that Mataafa and his leading chiefs be deported. It was a sad day for his friends and admirers among the natives and whites, especially for Stevenson, when Mataafa and thirteen of his leading chiefs were transferred to a German warship and taken to the island of Jaluit in the Marshall group which belonged to Germany. They spent lonely years on this low coral atoll, a mere strip of reef, almost devoid of vegetation; they had only brackish water to drink and the food given them was not what they were accustomed to.

They were homesick for their families, for their gracious people they longed for their beloved, distant native island, with its cool bright mountain rivers and fresh water and their favorite foods. To the credit of the Germans be it said the prisoners were well treated and were even supplied with some of their native dishes. The twenty-seven other rebel chiefs who were clapped in gaol in Apia were not so well cared for. The rest of the Mataafa faction were fined some 6,600 pounds.

Stevenson led the loud chorus of protest against the treatment accorded Mataafa and his followers; in fact he pointed an accusing finger at the "horrid white mismanagement in Samoa." "I tried standing by and looking on, and it became too much for me," he complained. In letters to the London *Times* and the *Pall Mall Gazette* and to members of the British Parliament, he unburdened his soul and cried out for justice. He heaped his greatest contempt upon the consular triumvirate: "They are such illogical fools . . . a commonplace unintellectual lot . . . an insane jealousy of the smallest kind . . . a desire to extend his little authority . . . no real sense of duty, no real comprehension . . . I could weep." "Politics," he asserted, "is a vile and bungling business. I used to think meanly of the plumber: but he shines beside the politician!" He denied that he was the firebrand that he had often been labeled; he admitted that he was a partisan of Mataafa, whom he considered the most honest man in all Samoa, not excepting the white officials.

In his letters to the English newspapers Stevenson reiterated his conviction that Samoa and Mataafa were unjustly treated by the three treaty powers and their white officials on the islands. Mataafa's only crime was that he took the Berlin Act seriously; it provided that selection of the king should be entrusted to the people of Samoa. Of course he had not read the infamous protocol, which, a "measure of German vanity, English cowardice, and American *incuria*—had not been and has *never yet* been translated into the Samoan language." The treaty powers feared light because their work was dark. He complained that the unfortunate Samoan islands were illegally and unjustly dominated by the consular triumvirate which had the ear of the foreign offices. At the instigation of the triumvirate and with the complicity of the warships, Mataafa was driven into "rebellion" and defeat and exile. Had the Three Powers at least acted a little sooner, with less vacillation, the atrocities committed on the unfortunate Mataafa party, the burning of houses, the severing of heads, would have been prevented.

Stevenson rebuked the consular triumvirate for permitting the King's forces "their bellyful of barbarous outrage," against the Mataafa people at Manono, Apolima and elsewhere. In spite of the solemn promises by the consuls and warship captains, there was no punishment, no inquiry, no protest; "not a word said to disown the act or disengage the honor of the Three Powers." What was even worse, there was no interference with the bestial practice of head-cutting. When the new chief justice, Ide, arrived from the United States, he took spirited action against this practice. He harangued the chiefs, informed them of the new law and threatened vengeance on offenders. Many of the natives were intimidated; others, more brave, said: "O! we have had chief justices before, we know what they are; I will take a head if I can get one." They believed that the white officials would not be supported by the consuls and would not dare lay a hand on this institution peculiar to Samoa. The consuls, not being very sentimental persons, pardoned the culprits and by so doing refused to support the honest and sincere Chief Justice Ide.

Finally, Stevenson criticized the punishment meted out to Mataafa as compared with that given several years before to Tamasese who also instigated a rebellion. Tamasese carried a gun; he himself fired it; he received heads; he threatened the white population. Mataafa, on the other hand, a famous old chief and once appointed king, had, of his own accord forbidden the taking of heads; he never ceased to reassure the whites that their lives and property would be respected. Yet how much more cruelly was Mataafa treated, largely because he antagonized the Germans while Tamasese had been their puppet. Stevenson did not begrudge Tamasese his more happy fate, he was distressed to see the unfair punishment inflicted on his friend, Mataafa. In the eyes of the Samoans exile was a punishment only less terrible than death, especially exile to an alien strip of land where the food and water were unpalatable even to whites. Moreover, these fourteen chiefs had been deprived of their families, some members of which had begged to be sent away with their husbands and fathers whom they could nurse when ill. The young beautiful wife of old and ill High Chief Faamuina had been refused permission to join her husband, who had been popular with the whites because of his services to them. Even Stevenson had not been permitted to send one stick of tobacco or one pound of *kava* to his good friends in exile. When he wanted to send the prisoners a package, an officer of the warship remarked: "Oh, you see, you like Mataafa; we don't." Stevenson pleaded also in behalf of the twenty-seven chiefs who were being held in the gaol without proper food. The government made no attempt to feed them, depending on their families to aid them and on the charity of sympathizing whites, especially Stevenson. Yet the prisoners refused to escape when the guard deserted, fearing it might hurt the cause of their leader.

Stevenson realized that writers of fiction, when they deal with matters of fact, are apt to be suspected of unreliability. Moreover, most readers of the *Times* refused to take his letters about Mataafa, printed in that newspaper, seriously. They were merely amused to observe this eminent author riding his hobby, concern for the welfare of a few far-away South Pacific savages, so furiously. But he, on his part, passionately protested against the gross injustice he believed had been done this gentle, brown-skinned people.

He appealed to a member of the British Parliament to help obtain permission for Mataafa to return at least to Fiji, where he could have fresh water and the food he had been accustomed to since childhood, and where "some of us could see him" and where he might pass a tolerable old age. "In a small way this is another case of Toussaint L'Overture, not so monstrous if you like, not on so large a scale, but with circumstances of small perfidy that make it almost odious."

The newspapers and the members of Parliament to whom Stevenson addressed his pleas expressed sympathy for the cause he was so persistently advocating. Occasionally editorials appeared and questions were asked in the House of Commons touching upon the Samoan imbroglio. One member of the Foreign Office, after reading Stevenson's letter in the *Times,* wrung his hands, exclaiming: "I'm sure I wish they would give him (Stevenson) Samoa, and let him do what he likes with it!"

Stevenson was greatly relieved when he received a letter from Mataafa stating that he was now well treated and had good food. Moreover, the author was finally permitted to send his friend many packages. It was not, however, until some three years after Tusitala's death that Mataafa was brought back to his homeland and could pay homage at the tomb of his great benefactor on the Summit of Mt. Vaea.

CHAPTER XVII

THE SILVER THISTLE

WHEN GRAHAM BALFOUR prepared to sail for the Line Islands by way of Hawaii, Stevenson announced that for his "health's sake he would accompany his cousin to Honolulu." A fortnight at sea, he believed, would do him much good, though he did not relish crowded steamers.

The day before his departure for Honolulu, September 11, 1893, Stevenson recorded as one of the "brightest in the annals of Vailima." With the permission of Captain Bickford the band of the British cruiser *Katoomba* was invited to a special party at the writer's home. Early in the afternoon fourteen white-capped bluejackets, with drum, fife, cymbals and bugles, followed by a host of children from the neighboring village, arrived at the gate where they were greeted by Major-domo Henry Simele in a white shirt, *lava lava* and black coat. When the smiling sailors appeared on the lawn they saluted the host and hostess and struck up a march.

The Laird of Vailima did all he could to make the visit a pleasant one. The sailors found the great hall decorated with flags and fragrant flowers and ferns. The tables were loaded with quantities of chicken, ham sandwiches, fruit, cake, coffee, lemonade and beer. The sparkling eyes of native girls added to the pleasure of the guests. The sailors ate and drank, played and danced and tumbled—to the great amusement of the natives. In appreciation, the garlanded male servants performed a war dance, and flower-bedecked native "Helens" climaxed the occasion with song and dance, gracefully swaying their voluptuous bodies to the great delight of the homesick bluejackets. At the end of the great day the sailors gave three cheers for Stevenson and Fanny and marched back to the ship with the band playing. Their exemplary behavior and good manners greatly pleased the Laird of Vailima and his wife both of whom were proud of the British navy that was doing such a fine job training these youngsters.

When Stevenson revisited Hawaii, after an absence of over three years, he found there, too, the political conditions sadly disturbing. His friend, champagne-bibbing King Kalakaua, with whom he had spent many a pleasant hour dreaming of a great Polynesian federation, had gone to his ancestors in January, 1891. Kalakaua's sister, Liliuokalani, who succeeded to the throne, had been deposed in January, 1893 by the American plantation owners. In place of the Polynesian Kamehameha dynasty, Hawaii was ruled by a Provisional Government of American plantation owners knocking at the door of the United States for annexation. His friends, the royalists, were now powerless and embittered. It was painful to Stevenson to realize that Polynesia was unable to withstand the onrush of white civilization and that the last experiment in native government had come to an untimely, tragic end, and with it would go the unspoiled, easy life of the people, a life of flowers, song, dance and laughter.

It was a sad and "most impressive" interview that Stevenson had with deposed Queen Liliuokalani, soon after his arrival in Honolulu. Wistfully they recalled the glorious days of the monarchy and the sumptuous banquets and entertainments when Stevenson had visited her in 1889. The proud ex-queen wept when she related her recent misfortunes. Nor were Stevenson's visits with his old friend and brother Scot, Cleghorn, happier. Here he recalled the pleasant hours he had spent with the lovely and dainty little Princess Kaiulani before she had left to attend school at Edinburgh, the native home of her father, Cleghorn. Now gone was the hope that this princess might some day succeed to the throne. He even feared she would not be able to survive the rigorous climate of wintery Scotland.

Though fully in sympathy with the royalist cause in Hawaii, Stevenson warned his interviewers in Honolulu: "It must be understood that I cannot express an opinion on local matters; it takes a bony head to keep the pace of a spry tongue. This much I have learned from my experience of Samoan politics, and I do not intend to get into politics—and consequently into trouble—while I remain here." Only in the presence of royalist friends did he express himself freely on the subject. When urged to give his opinion on the Hawaiian situation, he at first hesitated, then said: "There are several prudent reasons why I should use discretion on this point at the present. I am not yet sure that I have not erred with my meddling in Samoa, but my excuse is that my heart and head both pushed me to the defence of those poor people. But in Hawaii it is different. Here you have a homogeneous civilization . . . largely Anglo-Saxon, or Anglo-American. . . ." He was afraid that any interference on his part might do little good for the natives. He admitted that he had the will to intercede on behalf of the Hawaiians, if it were prudent. "Don't forget this—that I am a royalist at heart, with much pity for these poor Polynesians." He expressed the hope that the United States would "restore the poor Queen to the throne of her ancestors, not for her sake, guilty as I am informed she is by the leading men of her party . . . but for the sake of her poor oppressed people, who have done no wrong."

To Colvin he wrote: "Had a rather annoying lunch on board the American man-of-war, with a member of the P.G. (provisional government); and a good deal of antiroyalist talk, which I had to sit out—not only for my host's sake, but my fellow guests. At last, I took the lead and changed the conversation." When accused of being critical of the missionaries and white planters resident in Hawaii, he insisted that he was opposed to them not as men but as politicians. When invited to settle in Hawaii, he confessed that he could learn to like the country, "if it were not for your beastly cold weather—and your politicians." He accompanied his words with a grimace and a wave of the hand.

Of Samoan affairs Stevenson spoke quite freely. "I cannot see much risk in talking of Samoa, after the fat is already in the fire," he told his interviewer. Moreover he believed that "Hawaii is too far given over to the evils of civilization for salvation at any hand." But Samoa, ah, that was different, she was still unspoiled by such things as telephones. "God forbid that we should ever have such a thing . . . I want Samoa to be rid of such devilish inventions, which only disturb the mind, and can well be dispensed with!" The way to peace in Samoa was, in his opinion, to rescind the Berlin Act, to persuade the three treaty powers to withdraw, and to permit the natives to govern the islands according to their own customs. True, internal dissensions might affect commerce and the position of the foreigners, especially the Germans, but the interests of the poor natives must take precedence. At any rate, the natives will fight it out without the meddling of foreigners, particularly the Germans.

To Talolo, who had been chosen to accompany his master to Honolulu because of his superior knowledge of English, the visit to the metropolis was the greatest adventure in his entire life. He was proud to wear trousers; he was fascinated by the electric lights, street cars, pavement and ice cream. He visited kitchens and bakeries to learn new recipes and cooking methods. Long after his return to Samoa he continued to talk of his wonderful experiences in that wonderful Honolulu.

The white residents of Honolulu were aware of Stevenson's sympathies with the royalist cause and the Polynesians. They were inclined, however, to regard this as the eccentricity of a man of high talents, an eccentricity they were willing to overlook or condone. Besides, his literary successes were so great at this time that everyone felt flattered to bask in his light.

Shortly after he arrived at Honolulu he received an invitation from the Scottish Thistle Club to give an informal talk on any subject which he might choose. On the evening of the lecture, the Thistle Club was decorated with island flowers and ferns, Scottish thistles and tartan plaids. When Stevenson stood on the platform of the crowded hall he was greeted with warm applause. Smilingly he said: "Ladies and gentlemen, and Brither Scots . . . My one reason for consenting to talk before you tonight lies in that weakness, or strength, that binds

Scots' hearts together wherever they meet each other. I cannot sa
why they are proud to be Scotsmen; the fact remains that they are
It is not that our land is sunny, like these tropical isles, and its climat
is not even lovely. Scotland's history contains little that is not disgust
ing to people of humane feelings. That long brawl which is calle
Scottish history contains scarcely one object that Scots have an
patience with. First there was a long period during which the wil
Celts were cutting each other's throats, and trying the thickness o
each other's skulls . . . Following them came Robert the Bruce
a little humorous and certainly amiable. He was something of
rogue . . . the most offensive kind of a rogue is a politician. Bruc
figured at a time when the nobility were grasping at everything i
sight, each without regard for the right of property in his neighbor'
cow. . . . Coming to the Reformation they had two great character
—John Knox and Mary Queen of Scots—and I must confess to a foibl
for Mary in my sympathies. Take her all in all, Mary was quite a goo
fellow. It is true she blew up her husband, and committed other littl
eccentricities; still she was rather a good fellow. . . ." He conclude
nostalgically with the following: "I feel that when I shall come to di
out here among these beautiful islands, I shall have lost somethin
that had been my due—my native, predestinate, and forfeited grav
among honest Scots sods. And I feel that I shall never quite attai
to what Patrick Walker calls . . . my 'resting grave,' unless it wer
to be upon one of our purple hillsides, under one of our old, quaint
and half-obliterated table-tombstones slanting down the brae, and

> Where about the graves of the martyrs the
> whaups are crying,
> My heart remembers how!

The sentimental peroration brought tears to the eyes of many o
Stevenson's admirers. When the speaker smilingly resumed his place
a sad stillness settled over the entire audience. The flushed cheek
and consumptive appearance of their beloved author gave siniste
warning that his days were numbered. The chairman announced
"Lait's sang the'doaxology." All, including Stevenson, sang heartily
Auld Lang Syne.

Stevenson came to Honolulu just for a short visit and intended to return to Samoa by the steamer due from San Francisco. However his departure was delayed because of illness. When, with the careful nursing of Fanny who had come up from Samoa, Stevenson began to recover, he would sit for hours on the verandah of the Sans Souci Inn, a rambling bungalow facing the surf of Waikiki, listening to the wind and waves along the reef, watching the constant changes of the sea and clouds and the play of the breakers upon the reef. He never found the sea monotonous; even the calms were "truly poetic." When he read in a local newspaper a criticism of the Sans Souci Inn, accusing it of disorderliness and engaging in illicit liquor trade, he immediately jumped to its defense. In a letter to the press he asserted that there was no quieter haven than the Sans Souci. It was in one of its cottages that Allan Hutchinson made the cast for the "Hawaiian" bust of Stevenson which was later exhibited at the New Gallery in London. The artist also made a cast of the novelist's right hand and wrist which was later used by Mrs. St. Hill for her delineation of Stevenson's character.

The following two incidents clearly reveal Stevenson's personality and sympathies. At the dinner table at his hotel someone mentioned the name of William Stead, editor of the British *Review of Reviews* who had written exposing scandals in English high life and making unfavorable comments on a member of the English royal family. As a loyal Britisher and royalist Stevenson resented the criticism and, as soon as Stead's name was mentioned, he "opened the flood-gates of wrath" and for several minutes he continued to inveigh in strong language against that writer. Concluding his fierce tirade, he glared around the table as if to dare any one to reply. Then he swallowed the remainder of his food and wine and left the room. On the verandah, later on, he apologized to his neighbors for losing his temper.

At the Hawaiian Hotel an English tourist introduced himself to Stevenson and requested his permission to order drinks for the author and his friends. "Certainly, I will join you and my friend Talolo will also join us," replied Stevenson smilingly, while he embraced his Samoan valet. The tourist winced, and turning to the bartender he said: "He can't drink with us here. Give him something to drink over there." Resenting this rudeness, Stevenson turned to the Englishman:

"Sir," he said, "I do not even know your name, but if you say that Talolo cannot drink with me, I wish you to understand that I am not good enough to drink with you. Come, Talolo!" Arm in arm master and valet walked off to the dining room. People in the hotel were careful to note the extreme thoughtfulness which Stevenson displayed for his valet's welfare. It is clear why the natives at Vailima were so devoted to their master. Stevenson saw to it that Talolo had a chance to enjoy the sights of Honolulu. Fearing that a delayed lunch might cause the "boy" to miss his long-looked-for ride by rail, Stevenson burst into a torrent of protest which was finally stemmed by a soothing cup of black coffee and a cigarette.

On the day of his departure Stevenson made the rounds, bidding goodbye to his friends in Honolulu. When a friend expressed the hope that he would be able to visit Honolulu again, the author was silent for a moment; then he expressed his deeply-rooted conviction that he would not live much longer, not long enough, at any rate, for another visit. When Stevenson bade goodbye to Mr. Lindsay, chairman of the Scottish Thistle Club, the latter gently pinned on the lapel of his coat a silver Scottish Thistle, the Club's button badge. Stevenson, who was deeply touched by being elected honorary Chieftain of the Club, shook his friend's hand warmly. "Mr. Lindsay, I will never part with it; it is near enough to me heart now to be buried with me."

To Cleghorn his parting words on board the vessel were: "Now Cleghorn, if I can be of any service to the royalist cause in Hawaii, just drop me a line, and I will come right back here."

CHAPTER XVIII

THE GAY CAVALIER

EARLY IN NOVEMBER Stevenson was back at Vailima, "ruddier than the cherry," and refreshed physically and mentally. The succeeding thirteen months were the last and happiest of his entire career. His health had improved considerably, enabling him to enjoy the outdoors life he had so long prayed for. He had at last reached the zenith of his fame. When he heard that Charles Baxter had made arrangements with a publisher to bring out an Edinburgh edition of his works, he wrote to his friend: "I wish to assure you of the greatness of the pleasure that the Edinburgh Edition gives me." He reminded his good friend of their earlier dream of the future, of how years ago he had an intimation of "early death and aspirations after fame . . . If any one at that moment would have shown me the Edinburgh Edition, I suppose I should have died." He also recalled the days when they wandered down the Lothian Road; when they had searched their pockets vainly for a threepence to purchase two glasses of beer. And now, could it really be true: an annual income of from 4000–5000 pounds, and an Edinburgh edition of his works! But that was not all: he was happy to feel that his creative powers were not on the decline, for he considered the *Weir of Hermiston,* on which he was working feverishly, to be his masterpiece. In addition, he was planning a number of other projects.

To add relish to his life, there were the usual rounds of visits and entertainment. The 1893 birthday festival of Alii Vailima was typical, though perhaps a little more elaborate than former celebrations. About one hundred and fifty guests, most of them natives, were invited. After a hearty welcome by the host and hostess, the traditional *kava* was served. High Chief Seumanu of Apia gave Tusitala one of his names, and when the latter was called for *kava* he was addressed by that most exalted title, *Au mai taua ma manu-vao.* Surrounded by a host of chiefs and their dusky wives, Alii Vailima had the mien and appearance of a mediaeval lord.

When the *kava* ceremony was over, the guests, wearing colorful garlands of fragrant flowers, formed a procession for the march to the native house where the feast had been prepared. A debate ensued among the members of the household as to the correct native procedure. When Samoan etiquette was satisfied, the guests trooped away, led by Fanny and Tusitala, the latter wearing his wreath of white jasmine with great éclat. A fantastic sight greeted the guests when they emerged from the darkness into the blaze of torchlights. The native house had been decorated with leaves and flowers; the floor was covered with palm leaves, over which were spread many finely woven, tawny-colored mats. The uninitiated white guests found it difficult to believe that the colorful miscellaneous mass which was spread out before them on the ground, from one end of the house to the other and about five feet across, constituted the feast. Arranged on banana leaves were sixteen roast pigs—a huge one as centerpiece—chickens, 100 pounds of salt beef, 200 heads of *taro,* great branches of bananas, 800 pineapples—many weighing as much as fifteen pounds—oranges, tinned salmon and quantities of fish. Scattered around the "table" were clusters of scarlet and cream-colored hibiscus blossoms.

The food was eaten *faa Samoa* (à la Samoan) without knives forks or plates. Native boys knelt with basins of water and napkins beside the guests, who sat cross-legged on mats. The pretty native girls were amused when the white guests did not seem to relish some of the delicacies served, such as *taro*-root baked like potatoes and *taro*-root minced and whipped with coconut milk. The unique delicacy that puzzled and repelled some of the white guests was fried *palolo*. The banquet continued for some time. At intervals the servants brought fresh coconuts, with the tops removed, from which each guest took a drink. Fresh leaves were also brought in from time to time.

At the completion of the feast a chief proposed the health of his host; Tusitala replied in a short speech thanking his good friends of Samoa. Then the large *kava* bowl was placed before the chief, who filled a small cup made out of a polished coconut, and in a loud voice chanted his directions for serving. When the servitor brought the first cup to Tusitala he clapped his hands, held up the bowl and addressed himself to the guests: *Ia manuia!* (Here's to you!) Everyone replied, *soi fua!* (May you live long!) The cup was then passed to Fanny, then to Aunt Maggie, and so on. Each time the cup was passed, the same formula, the same ceremony, was repeated. One of the guests, a visiting white woman, Miss Frazer, was addressed *Mata-lanumoana* (the fair young stranger with blue eyes from over the seas).

After *kava* the guests returned to the verandah to smoke and chat until a delegation of excited, smiling house servants announced that the arrangements for a *siva* had been completed. The guests then adjourned to another native house to witness the performance. On a raised platform sat a dozen dancers in gala attire. Their oiled and shining bodies were decorated with garlands of hibiscus blossoms, and their hair was oiled and combed out. They were arranged in two rows, men and women alternately. Behind them sat a few musicians who beat drums and chanted verses about the guests. All the actors chanted and swayed their nimble bodies in rhythm, and waved their hands and arms in various movements and tempos, illustrating the themes of their songs. The principal actors rose and pantomimed a game of cricket, rowing, and suffering from starvation. The last scene was realistically portrayed; for when the starved one was finally successful in procuring a banana, he gave the impression of being too weak to eat it.

The natives would have continued the dances indefinitely had not Tusitala suggested that the hour was late. The guests gave the performers an enthusiastic cheer, thanking them for their splendid entertainment, and then departed. Even the departure was picturesque: dozens of slim, wiry horses brought by the guests and their servants, and gaily-attired natives flitted around in the glare of the torches that cast fantastic lights and shadows over the entire scene. Amidst considerable excitement and merriment, the mounted guests trotted out into the dark, shouting, "good night!" *To fa, soi fua* came ringing back from the Vailima hosts. In the distance could be heard some departing officers of the British warship stationed in Apia port calling to each other.

"Say, old man, where are you?"

"Oh, I don't know! Where are you?"

"Heaven knows, but my brute seems to know where every tree with prickles exists on the island."

Tusitala received many gifts from his admirers: fans, native baskets, rolls of tapa, *kava* bowls, coconut cups, an orator's staff, and a precious mat from one of the pretty native girls.

All these occasions for gaiety did not make Stevenson forget the less fortunate among his Samoan friends. His heart was heavy when he thought of his good friend Mataafa in exile in the distant Marshall Islands. He did not forget to send him and his fellow chiefs sacks of *kava* roots and material for shirts. Nor did he forget the twenty-three Mataafa chiefs in a prison camp located at the edge of a mangrove swamp between Apia and Mulinuu. The gaol was a wretched little building surrounded by a fence of corrugated iron, and consisted of one small room and six cells. But since it housed chiefs, it was called *maota* (palace). In charge of the gaol, fortunately, was Captain Wurmbrand, a kindly ex-officer of the Austrian army.

Considering himself a "sort of father of the political prisoners," Alii Vailima, Fanny, Lloyd and Belle drove out "in great style" in a hired carriage with a native outrider. They brought the prisoners a huge supply of *kava* and tobacco. In appreciation of the gifts the prisoners invited the Stevensons and the gaoler to drink *kava* with them. Although it was prepared in the old-fashioned way, elegantly called "spit *kava*," there was no escape; it had to be accepted.

On the way home Stevenson and Fanny reflected: "Could we

ever stand Europe again? Did we appreciate that if we were in London, we should be *actually jostled* in the street? And there was nobody in the whole of Britain who knew how to take *kava* like a gentleman. 'Tis funny to be thus of two civilizations—or, if you like, of one civilization and one of barbarism. And, as usual, the barbarism is the more engaging."

In gratitude for the numerous gifts which they had received from Vailima, the imprisoned chiefs invited Tusitala and his family to a Christmas party. When the Stevensons arrived they were welcomed by Captain Wurmbrand and eighteen gorgeously arrayed chiefs. After a group of lovely girls had prepared the *kava*, High Chief Auilua, a magnificent figure of a man, with the physique of an Ajax and a countenance expressive of both shrewdness and authority, acted as master of ceremonies. Since the affair was to be done in European style, the white guests were addressed by their English names, and in the order followed in Europe: Fanny, accordingly, was called first for the cup of *kava*.

When everyone was seated on the floor for the feast, the chiefs removed their *ulas* (necklaces) and placed them around the necks of their Vailima guests. The Stevensons politely resisted, protesting that this was too great an honor. Auilua, however, countered by insisting that they should not only accept the necklaces but wear them as they rode back to Vailima past the palace of King Malietoa. After the feast all returned to the *kava* house where the Tusitala family was presented with numerous gifts: thirteen pieces of tapa of unusual quality; thirty fans of every shape and color; a *kava* cup and other valuables. Chief Auilua informed "their only friend," Tusitala, that he and his comrades were in virtual slavery, that they had no money and that all the gifts had been made by members of their families. Then with an overtone of triumph in his voice, he added: "This is a gift from the poor prisoners to the rich man." As he presented a little basket to the guests, Auilua's gravity yielded to a humorous expression and he said: "Here is a little basket for Tusitala to put sixpence in, when he could get hold of one." While Tusitala was expressing his thanks, he heard the crier calling out the gifts. The chiefs urged Stevenson to carry the presents through Mulinuu, so that King Malietoa and his people would see them and "make 'em jella." The reason for the gifts, thought Stevenson, was "one half, gratitude to me—one half, a wipe at the King."

Stevenson realized that his visit to the gaol was risky. He was afraid that it might have been a put-up affair to connect him with the current Tamasese rebellion, thus using him and his family as pawns in the game of political intrigue. There were many of the King's men around. No wonder the captain of the gaol, fearing trouble, was nervous and anxious to see the Vailima guests depart. Decorated with their colorful necklaces and garlands of flowers, followed by the load of presents, the Vailima cavalcade crossed through the whole length of Apia, through the sentries and howling crowds, and past the King's palace at Mulinuu. It was a triumphal procession amidst admiring exclamations of *manaia!* (beautiful). It was exciting; it was like riding in a circus parade. Tusitala was proud, for no such feast had ever honored any other white family.

Tusitala was the friend of all natives and all natives were his admirers. Only King Malietoa still felt aggrieved at this championing of his enemy Mataafa. By 1894, however, when his rival was far away in exile and the rebel chiefs were in prison, King Malietoa decided to "pay a secret visit of reconciliation" to Alii Vailima. With the aid of an interpreter the two discussed several problems. Then the King expressed a wish for a revolver out of Alii Vailima's considerable arms collection. To accommodate his royal visitor Stevenson took from his safe a shiny, loaded revolver, emptied it of the cartridges and handed it to Fanny for inspection. Thinking that something was wrong with the trigger, Fanny tried it several times. Four times the weapon clicked. The King, being curious, leaned forward to examine it. Just as he was peering into the barrel, Fanny, yielding to an unaccountable impulse, decided to inspect the pistol again. To her great horror there was a loaded cartridge in the fifth chamber. Had she pressed the trigger the fifth time, she might have blown out the King's brains. One may well speculate as to what might have been the consequence to Alii Vailima and Samoa of such a misfortune.

Though Apia was small, it was a cosmopolitan town. Its social life was considerably enlivened by the presence of foreign officials and the personnel of visiting British, German and American warships. As a man of the world the Laird of Vailima enjoyed the cheery company of all, irrespective of nationality. As a Britisher, however, he was especially fond of the officers and men of His Majesty's warships, above all if they happened to be Scotsmen. Stevenson was a loyal Scot, and proud of it. On their part Scotch officers and men on their first day of leave invariably made for Vailima "like homing pigeons." One midshipman, who had spent some time at Vailima, confessed that only while browsing in the library it "came over him all of a heap" —*He's* the "josser that wrote *Treasure Island.*"

Of all the personnel of the British warships visiting Apia, Stevenson was on the most friendly terms with the officers and men of the *Curaçoa,* which was stationed in Apia for about seven months during the year of 1894. He wrote to Henry James that he had known many naval officers, "and somehow had not learned to think entirely well of them, and perhaps sometimes ask myself a little uneasily how that kind of men could do great actions? and behold! the answer comes to me, and I see a ship that I would guarantee to go anywhere it was possible for men to go, and accomplish anything it was permitted man to attempt." He assured his friends that the *Curaçoa* "is really a model ship, charming officers and charming seamen."

Owing to the good company of the men of the *Curaçoa* and to the jovial residents of the island, Stevenson found the second half of 1894 "particularly cheery." There were many occasions for social gatherings at Vailima and Apia, and on board the warship. In fact, the road to Vailima became known as the "Curaçoa track" and the front verandah as the "Curaçoa Club." Late in June Stevenson made a trip on board the *Curaçoa* to the neighboring islands of Manu'a which, though a part of the Samoan archipelago, were considered independent. He was amused to find the three tiny islands jealous of their independence and ruled by a twenty-year-old half-caste girl, dressed in a pink gown, who was having a dull time living in a European house, gazing out at the unresponsive palm trees and listening to the everlasting pounding of the surf. Had she attempted to move, for diversion, to another village, the people in the "capital" would have become jealous. From the moment she left the house to enter another one, a stalwart native had to keep blowing on a conch shell at the top of his lungs until bystanders feared that he might burst a blood vessel. When the customary *kava* was served, Stevenson's name was called after the Captain's, and several of the chiefs drank to him by name, which was in accordance with Samoan practice. Although he greatly enjoyed his stay at Manu'a, the adventure-loving author was even more delighted with the treatment he received, and with the good will evinced, by all those on board the warship. He felt that he had now gained enough maritime experience and had collected a sufficient vocabulary of technical terms and ship's slang to furnish forth a sea story.

An examination of Stevenson's letters and the diary of his stepdaughter, Isobel, will show how crowded was the Vailima social calendar, curtailing the time at his disposal for writing. On July 3, accompanied by Lloyd and Belle, Stevenson attended the officers' ball on the *Curaçoa,* which was "very rackety and joyous and naval." On the following day a corporal of the marines, heading a delegation from the *Curaçoa,* arrived at Vailima, saluted and announced: "Me and my shipmates inwites Mr. and Mrs. Stevens, Mrs. Strong, Mr. Austin and Mr. Balfour [who had returned from his travels] to a ball to be given tonight in the self same 'all'."

The affair was a grand success: Belle waltzed with a gallant bluejacket and Stevenson danced a polka and the Highland schottische. A beachcomber watching the dancing, remarked: "It's a nice sight this some way, to see the officers dancing like this with the men, but I tell you, sir, these are the men that'll fight together!" Stevenson's own remark was, "The *Curaçoa* revives my faith in human nature." The climax of most of these entertainments was reached with the Highland schottische and the singing of *Auld Lang Syne.*

The following day the Vailima family rode in the grand parade staged by the Germans, called the *Blumen Corso* or Flower Fete, the sort of festival that is known in Southern France as a *Bataille de fleurs.* All the horses and carriages were beautifully decorated; bouquets were thrown back and forth, just as in Nice. In Samoa the exotic beauty of the flowers gave a tropical character to the scene. A luncheon on the *Curaçoa* followed the *Blumen Corso,* and then a breakfast at President Schmidt's, and an evening *Bierabend* (literally, Beer Evening) at Dr. Funk's. Then there was a dinner party at Vailima for twenty guests, among whom were the captain of the *Curaçoa,* President Schmidt, and Count and Countess Rudolf Festetics. The Count was a pleasant young Austrian officer, and his wife, the Countess, the daughter of an American millionaire. They were visiting Samoa in their own yacht. The big hall was brilliantly lighted; the silver and glass were displayed with dazzling effect; the food was excellent; and the Laird of Vailima was in splendid health and high spirits.

Stevenson's health was so good during this last year of his life that, despite the welter of social activities and his intense concentration on the *Weir of Hermiston,* he seems to have had a surplus fund of energy he felt needed to be worked off in physical exertion. For years he had wished to take part in the old English sport of fox hunting; now, when he had become strong enough to follow the hounds, he discovered that there were no foxes in Samoa, not to speak of fox hounds. As a substitute he proposed the paper chase to his friend, the ex-Hussar, Count Festetics. This might be even more fun, since the participant had to be both hunter and hound.

On Sunday, August 5, Stevenson, Lloyd, Festetics and a number of clerks from the German plantation engaged in an exciting paper chase at Vailele Plantation. Stevenson came in third on his faithful Jack, but the "old sensations of exhilaration, discovery, and appeal to savage instinct" made him feel about seventeen again, a "pleasant experience."

Unfortunately, the careening of a number of horsemen through native villages at the hour of worship on the Sabbath Day aroused the indignation of the native pastors and the white missionaries. To think that a son of a Covenanter and a Sunday school teacher should desecrate the Lord's Day! Even before the paper chase Stevenson realized that he would risk criticism. "I am now a pariah among the English," he wrote. To make amends he invited his friends, Reverend and Mrs. Clarke, to dine at Vailima. The Reverend's anger was so great that he declined the invitation; his wife, however, came. The good missionary lady argued with her host: "I have no doubt you can easily silence me in an argument," she exclaimed, "but I am astonished that you attempt any justification. You know quite well that you did wrong. What would Samoa be like without a Sabbath? And have you no thought of the effect of your conduct upon the natives who regard you as a Christian man, and as our friend." During this outburst Stevenson stood tugging at his moustache. After musing for a few minutes, he held out his hand, exclaiming: "Forgive me, Mrs. Clarke, you are quite right, and I was altogether wrong. I regret it with all my heart." Before night it was known all over Apia, on the German plantation and in the wardroom of every warship in the harbor, that Tusitala had openly expressed his penitence for violating the Sabbath.

While Stevenson was willing to conciliate the lady on this matter, he was not ready to accept the missionary point of view on other matters of conduct and morality. To one of them who protested against the abbreviated dress of the native women, he blazed: "Woman! is your mind so base that you cannot see and admire what is beautiful in the form God Almighty has created? Do you not understand that their own dress is right for the climate and their simple way of living? And do you not see that the first thing you do on landing on the beautiful island is to pollute their minds and sully their modest thoughts?"

When in the fall of 1894 the friendly intervention of Tusitala finally effected the release of the imprisoned chiefs, the freed men, instead of hurrying home at once to their families, spent all day Sunday drinking *kava* and discussing what they were to do for their great benefactor at Vailima. The following day Tusitala was informed by his cook that the liberated chiefs were coming to consult him on an important matter. A few hours later, when he was busily working on the *Weir of Hermiston,* he saw a number of chiefs crossing his lawn toward the house. He was used to such consultations and to giving advice, which was frequently accepted with good results. He felt, however, that while these councils ministered "to a sense of dignity," they were not conducive to "peace of mind," and consumed interminable time, since they occurred always in the morning when he was busy writing. Nevertheless it was his fixed policy to give his help when the natives demanded it.

It was a picturesque scene: Tusitala, surrounded by Lloyd, Graham, Isobel and little Austin, facing nine chiefs squatted in a big circle on the dining room floor. After the usual courtesies had been exchanged the chiefs stated that during their long months in prison, when they had no other friend, Tusitala's name "was always in their prayers," and "his goodness to them . . . was their most cherished memory." As an expression of gratitude the men had agreed among themselves to construct a road, joining Vailima with the public highway. Though feeling flattered by this gesture, Stevenson at first feared that he would be burdened with considerable expense for tools, food, and gifts to a group of old and somewhat infirm chiefs. Imagine his happy surprise when they assured him the work was to be their gift; Tusitala would be expected to supply only tools, but no food, no presents. How it warmed Stevenson's heart! "Think of it!" he wrote to Colvin. "It is road-making—the most fruitful cause (after taxes) of all rebellions in Samoa, a thing to which they could not be wiled with money nor driven by punishment. It does give me a sense of having done something in Samoa after all."

Soon, early on a bright morning, Old Poe, father-in-law of Talolo and the guiding spirit of the noble project, arrived with a gang of sturdy young men ready for work. It was amusing to behold Old Poe who appeared to have been completely rejuvenated by the excitement of the enterprise. As he distributed the tools, he was in high spirits and jestingly damned the Malietoa government. It was a difficult undertaking, for the road to Vailima was to be built on a generous scale, some thirty feet wide, and many trees had to be felled and boulders removed. Nevertheless it was completed without a hitch by early in October. Tusitala suggested that it should be named, "The Road of the Grateful Hearts," but the chiefs insisted on, "The Road of the Loving Heart," *Alo Loto Alofa.*

The completion of the task was properly celebrated. To a large tree at the entrance of the road was nailed a board on which were inscribed the names of the *alofa* workmen and an explanation of the reasons for the enterprise. The inscription which the chiefs had drawn up read:

The Road of Gratitude

Considering the great love of Tusitala in his loving care of us in our distress in the prison, we have therefore prepared a splendid gift. It shall never be muddy, it shall endure forever, this road that we have dug.

Tusitala used this occasion to combine a complimentary function with the expression of good advice to the Samoan people. "I wanted to pitch it in hot," wrote Stevenson to Sidney Colvin. It was an elaborate affair to which a number of guests were invited. Though some declined the invitation, fearing that it might be used as an occasion for political speeches rousing native hostilities, nevertheless, the élite of Apia were present. Among the guests were Chief Justice Ide, President Schmidt, Consul Mulligan, Land Commissioners Haggard and Chambers, Advocate Gurr and a number of naval officers of the British warship *Curaçoa.* There also were a number of chiefs, with High Chief Seumanutafa representing King Malietoa. The ceremony was opened with the usual *kava* prepared by three lovely *Taupos* and presented by the proper people in correct Samoan fashion to the guests who were seated on mats on the floor of the verandah. After the photographer had taken several pictures of the assembled guests, Tusitala delivered in English his carefully prepared and beautifully phrased address with great deliberation.

He began with an explanation to his *papalangi* (white) guests of the circumstances which occasioned the celebration. He related that when the chiefs were in gaol he had on several occasions done them certain favors. When his friends were finally freed they offered, of their own free will, to construct the road as a token of their appreciation for his friendship. Knowing how poor their families were because of a long period of disorganization and absence of direction by the family heads, he wanted to decline the kind offer. He finally accepted it, however, because he thought the lesson of the road might be more useful to the natives than a thousand breadfruit trees. For him it was an exquisite pleasure to receive this offering made by chiefs with their own hands, though some of them were old and ill. And now that the project had been completed, he had the names of those who had participated in the enterprise inscribed, *in perpetuam memoriam.*

Then addressing himself to the chiefs of Samoa, he said: "I will tell you, Chiefs, that when I saw you working on that road, my heart grew warm; not with gratitude only, but with hope. It seemed to me that I read the promise of something good for Samoa; it seemed to me, as I looked at you, that you were a company of warriors in a battle, fighting for the defence of our common country against all aggression.

For there is a time to fight, and a time to dig. You Samoans may fight, you may conquer twenty times, and thirty times, and all will be in vain. There is but one way to defend Samoa. Hear it before it is too late. It is to make roads, and gardens, and care for your trees, and sell their produce wisely, and, in one word, to occupy and use your country. If you do not, others will. . . .

"I do not speak of this lightly, because I love Samoa and her people. I love the land; I have chosen it to be my home while I live, and my grave after I am dead; and I love the people, and have chosen them to be my people to live with and die with. And I see that the day is come now of the great battle; of the great and last opportunity by which it shall be decided, whether you are to pass away like these other races of which I have been speaking, or to stand fast, and have your children living on and honouring your memory in the land you received of your fathers."

He reminded the assembled chiefs that their great leader, Mataafa, who was at that time in exile far away, "saw the day was come when Samoa had to walk in a new path, and to be defended not only with guns and blackened faces, and the noise of men shouting, but by digging and planting, reaping and sowing." Consciously or unconsciously, Tusitala assumed the traditional role of a native high chief whose last deed while bidding farewell to life, was to summon chiefs and talking-men to his death-bed in order to recount to them the history of their ancestors and to urge them to labor for the good of their people.

When Tusitala had finished, Lloyd read a translation of the speech into the language of the high chiefs, a translation carefully prepared by one of the missionaries. Chief Poe, in response, expressed the great appreciation of the natives for the courtesies accorded them by Tusitala and the sentiments that had been expressed in his address to which they had listened with genuine pleasure and undivided attention. Following the speeches the guests repaired to a banquet spread out in *faa Samoa* fashion on another portion of the verandah. When the feast was over all the guests agreed that the ceremony had been a beautiful and memorable one. None of those present realized that this was destined to be Tusitala's farewell address to his beloved Samoans and to the entire Polynesian race.

CHAPTER XIX

HOME IS THE SAILOR

SEEMING TO SENSE that he was approaching his last "Port of Call," Robert Louis Stevenson embarked with renewed vigor and freshness upon what was to be his final literary work. This indefatigable sailor, this incorrigible lover of the sea had found his haven in Vailima. But he needed more than the life about him, its politics and its play to absorb him completely.

He seemed to be spurred on now by a feverish urgency. He seemed fired with inspiration as he sketched the *Weir of Hermiston.* He shaped each character with the sharpness of a sculptor's chisel. Never before had he shown greater vigor. Never before was his narrative more authentic, more firmly charted in its course.

With only a few lines before him he dictated to Belle as clearly and as steadily as though he were reading from a carefully prepared manuscript. His lively imagination was unfolding the relentless tragedy of the Weir. This was to be his masterpiece; its own tragic foreboding mood seemed to foreshadow the sudden, untimely fate of its author.

One evening after dinner, with the family around him, he read from his new work. His resonant voice dramatized the introduction to his Sophoclean-Scotch tragedy.

"In the wild end of a moorland parish, far out of the sight of any house, there stands a cairn among the heather, and a little by east of it, in the going down of the braeside, a monument with some verses half defaced. It was here that Claverhouse shot with his own hand the Praying Weaver of Balweary, and the chisel of Old Mortality has clinked on that lonely gravestone. Public and domestic history have thus marked with a bloody finger this hollow among the hills; and since the Cameronian gave his life there, two hundred years ago, in a glorious folly, and without comprehension or regret, the silence of the moss has been broken once again by the report of firearms and the cry of the dying. . . .

"The Deil's Hags was the old name. But the place is now called Francie's Cairn. For a while it was told that Francie walked. Aggie Hogg met him in the gloaming by the cairnside, and he spoke to her, with chattering teeth, so that his words were lost. He pursued Rob Todd (if any one could have believed Robbie) for the space of half a mile with pitiful entreaties. But the age is one of incredulity; these superstitious decorations speedily fell off; and the facts of the story itself, like the bones of a giant buried there and half dug up, survived, naked and imperfect, in the memory of the scattered neighbours. To this day, of winter nights, when the sleet is on the window and the cattle are quiet in the byre, there will be told again, amid the silence of the young and the additions and corrections of the old, the tale of the Justice-Clerk and of his son, young Hermiston, that vanished from men's knowledge; of the Two Kirsties and the Four Black Brothers of the Cauldstaneslap; and of Frank Innes, 'the young fool advocate,' that came into these moorland parts to find his destiny.

"The Lord Justice-Clerk was a stranger in that part of the country; but his lady wife was known there from a child, as her race had been before her. The old 'riding Rutherfords of Hermiston,' of whom she was the last descendant, had been famous men of yore, ill neighbours, ill subjects, and ill husbands to their wives though not their properties. Tales of them were rife for twenty miles about; and their name was even printed in the page of our Scots histories, not always to their credit. . . .

"Mrs. Weir sat at the head of the table whimpering without disguise; and his lordship opposite munched his bread and cheese in ostentatious disregard. Once only Mrs. Weir had ventured to appeal. He was passing her chair on his way into the study.

" 'O Edom!' she wailed, in a voice tragic with tears, and reaching out to him both hands, in one of which she held a sopping pocket-handkerchief.

"He paused and looked upon her with a face of wrath, into which there stole, as he looked, a twinkle of humour.

" 'Noansense!' he said. 'You and your noansense! What do I want with a Christian Faim'ly? I want Christian broth! Get me a lass that can plain-boil a potato, if she was a whüre off the streets.' And with these words, which echoed in her tender ears like blasphemy, he has passed on to his study and shut the door behind him. . . .

"Dressed as she was for her last walk, they had laid the dead lady on her bed. She was never interesting in life; in death she was not impressive; and as her husband stood before her, with his hands crossed behind his powerful back that which he looked upon was the very image of the insignificant.

" 'Her and me were never cut out for one another,' he remarked at last. 'It was a daft-like marriage.' And then, with a most unusual gentleness of tone, 'Puir bitch,' said he, 'puir bitch!' Then suddenly: 'Where's Erchie?'

"Kirstie had decoyed him to her room and given him 'a jeely-piece.'

" 'Ye have some kind of gumption, too,' observed the Judge, and considered his housekeeper grimly. 'When all's said,' he added, 'I micht have done waur—I micht have been marriet upon a skirling Jezebel like you!'

" 'There's naebody thinking of you, Hermiston!' cried the offended woman. 'We think of her that's out of her sorrows. And could *she* have done waur? Tell me that, Hermiston—tell me that before her clay-cauld corp!'

" 'Well, there's some of them gey an' ill to please,' observed his lordship."

The author had finished. His family sat spellbound. The almost hypnotic spell that gripped them was finally broken by their applause.

Only Lloyd remained silent. Poised with pencil and paper, he had come to take notes, but he was so overcome by the beauty, power, and masterful craftsmanship of what he had heard that he was unable to express an opinion. He could not shake himself from this dream; all he could do was to pour himself a whiskey and soda and gulp it down. For a while he remained staring at the ceiling, then, when the family dispersed for bed, he rose, said "Good night, Louis!" and turned to go to his cottage a short distance from the hall. Before he reached the threshold Stevenson grabbed his arm and in a trembling, agitated voice cried: "My God, you shall not go like that! What! Not a single note, not a single word, not even the courtesy of a lie! You, the only one whose opinion I depend on, and all you can say is: 'Good night, Louis!' So that is your decision is it? Just 'Good night, Louis,'—like a blow in the face!" He went on with great passion, "I am no child who has always to have my lollypops; I can brace myself for any criticism, no matter how damning."

Though stung by this outburst Lloyd felt that he deserved it; his inexcusable "idiotic silence" had deeply wounded Stevenson. He protested, "This is no lack of appreciation"; rather the hypnotic impression which the novel had made on him; its power and its beauty had so enraptured him that words became inadequate. He was convinced that the *Weir of Hermiston* would not only be the author's masterpiece, but promised to be "the greatest novel in the English language." These assuring words moved Stevenson to tears. For hours the two sat in the dark, talking. Never before had the frail but "happy warrior" opened his heart so fully. He spoke of his "rather bitter, blighted youth," of his unhappy relations with his father, of his physical ailments and the "physical dishonor" which kept him in "perpetual torment," of moments when he longed for death. As a young man he prayed for three things: health, a modest income, and friends. He was happy that his wishes were now realized abundantly. When and where except in Samoa could he have engaged in such strenuous sports as riding, hiking, and even a paper chase? Yet the thought that he dared not live anywhere else, not even visit his homeland and his friends, weighed heavily upon him; he was after all an exile.

Though Stevenson never appeared as well as he had during the last few months of his life, yet he frequently talked as if he had a premonition, saying on one occasion, "It will not be for long." "O, it is bad to grow old. For me it is practically hell," he complained. A number of times he expressed the wish to be buried on the peak of Mount Vaea. Often, when the evening stars sparkled over the peak, he would stand and gaze in that direction. How frequently and sadly he expressed the regret: "Oh, it's a wrench not to be planted in Scotland. If I could only be buried in the hills, under the heather and a table tombstone like the martyrs, where the whaups and plovers are crying!"

The return of the rainy season with its sticky, oppressive weather dampened the spirits at Vailima. To the great regret of the Stevensons, the *Curaçoa* had been ordered home. Saturday, before the ship's departure, Vailima gave a large dinner for the officers who, during their seven-month stay in the port of Apia, had almost become members of the household. It was a gay dinner, and before parting a lieutenant of the Marines played the piano and all joined heartily in *Auld Lang Syne.* On Sunday the Stevensons and many people from Apia came to bid farewell to their departing friends. The scene was impressive: the harbor was filled with boats, canoes and rafts. The *Curaçoa* steamed round the two other warships at that time in the port. Then, with her homeward-bound flag flying, "her band playing *Home, Sweet Home,* and Samoa's poignant song of farewell, *To Fa My Feleni,*" she steamed out. On shore friends waved their hats, handkerchiefs and flags, shouting *To fa Curaçoa!* And a chorus of voices from the departing ship replied, *Soi Fua Samoa* (Goodbye, May you live). "Life is a series of farewells, even in art," mused Stevenson.

A few gay parties were still left for Tusitala to enjoy. Fortunately the rain ceased on the thirteenth in time to enable Vailima to celebrate the master's birthday. As usual it was an elaborate affair and, of the one hundred guests, the greater number were native chiefs and their families. Trusty Talolo supervised the preparation of the food: a heifer roasted whole, twenty pigs, fifty chickens, seventeen pigeons, four-hundred and thirty *taro* roots, thirteen yams, eighty arrowroot puddings, eight-hundred pineapples, twenty bunches of bananas and many baskets of oranges. The oranges were brought by Stevenson's favorite, Faauna, and her girl friends. The guests came bearing choice gifts of tapa, *kava* bowls, fans, baskets, and carved clubs. When the mass of food was spread on banana leaves, Tusitala sat at the head of the "table" with Fanny on his right and Anne Ide on his left. The meal was served and eaten in strictly Samoan fashion, *sans* knives and forks.

The feast was followed by songs and a *siva.* At first a group of Tongans performed war-like dances. They were followed by Samoans who sang in honor of Tusitala and acted various scenes of native life. Before departing the American consul-general, Mulligan, proposed a toast to Tusitala's health on this, his forty-fourth birthday.

The last festival that Stevenson lived to celebrate was the Thanksgiving dinner, November 29, 1894. It was a holiday that stemmed from Fanny's native land; the guests and the dishes were, therefore, largely American. The old mahogany table in the great hall was festive with roast turkey embellished with a small red berry to simulate the cranberry, sweet potatoes replaced the pumpkin in the traditional pie, and real American apples had arrived by steamer the day previous. On the table were also bottles of Madeira, sherry, port and Bordeaux, wines that Stevenson's parents and grandparents had stored in Scotland and that now filled the Vailima cellar. In sparkling glasses was served *Eau de Vie de Danzig,* a liqueur imported from Holland. The light from the large swinging lamps picked out the brilliance of the glass and silverware on the table.

The conversation was gay and amusing, as one would expect from Tusitala, the brilliant Laulii and the witty Irish Judge Mulligan, the new American Consul-General. To everyone's surprise, Talolo brought in for dessert champagne with real ice which he had secured from a steamer in Apia Harbor. When the glasses were filled the Laird of Vailima spoke in honor of the Thanksgiving celebration and of his mother and wife:

"There on my right sits she who has but lately from our own loved native land come back to me—she to whom, with no lessening of affection to those others to whom I sing, I love better than all the world besides—my mother. From the opposite end of the table, my wife, who has been all in all to me, when the days were very dark, looks tonight into my eyes—while we have both grown a bit older—with undiminishing affection." Nor did he overlook the other members of his family. "Childless," he went on, "yet on either side of me sits that good woman, my daughter, and the stalwart man, my son, and both have been and are more than son and daughter to me, and have brought into my life mirth and beauty." Then he turned to Belle's young son, Austin: "There sits the bright boy dear to my heart, full of the flow and the spirits of boyhood, so that I can even know that for a time at least we have still the voice of a child in the house." Judge Mulligan's response was eloquent and witty; the whole company was delighted and amused.

For those who are always on the brink of death each day granted comes like a welcome reprieve. Lloyd frequently observed that in the late afternoons, toward the end of his life, Stevenson would walk the verandah, lost in reverie, gazing up at the peak of Mount Vaea where he desired to be buried. The expression on his face at such solemn moments disquieted his stepson, who began to suspect that the buoyancy and unconquerable spirit of the brave fighter was perhaps breaking.

In a letter to Meredith Stevenson spoke of his years of suffering: "For fourteen years I have not had a day's real health; I have wakened sick and gone to bed weary; and I have done my work unflinchingly. I have written in bed, and written out of it, written in hemorrhages, written in sickness, written torn by coughing, written when my head swam for weakness; and for so long, it seems to me I have won my wager and recovered my glove. I am better now, have been, rightly speaking, since first I came to the Pacific; and still, few are the days when I am not in some physical distress."

As the end of the long struggle drew near the undaunted, indomitable optimist at last sounded a note of pessimism. Two days before his dramatic exit, Stevenson wrote to his friend, Edmond Gosse:

> " 'I yearn not for the fighting fate,
> That holds and hath achieved;
> I live to watch and meditate
> And dream—and be deceived.'

"You take the change gallantly. Not I, I must confess. It is all very well to talk of renunciation, and of course it has to be done. But, for my part, give me a roaring toothache! I do like to be deceived and to dream, but I have very little use for either watching or meditation. I was not born for age. . . . You are going on sedately travelling through your ages, decently changing with the years to the proper tune. And here am I, quite out of my true course, and with nothing in my foolish elderly head but love-stories. This must repose upon some curious distinction of temperaments. I gather from a phrase, boldly autobiographical, that you are—well, not precisely growing thin. Can that be the difference?

"It is rather funny that this matter should come up just now, as I am at present engaged in treating a severe case of middle age in one of my stories—*The Justice-Clerk*. The case is that of a woman, and I think that I am doing her justice. You will be interested, I believe, to see the difference in our treatments. *Secreta Vitae* comes nearer to the case of my poor Kirstie. Come to think of it, Gosse, I believe the main distinction is that you have a family growing up around you, and I am a childless, rather bitter, very clear-eyed, blighted youth. I have, in fact, lost the path that makes it easy and natural for you to descend the hill. I am going at it straight. And where I have to go down it is a precipice."

A few days later Tusitala read to his family a prayer he had written: "When the day returns, call us up with morning face and with morning hearts, eager to labor, happy, if happiness be our portion, and if the day be marked for sorrow, strong to endure it." This was the last prayer he wrote; a few days later it was appropriately read at his funeral.

The rain continued to pour down day after day with its depressing effect upon the Vailima household. After dinner, December 2, Stevenson, who seemed to be the only one in good spirits, declared: "We are getting horribly dull up here. Everybody sticks round a lamp, with a book, and it's about as gay as a Presbyterian mission for seamen. Let's play a game I have just thought of." He suggested that each one in turn enter the room and by means of pantomime or any other device, portray some friend for the others to recognize. Though at first none but Stevenson was interested, it soon became a hilarious pastime which continued for hours, much later than the customary bedtime hour. The most amused and amusing was Stevenson, who impersonated Harry Lauder.

The following morning, the fatal December 3, 1894, Tusitala

woke up early, as usual, had his breakfast, smoked his cigarette, and began making notes. When Belle came he began to dictate the beginning of chapter nine of the *Weir of Hermiston.* He seemed to be buoyant and happy. He was working on a gripping scene in the novel: Archie and Kirstie, the two lovers, meet on the moors at the Praying Weaver's Stone, where Archie's mother, Jeannie used to pray with him in his childhood days. Archie tells Kirstie that people have been talking about their relations and that for his father's sake they must see less of one another. Kirstie bursts into bitter tears:

"Poor Archie stood dumbfounded. She had moved some steps away from him before he recovered the gift of articulate speech.

" 'Kirstie!' he cried. 'Oh, Kirstie woman!'

"There was in his voice a ring of appeal, a clang of mere astonishment that showed the schoolmaster was vanquished.

"She turned round on him. 'What do ye Kirstie me for?' she retorted. 'What have ye to do wi' me? Gang to your ain freends and deave them!'

"He could only repeat the appealing 'Kirstie!'

" 'Kirstie, indeed!' cried the girl, her eyes blazing in her white face. 'My name is Miss Christina Elliott, I would have ye to ken, and I daur ye to ca' me out of it. If I canna get love, I'll have respect, Mr. Weir. I'm come of decent people, and I'll have respect. What have I done that ye should lightly me? What have I done? What have I done? Oh, what have I done?' and her voice rose upon the third repetition. 'I thocht—I thocht—I thocht I was sae happy!' and the first sob broke from her like the paroxysm of some mortal sickness.

"Archie ran to her. He took the poor child in his arms, and she nestled to his breast as to a mother's, and clasped him in hands that were strong like vises. He felt her whole body shaken by the throes of distress, and had pity upon her beyond speech. Pity, and at the same time a bewildered fear of this explosive engine in his arms, whose works he did not understand, and yet had been tampering with. There arose from before him the curtains of boyhood, and he saw for the first time the ambiguous face of woman as she is. In vain he looked back over the interview; he saw not where he had offended. It seemed unprovoked, a wilful convulsion of brute nature. . . ."

He continued to dictate until the late afternoon when he paused to listen to the news which Lloyd had just brought from Apia. The sense of successful effort had made him happy and buoyant. Yet at times he appeared to be brooding and looked strangely toward the peak of Mount Vaea. At sunset he came downstairs to help his wife with the salad, one of his specialties. To celebrate the good progress of his great novel, to make up for an earlier outburst which had taken place between him and Fanny, and to help shake off her anxious forebodings, he brought up a bottle of burgundy. According to Fanny, who was the only one with him at the fatal moment, he was talking to her when suddenly he cried out: "My head—oh, my head! Do I look strange?" and fell unconscious to the floor. The members of the family placed the dying man in an arm chair, fanned him, poured brandy between his lips, spoke to him, but in vain. He never regained consciousness. The reddened face and the heavy breathing with the unseeing, wide open eyes, were stark evidence of an apoplectic stroke.

Immediately Lloyd saddled the fastest horse at Vailima. Hatless and coatless he sped to Apia for medical aid. He persuaded Dr. Funk, the thick-set Von Tirpitz-like German practitioner, to mount the horse while he helped himself to a tethered horse near the town bar. As the two galloped up the "Road of the Loving Heart," Lloyd described the condition of his "father." The doctor muttered "Ach, ach!" in a tone not too encouraging. When Dr. Funk and Dr. Anderson of the British warship *Wallaroo* arrived, the stricken man was still breathing but it was a stertorous sort of breathing. The physicians looked at him, shook their heads. Tusitala was dying from a blood clot on the brain. It was a tragic scene: the dying man was breathing, ever more faintly and with greater difficulty; he never regained consciousness. His heartbroken mother was clasping the hand of her beloved son; his wife was sitting in a stupefaction of grief; his faithful servants were crouching prostrate at his feet. At about eight o'clock Tusitala breathed his last.

The sudden shock stunned the members of the entire household. They went about their tasks with heavy hearts and tear-dimmed eyes. Only Tusitala lying on the bier in his favorite great hall seemed absolutely serene. Late that night his body was washed and dressed in his favorite evening attire—a soft white linen shirt, a white tie and a dark blue sash, black evening trousers and patent leather shoes, his hands peacefully folded. On one finger was his silver wedding ring; on his chest was pinned the silver thistle brooch given to him by the

Thistle Club at Honolulu which he had always worn as a memento of his native Scotland. Over his body was placed his favorite Union Jack which had flown on his cruises in the South Seas and later over his Vailima home. Around the bier were placed lighted candles; numerous wreaths lay on a table nearby. A number of precious Samoan mats covered the bed on which he rested. The ever-faithful Talolo and Sosimo kept uninterrupted watch throughout the night. The Roman Catholic boys of the household asked permission to "make a church," and the room echoed their sweet and powerful chanting. The Latin words coming from the lips of the Polynesians sounded strangely impressive.

The terrible news spread quickly throughout the island: "Tusitala has passed away." When Reverend Clarke was informed by a messenger, he immediately rushed to Vailima. All through the night commoners and high chiefs came over great distances to bid farewell to their beloved friend. They came with their tributes of flowers and highly-valued mats, heirlooms, some as soft as silk, to lay on the bier. These were the offerings that had been customary in the old heathen days, and they kept their vigil chanting funeral dirges to drive away the evil spirits. It was a touching scene when the high chiefs entered bowing and sobbing, "talofa, Tusitala!" Then, after kissing the dead and sitting a moment in silence, they went out bowing and murmuring sadly, "tofa, Tusitala." A Mataafa man cried: "Mataafa is gone, and Tusitala is gone, and we have none left." An eloquent orator intoned the exalted phrase: "Samoa ends with you, Tusitala, when death closed the eyes of our best and greatest friend; we know as a race that our day is done."

Before he departed, Doctor Funk instructed Lloyd to bury the body before three the following day; quick burial is imperative in a tropical climate. Stevenson had begged Lloyd many times to cut out a pathway to the top of Mount Vaea. His stepson, however, had felt an understandable aversion to such a task—building a path the sole use for which would be to carry the body of his beloved stepfather to its last resting place; and therefore he kept postponing the unpleasant undertaking. Now the unhappy time had come and he was faced with the difficult problem of getting the coffin carried to the summit of the steep mountain.

Lloyd sent messages to a number of friendly chiefs, begging them to come at once to assist in the arduous task that had to be accomplished by early morning. In Apia he secured some two hundred axes, bush-knives, picks, and spades and white singlets and black cotton cloth to make *lava lavas* for the retainers. He held a council with the chiefs and their workers and during the remainder of the night and early morning the enveloping stillness was broken only by the sound of the swinging axes and the thud of falling trees. These chiefs and their axes that only a short time ago were joyfully building the "Road of the Loving Heart," were now sadly hacking the "Road of the Sorrowing Heart."

Reverend Clarke, the missionary who was among the first to greet Stevenson upon his arrival in Samoa, was entrusted by the family with the funeral arrangements and the burial service. He ordered the coffin and invited the white and native guests. The preparations were complete. About two o'clock in the afternoon twelve strong natives gently lifted the coffin to their shoulders. Directly behind them marched some thirty or forty other natives who at intervals changed places with the bearers. As an act of reverence the pallbearers carried their beloved Tusitala shoulder high. Owing to the difficult terrain and the steep ascent, the bearers could do no more, in some places, than retain their hold on the casket while by means of ropes around their waists, their comrades hauled them upward.

Some nineteen whites and sixty natives assembled before the open grave which had been dug on the summit by the outside boys. There, at the picturesque spot and in the serene mountain solitude, Reverend Clarke read the solemn service, the prayer which Tusitala had written and had read aloud to his household the evening before his death:

"We beseech Thee, Lord, to behold us with favour, folk of many families and nations gathered together in the peace of this roof, weak men and women subsisting under the covert of Thy patience. Be patient still; suffer us yet awhile longer;—with our broken purposes of good, with our idle endeavours against evil, suffer us awhile longer to endure, and (if it may be) help us to do better. Bless to us our extraordinary mercies; if the day come when these must be taken, brace us to play the man under affliction. Be with our friends, be with ourselves. Go with each of us to rest; if any awake, temper to them the dark hours of watching; and when the day returns, return to us, our sun and comforter, call us up with morning faces and with morning hearts—eager to labour—eager to be happy, if happiness shall be our portion—and if the day be marked for sorrow, strong to endure it.

"We thank Thee and praise Thee; and in the words of Him to whom this day is sacred, close our oblation."

Reverend Newell made a short address in Samoan; then another prayer concluded the service. As the coffin was being lowered into the grave, with wreaths and crosses tossed in till it was hidden from view, the minister pronounced the Lord's Prayer: "Thy Kingdom come, Thy will be done." Then the houseboys seized the spades from the outside boys who had dug the grave; no hands but their own should fill the resting place of their beloved Tusitala. When Tusitala lay at rest and the mourners began to descend, an old chief looked back and cried: *Tofa Tusitala, Tofa Tusitala.*—"Sleep, Tusitala."

On the day of the funeral the chiefs of Upolu proclaimed one of their important tabus: no firearms were to be used on the hillside where Tusitala lay, that birds might live there undisturbed and sing above his grave the songs he used to love to hear. For many years no one was permitted to shoot woodland birds in the vicinity. For months after the death of Tusitala native parties headed by their chiefs would arrive in Vailima bringing precious mats and offer their condolences to the family. On his birthday, November 13, the natives would decorate Tusitala's tomb with flowers and sing a most heartfelt and most eloquent dirge, composed at the time of Stevenson's death by one of their chiefs: *

Listen oh! this world as I tell of the disaster,
That befell in the late afternoon,
That broke like a wave of the sea,
Suddenly and swiftly blinding our eyes.

Alas! for Lois who speaks, tears in his voice,
Refrain, groan, and weep, oh, my heart in its sorrow!
Alas! for Tusitala who rests in the forest.

Aimlessly we wait and wonder, Will he come again?
Lament, oh Vailima, waiting and ever waiting;
Let us search and inquire of the Captains of Ships,

* Translation by Lloyd Osbourne.

"Be not angry, but has not Tusitala come?"
Tuila, sorrowing one, come hither,
Prepare me a letter, I will carry it.

Let her Majesty, Queen Victoria, be told,
That Tusitala, the loving one, has been taken home.
Refrain, groan, and weep, oh, my heart in its sorrow!
Alas! for Tusitala who rests in the forest.

Alas! my heart weeps with anxious pity,
As I think of the days before us,
Of the white men gathering for the Christmas assembly;
Alas! for Alola,* left in her loneliness,
And the men of Vailima, who weep together,
Their leader being taken;
Refrain, groan, and weep, oh, my heart in its sorrow!
Alas! for Tusitala, who sleeps in the forest.

Alas! oh, my heart, it weeps unceasingly,
When I think of his illness,
Coming upon him with so fatal a swiftness,
Would that it had waited a word or a glance from him,
Or some token from us of our love.
Refrain, groan, and weep, oh, my heart in its sorrow!
Alas! for Tusitala, who sleeps in the forest.

Grieve oh, my heart! I cannot bear to look on,
At the chiefs who are assembling.
Alas! Tusitala, thou art not here;
I look hither and thither in vain for thee,
Refrain, groan, and weep, oh, my heart in its sorrow!
Alas! for Tusitala, he sleeps in the forest.

Twelve years later Mataafa wrote: "It is impossible for my heart to forget the great love of this Chief Tusitala."

Thus Robert Louis Stevenson made his dramatic exit at the age of forty-four. It was a leave-taking, "just as he wished, sudden and painless, swift and clean," while enthusiastically at work on his masterpiece, at the peak of his fame, and mourned by his family, retainers and a host of admirers, white and colored, by all who knew him.

* Alola—literally, the "loved one."

On December 10, 1896 Edinburgh held a great meeting to establish a memorial in honor of the city's famous son, whom once it held in small esteem. When Mother Stevenson arrived late, Lord Rosebery, the presiding chairman, announced, "His mother is with us." The packed hall gave the good lady a sincere ovation, which warmed her heart.

Five months later, on May 14, 1897 Mother Stevenson died of pneumonia. At the end imagining she saw her beloved son at the foot of her bed, she cried, "There is Louis! I must go."

Fanny outlived her husband some twenty years. On February 18, 1914, in a week of a raging storm, she, too, passed away suddenly. About a year later Isobel took her ashes to Samoa to be placed in the tomb of her husband. Upolu had been in the meantime captured from the Germans by the New Zealand forces during the war, and Vailima, now used as a government house, was flying Stevenson's beloved Union Jack.

Over the remains of Louis and Fanny rests a huge block of concrete shaped like a native chief's rock monument. On either side is a bronze plate. On one are inscribed the words in Samoan, "The Tomb of Tusitala," followed by the pathetic plea of Ruth to Naomi: "Whither thou goest, I will go; and where thou lodgest, I will lodge: thy people shall be my people, and thy God my God; where thou diest, I will die, and there will I be buried." Beside this Biblical inscription are a thistle and a hibiscus flower, the respective emblems of Scotland and Samoa. The plate bearing Fanny's name has on it the design of a tiger-lily, symbolic of the strong, hot-blooded woman. On another panel are the well-known words of Stevenson's *Requiem* in English:

Under the wide and starry sky,
Dig the grave and let me lie.
Glad did I live and gladly die
And I laid me down with a will.

This be the verse you grave for me:
Here he lies where he longed to be,
Home is the sailor, home from the sea,
And the hunter home from the hill.

BIBLIOGRAPHY

ADAMS, Henry *Letters of Henry Adams (1858–1891)*, 2 Vols., Edited by Worthington Chauncey Ford. Boston, Houghton Mifflin Company, 1930.

ALEXANDER, W. D. "The Origins of the Polynesian Race," in *Seventh Annual Report of the Hawaiian Historical Society*, 1910.

ALLEN, Maryland "South Sea Memories of R. L. S.," *Bookman*, August, 1916.

Anonymous "Literary Leprosy," *Saturday Review*, November 30, 1901.
"Stevenson From a New Point of View," *Current Opinion*, December, 1924.
"Stevenson Unwhitewashed," *Atlantic Monthly*, March, 1900.

ARNOLD, William Harris "My Stevensons," *Scribner's*, January, 1922.

BAILEY, Millard "Some Rare Glimpses of Stevenson," *Bookman*, January, 1909.

BALFOUR, Graham *The Life of Robert Louis Stevenson*, New York, Charles Scribner's Sons, 1901.

BERMANN, Richard A. *Home From the Sea. Robert Louis Stevenson in Samoa*, Translated by Elizabeth Reynolds Hapgood. Indianapolis, The Bobbs-Merrill Company, 1939.

BOK, Edward W. *The Americanization of Edward Bok*, New York, Charles Scribner's Sons, 1922.

BOK, Edward W. "The Playful Stevenson," *Scribner's*, August, 1927.

BOUGAINVILLE, Louis Antoine de *Voyage autour du monde*, 2 Vols., Paris, 1771–72.

BRANDENBURG, Erich *From Bismarck to the World War. A History of German Foreign Policy, 1870–1914*, Translated by Annie Elizabeth Adams. New York, 1927.

BRIGHAM, W. T. "Index to the Pacific Islands," in *Memoirs B. P. Bishop Museum*, Vol. I, No. 2, 1900.

British Possessions in Oceania, Handbook prepared under the direction of the Historical Section of the Foreign Office, No. 144, London, 1920.

BROWN, George *Melanesians and Polynesians: Their Life Histories Described and Compared*, London, Macmillan and Company, 1910.

BROWN, George *Pioneer Missionary and Explorer. An Autobiography*, London, Hodder and Stoughton, 1908.

BROWN, George E. *A Book of R. L. S. Works, Travels, Friends, and Commentators,* London, Methuen & Company, 1919.
BUCK, P. H. *Vikings of the Sunrise,* New York, 1938.
BUELL, Llewellyn M. Eilean Earraid: "The Beloved Isle of Robert Louis Stevenson," *Scribner's,* February, 1922.
BURGESS, Gelet "An Interview with Mrs. Robert Louis Stevenson," *Bookman,* September, 1898.

CARRÉ, Jean-Marie *The Frail Warrior,* Translated from the French by Eleanor Hard. New York, Coward-McCann, Inc., 1930.
CARRINGTON, James B. "Another Glimpse of R. L. S.," *Scribner's,* August, 1927.
CHESTERTON, G. K. *Robert Louis Stevenson,* New York, Dodd, Mead & Company, 1928.
CHURCH, J. W. "A Vanishing People of the South Seas," *National Geographic Magazine,* October, 1919.
CHURCHILL, William "Stevenson in the South Seas," *McClure's Magazine,* December, 1894.
CHURCHILL, William "Stevenson in the South Seas," *McClure's Magazine,* February, 1895.
CHURCHWARD, William B. *My Consulate in Samoa: A Record of Four Years' Sojourn in the Navigators Islands, with Personal Experiences of King Malietoa Laupepa, His Country, and His Men,* London, Richard Bentley & Son, 1887.
CLARKE, W. E. "Robert Louis Stevenson in Samoa," *Yale Review,* January, 1921.
COLBY, Frank Moore "A Debated Charm," *Bookman,* February, 1902.
COOPER, Lettice *Robert Louis Stevenson,* The English Novelists Series, London, Home & VanThal, 1947.
COPELAND, Charles Townsend "Robert Louis Stevenson," *Atlantic Monthly,* April, 1895.
CROCKETT, S. R. Robert Louis Stevenson, *McClure's Magazine,* February, 1895.
CROSSLAND, C. "The Islands of Tahiti," *Geographical Journal,* Vol. 71, No. 6, 1928.

DAICHES, David *Robert Louis Stevenson. The Makers of Modern Literature,* Norfolk, Connecticut, New Directions Books, 1947.
DALGLISH, Doris N. *Presbyterian Pirate. A Portrait of Stevenson,* London, Oxford University Press, 1937.
DANKS, Benjamin "Samoa," in *A Century of the Pacific,* Edited by J. Colwell. London, 1914.
DAWSON, W. J. "The Religion of Robert Louis Stevenson," *Bookman,* September, 1896.
DIXON, R. B. *The Racial History of Man,* New York, 1923.
DOYLE, Conan A. "Mr. Stevenson's Methods in Fiction," *Living Age,* February 16, 1890.

DUNCAN, Jr., William Henry "Stevenson's Second Visit to America," *Bookman,* January, 1900.

ELLIS, W. *Polynesian Researches,* 4 Vols., London, 1836.

ELLISON, Joseph W. "The Adventures of an American Premier in Samoa, 1874–1876," *Pacific Northwest Quarterly,* October, 1936.

ELLISON, Joseph W. *Opening and Penetration of Foreign Influence in Samoa to 1880,* Oregon State College, Monographs in History, No. I, 1938.

ELLISON, Joseph W. "The Partition of Samoa: A Study in Imperialism and Diplomacy," *The Pacific Historical Review,* September, 1939.

FIELD, Isobel Osbourne Strong (with Lloyd Osbourne) *Memories of Vailima,* New York, Charles Scribner's Sons, 1902.

FIELD, Isobel Osbourne Strong *Robert Louis Stevenson,* Saranac Lake, New York, Stevenson Society of America, 1920.

FIELD, Isobel Osbourne Strong *This Life I've Loved,* New York, Longmans, Green & Company, 1937.

FISHER, Anne B. *No More A Stranger,* Stanford University, Stanford University Press, 1946.

FLETCHER, C. Brundson *Stevenson's Germany. The Case Against Germany in the Pacific,* London, William Heinemann, 1920.

Foreign Office *Former German Possessions in Oceania,* Handbooks prepared under the direction of the Historical Section of the Foreign Office, No. 146.

FORNANDER, Abraham *An Account of the Polynesian Race: Its Origin and Migrations and the Ancient History of the Hawaiian People to the Time of Kamehameha,* I., 3 Vols., London, 1885.

FOSTER, John W. *American Diplomacy in the Orient,* Boston, 1903.

FOSTER, Rhea Dulles *America in the Pacific,* Boston and New York, 1922.

FRASER, Marie *In Stevenson's Samoa,* Preface by James Payn. London, Smith, Elder & Company, 1895.

GENUNG, John Franklin *Stevenson's Attitude to Life,* New York, Thomas Y. Crowell, 1901.

GILDER, Jeannette L. "Stevenson—and After," *Review of Reviews,* February, 1895.

GORDON-CUMMING, C. F. *A Lady's Cruise in a French Man-of-War,* Edinburgh, 1882.

GOSSE, Edmund "Personal Memories of Robert Louis Stevenson," *Century,* July, 1895.

Great Britain, Parliament *Samoa.* No. I (1890), No. I, (1893), No. I, (1899). *Further Correspondence Respecting the Affairs of Samoa (In continuation of "Samoa" No. I* (1889), C. 5629.) London, Her Majesty's Stationery Office.

GREEN, Roger Lancelyn "Stevenson in Search of a Madonna," *Essays and Studies:* 1950, Edited by G. Rostrevor Hamilton. London, John Murray, 1950.

GREEN, W. "Social Traits of Samoans," *Journal of Applied Sociology,* November–December, 1924.

GREGORY, H. E. "Geography of the Pacific," in *Problems of the Pacific,* Chicago, 1928.

GRIFFIN, A. P. C. *A List of Books on Samoa and Guam,* compiled for the Library of Congress, 1901.

GROSE, William M. *American Samoa, A General Report by the Governor,* 1913. (Navy Department)

GWYNN, Stephen "Mr. Robert Louis Stevenson," *Living Age,* January 12, 1895.

HAMILTON, Clayton *On the Trail of Stevenson,* New York, Doubleday, Page & Company, 1916.

HAMMERTON, J. A. (Editor) *Stevensoniana: an Anecdotal Life and Appreciation of Robert Louis Stevenson.* Edinburgh, John Grant, 1910.

HANDY, E. S. C. "The Insular Pacific," *Pacific Affairs,* June, 1932.

HANDY, E. S. C. "The Native Culture in the Marquesas," *B. P. Bishop Museum Bulletin,* 9, Honolulu, 1923.

HELLMAN, George S. "R. L. S. and the Streetwalker," *American Mercury,* July, 1936.

HELLMAN, George S. "Stevenson and Henry James," *Century,* January, 1926.

HELLMAN, George S. "The Stevenson Myth," *Century,* December, 1922.

HELLMAN, George S. *The True Stevenson: A Study in Clarification,* Boston, Little, Brown & Company, 1925.

HINKLEY, Laura L. *The Stevensons: Louis and Fanny,* New York, Hastings House, 1950.

ISSLER, Anne Roller *Happier for His Presence, San Francisco and Robert Louis Stevenson,* Stanford University Press, 1949.

JOHNSTONE, Arthur *Recollections of Robert Louis Stevenson in the Pacific,* London, Chatto & Windus, 1905.

KEESING, Felix M. *Modern Samoa: Its Government and Changing Life,* London, George Allen & Unwin, Ltd., 1934.

KEIM, Jeannette *Forty Years of German-American Political Relations,* Philadelphia, 1919.

KIMBERLY, L. A. "Samoa and the Hurricane of March, 1889." Vol. XII, *Military Historical Society of Massachusetts.*

KRÄMER, A. K. *Die Samoa-Inseln,* 2 Vols., Stuttgart, 1902.

KUYKENDALL, R. *The Hawaiian Kingdom,* 1778–1854. New York, 1938.

LA FARGE, John *Reminiscences of the South Seas,* Doubleday Page, Garden City, 1912.

LANG, Andrew "Recollections of Robert Louis Stevenson," *North American Review,* February, 1899.

LANIER, Charles D. "Robert Louis Stevenson," *Review of Reviews,* February, 1895.
LEPSIUS, Johannes; Mendelsohn, Albrecht Bartholdy, and Friedrich Thimme, (Editors) *Die Grosse Politik, der Europäischen Kabinette, 1871–1914,* Berlin, 1922–1926.
LOVETT *History of the London Missionary Society,* 2 Vols., London, 1896.
LOW, Will H. "A Chronicle of Friendship," *Scribner's,* July, 1908.
LUNDIE, G. A. *Missionary Life in Samoa,* Edinburgh, 1846.

MACALLUM, Thomas Murray *Adrift in the South Seas, Including Adventures with Robert Louis Stevenson,* Los Angeles, California, Wetzel Publishing Company.
MACLAREN, Ian "In Memoriam: R. L. S.," *McClure's Magazine,* February, 1895.
MARTIN, K. L. P. *Missionaries and Annexation in the Pacific,* London, 1924.
MASSON, Rosaline *I Can Remember Robert Louis Stevenson,* Edinburgh, W. & R. Chambers, 1922.
MASSON, Rosaline *A Life of Robert Louis Stevenson,* New York, Frederick A. Stokes Co., 1923.
MASTERMAN, Sylvia *Origins of International Rivalry in Samoa, 1845–1884,* Stanford University Press, Stanford University, 1934.
McCLURE, Samuel S. *My Autobiography,* New York, Frederick A. Stokes Company, 1914.
MEAD, Margaret *Coming of Age in Samoa,* New York, 1928.
MILL, H. R. (Editor) *International Geography,* 1922.
MOORS, Harry Jay *With Stevenson in Samoa,* Boston, Small, Maynard and Company, 1910.
MURRAY, A. W. *Forty Years' Mission Work in Polynesia and New Guinea, 1835–1875,* London, 1876.

New York Tribune "War Ships Sunk in Samoa," *Tribune Association,* Vol. k, March 30, April 15, 1889.

OSBOURNE, Lloyd *An Intimate Portrait of R. L. S.,* New York, Charles Scribner's Sons, 1924.
OSBOURNE, Lloyd "Mr. Stevenson's Home Life at Vailima," *Scribner's,* October, 1895.
Outlook October, 1916 (114).

PEARS, Sir Edmund Radcliffe "Some Recollections of Robert Louis Stevenson," *Scribner's,* January, 1923.
PHELPS, William Lyon *Essays on Modern Novelists,* New York, Macmillan Company, 1910.
PRITCHARD, W. J. *Polynesian Reminiscences,* London, 1866.

REINECKE, F. *Samoa,* Berlin, 1901.

RICHARDSON, J. D. *A Compilation of the Messages and Papers of the Presidents, 1789–1897,* Vol. 7, Washington, 1896–1899.

RIVENBURGH, Eleanor "Stevenson in Hawaii," *Bookman,* October–November, December, 1917.

ROWE, N. A. *Samoa Under the Sailing Gods,* London, 1930.

RUSSELL, M. *Polynesia, or an Historical Account of the Principal Islands in the South Sea including New Zealand,* New York, 1843.

RUSSELL, M. *Polynesia,* Edinburgh, 1845.

RYDEN, G. H. *The Foreign Policy of the United States in Relation to Samoa,* New Haven, 1933.

Samoa *A Handbook of Western Samoa,* Wellington, 1925.

SANCHEZ, Nellie Van de Grift *The Life of Mrs. Robert Louis Stevenson,* New York, Charles Scribner's Sons, 1920.

Saturday Review of Literature September 25, 1937.

SCHOLEFIELD, Guy H. *The Pacific, Its Past and Future, and the Policy of the Great Powers from the Eighteenth Century,* London, 1919.

SIMPSON, Eva Blantyre "Robert Louis Stevenson's Hills of Home," *Living Age,* April 20, 1901.

SMITH, Janet Adam (Editor) *Henry James and Robert Louis Stevenson. A Record of Friendship and Criticism,* London, Rupert Hart-Davis, 1948.

STAIR, John B. (Rev.) *Old Samoa or Flotsam and Jetsam From the Pacific Ocean With an Introduction by Bishop of Ballarat,* The Religious Tract Society, 1897.

State Department *Foreign Relations,* 1889–1894.

STEINBERGER, A. B. "Report on Samoa or Navigators Islands." *H. Ex. Doc. No. 161,* 44 Congress, 1 Session (Serial 1691).

STEPHEN, Leslie "Robert Louis Stevenson," *Living Age,* February 22, 1902.

STEVENSON, Fanny Van de Grift Osbourne *The Cruise of the* Janet Nichol *Among the South Sea Islands. A Diary by ——,* New York, Charles Scribner's Sons, 1914.

STEVENSON, Margaret Isabella (Balfour) *From Saranac to the Marquesas and Beyond* (Letters written by —— during 1887–1888, to her sister.) *Letters from Samoa, 1891–1893,* Edited by Marie Clothilde Balfour. New York, Charles Scribner's Sons, 1906.

STEVENSON, Robert Louis *The Complete Poems,* New York, Charles Scribner's Sons, 1923. *David Balfour: A Sequel to "Kidnapped,"* South Seas Edition, New York, Charles Scribner's Sons, 1925. *In the South Seas,* South Seas Edition, Vol. XX. New York, Charles Scribner's Sons, 1925. *The Letters of Robert Louis Stevenson,* Edited by Sidney Colvin, South Seas Edition, Vol. XXIX, XXX, XXXI, XXXII. New York, Charles Scribner's Sons, 1925. *The Ebb-Tide* and *Some Unfinished Stories,* South Seas Edition, Volume XXIV. New York, Charles Scribner's Sons, 1925. *The Master of Ballantrae: A Winter's Tale,* South Seas Edition, Vol. XVIII. New York, Charles Scribner's Sons, 1925. *Weir of Hermiston,* South Seas Edition, Vol. XXVIII. New York, Charles Scribner's Sons, 1925. *The Wrecker,* South

Seas Edition, Volume XXI. New York, Charles Scribner's Sons, 1925. *Vailima Papers* and *Footnote to History,* South Seas Edition, XXVI. New York, Charles Scribner's Sons, 1925. *St. Ives,* South Seas Edition, Vol. XXV. New York, Charles Scribner's Sons, 1925. *Virginibus Puerisque and Other Papers,* The Biographical Edition of the Works of Robert Louis Stevenson. New York, Charles Scribner's Sons, 1921.

STODDARD, Charles Warren *Exits and Entrances,* Boston, Lothrop Publishing Company, 1903.

STONEHEWER, Cooper H. *Coral Lands,* 2 Vols. London, 1880.

STUBBS, Laura *Stevenson's Shrine: The Record of a Pilgrimage,* London, Alexander Mering, 1903.

SWINNERTON, Frank *R. L. Stevenson. A Critical Study,* New York, George H. Doran Co., 1923.

TOWNSEND, Mary Evelyn *The Rise and Fall of Germany's Colonial Empire 1884–1918,* New York, 1930.

TRIGGS, W. H. "R. L. Stevenson, as a Samoan Chief," *Cassell's Family Magazine,* February, 1895.

TURNER, George *Samoa: A Hundred Years Ago and Long Before,* London, Macmillan and Co., 1884.

TURNER, George *Nineteen Years in Polynesia,* 1865.

WAKEMAN, W. *Report on the Navigator Islands.* New York, 1871.

WILKES, Charles *Narrative of the United States Exploring Expedition During the Years, 1838, 1839, 1840, 1841, and 1842,* 5 Vols., Philadelphia, 1845.

WILLIAMS, John *A Narrative of Missionary Enterprises in the South Sea Islands,* 1873.

WILLIAMSON, R. W. *The Social and Political Systems of Central Polynesia,* 3 Vols., Cambridge, 1924.

YOUNG, W. Allen *Christianity and Civilization in the South Pacific Ocean,* London, 1922.

ZIMMERMANN, Alfred *Geschichte der Deutschen Kolonial Politik,* Berlin, 1914.

INDEX